BEAUTY AND THE BEASTS

D0190255

Property of Cultural Resource Management Program

DO NOT REMOVE

CULTURAL RESOURCE MANAGEMENT PROGRAM
Division of Continuing Studies
University of Victoria
PO Box 3030 STN CSC
Victoria, BC V8W 3N6 Canada

Stephen E. Weil

BEAUTY AND THE BEASTS

ON MUSEUMS, ART, THE LAW, AND THE MARKET

Smithsonian Institution Press
Washington, D.C.

© 1983 Smithsonian Institution. All rights reserved.
Printed in the United States of America.

Library of Congress Cataloging in Publication Data
Weil, Stephen E.
    Beauty and the beasts.
    Supt. of Docs. no.: SI 1.2:B38
    1. Museums—Law and legislation—United States—
Addresses, essays, lectures. 2. Law and art—Addresses,
essays, lectures, 3. Museums—United States—
Addresses, essays, lectures. I. Title.
KF4305.A75W44   1983   344:73'.093   82-600394
ISBN 0-87474-958-1   347.30493
ISBN 0-87474-957-3 (pbk.)

97 96 95 94 93 92 91 90   5 4 3

⊗The paper in this book meets the requirements of the
American National Standard for Permanence of Paper
for Printed Materials Z39.48-1984.

For Rachel, David and Michael

Contents

Acknowledgments

Inasmuch as this book is a mosaic, I am deeply indebted not only to my many talented colleagues in and around the Smithsonian Institution who made possible its final assembly but also to the host of people across the country and beyond who, over a period of nearly twelve years, helped me shape the motley tesserae from which it was composed.

Among the latter, I owe particular thanks to: Thomas H. Garver and the late Mary French for "The Multiple Crises in Our Museums"; Dore Ashton for "An Inventory of Art Museum Roles"; Linda Evans for "Toward Greater Museum Integrity" and "'If Men Were Angels . . .'"; Patricia Joan McDonnell and Ann Hofstra Grogg for "MGR: A Conspectus of Museum Management"; Roberta Faul for "The Filer Commission Report: Is It Good for Museums?"; Ellen Cochran Hicks for, among the several pieces she so expertly edited, the review of *The Endangered Sector;* Paul Wolkin and my fellow members of the Museum Law Conference planning committee—Marie G. Malaro, Suzanne Dupré Murphy, Peter Powers, Alan D. Ullberg, and Nicholas D. Ward—for "No Museum Is an Island," "Vincible Ignorance: Museums and the Law," and "Custody Without Title"; Judge Shoshana Berman, Deborah dePorter, Laura Werner, and, again, Roberta Faul and Alan D. Ullberg for "Breaches of Trust, Remedies, and Standards in the American Private Art Museum"; Signe Larsen for "Beauty and the Beast"; Pamela Lajeunesse for "Some Thoughts on 'Art Law'"; Bruce Wolpe, Milton Esterow, and Sylvia Hochfield for "Resale Royalties: Nobody Benefits" and "The 'Moral Right' Comes to California"; Brian O'Doherty for "Prices—Right On!"; and finally, but not least (because she was the first person to ask me to write about the art market), Judith Goldman for the reviews of *Money and Art* and *The Economics of Taste*.

At the Smithsonian, Nancy Grubb and Glen B. Ruh initially championed the possibility that these pieces might be assembled into a coherent design. Felix Lowe, the director of the Smithsonian Institution Press, was not only an early supporter but, as important, proved a master at untangling whatever snarls we encountered along the way. Others at the press who made important contributions were Maureen Jacoby, Bradley Rymph, and Alan Carter. The work of Felicia Robb, my volunteer researcher, and the expert assistance of Laura Lewis Mandeles were also invaluable.

That I have been able to pursue the various interests reflected in this book has been possible only because each of the three museum directors for whom I have had the privilege to work— Lloyd Goodrich, John I. H. Baur, and Abram Lerner—was so deeply committed to the field and wonderfully generous in permitting the members of his staff to follow their own professional involvements. I am profoundly grateful to them all.

My deepest gratitude, however, is reserved for the three people who ultimately made this book possible: my secretary Carole Clore, whose uncanny ability throughout many years to pursue wayward facts and decode my crabbily interlineated drafts has been nothing short of miraculous; Carole Jacobs, an editor of the rarest gifts whose tactful prodding and straight-on-the-mark questions were responsible for much of what is contained in the ten "afterwords" scattered throughout the book; and my wife, Elizabeth A. C. Weil, whose monumental patience and gentle support through all of the evenings, weekends, sulks, mess, and nasty grumps that this book entailed can never be adequately acknowledged.

For whatever errors or omissions the reader may discover hereafter, I have no one to thank but myself.

S.E.W.

Introduction

M y first conversations with the Smith-sonian Institution Press about this book took place in the summer of 1979. At issue from the start was whether the pieces it was to comprise ought to be revised to be more consistent both in substance and style, or whether they should be reprinted as originally written.

The first approach was attractive for several reasons. Rereading what I had written over many years, and particularly about museums, it was clear that my attitude had changed toward a number of things, especially the proper ordering of museum priorities and the role of trustees. In some instances these changes could be traced as evolutionary. In others they appeared as inconsistencies. Then, too, some material had been overtaken by events and no longer was timely. Given the chance to revise, I might have hoped to weave these disparate strands into an apparently seamless whole and to present myself in public with at least a reasonable semblance of authority.

On reflection, though, this revisionary alternative seemed to me somehow inappropriate—particularly for a book intended to deal extensively with museums. If I was to insist so strongly that the central obligation of the museum is to preserve the material evidence of the past for the uses of the future, did I not have some similar obligation toward the fragments from which this book was to be composed? These fragments were integral to the times in which they were written. Their integrity—their value as evidence—could better be preserved by leaving them intact. Whatever I might lose in the appearance of authority could be more than compensated for by my added value as a witness.

I began to write about museums in the early seventies, not a long time ago in years but—for those of us who then worked in the art museums of New York City—a time as distant as the far side of the moon. In the turmoil that followed the assassinations of Martin Luther King, Jr., and Robert F. Kennedy, the incursion into Cambodia, and the killings at Kent State, many artists and other creative people in New York were overwhelmed by a rage for which few outlets were available. The Nixon government was in Washington, distant and imperturbable. The museums—perceived by the artists as surrogates for power—were immediately at hand, and immensely perturbable. Rage crystallized into hostility, and the local museums were among its targets.

My most vivid memory is of June 1, 1970, the first day of the American Association of Museums's annual meeting, held that year at the Waldorf-Astoria Hotel in New York. The meeting had scarcely begun when members of two protest groups—the Art Workers Coalition and the New York Art Strike—overran the podium and commandeered the microphones. Most of the delegates came from distant parts of the country and represented either history or natural history museums. Few had any notions of who the protesters were, and their initial responses were largely ones of astonishment. For some of us, though, the dismay of the moment had an added dimension. Many of the artists, dancers, and writers who were jeering at us from the podium had been our friends and more—our colleagues in an effort to establish a larger acceptance for contemporary art.

What these protesters were demanding was that the museums of the country abandon their traditional concerns and pledge, then and there, that their resources would henceforth be devoted to wiping out war, racism, sexism, and repression. To question how museums might do this—or even to ask under what authority the roomful of puzzled delegates could bind their institutions in such a way—was abruptly dismissed as pettifogging. The time for talking was past. The time for action was now. Atrocities were being committed. The establishment was to blame. Museums were part of the establishment. Museums were guilty as accomplices. Repent, or be trashed.

Following a reception at the Brooklyn Museum that evening, another such scene was played. Two days later, when New York Governor Nelson Rockefeller came to address the meeting, still a third confrontation took place. If the preceding period had been one of general goodwill toward museums—and I thought it was when I first went to work at the Whitney Museum in 1967—that sense of goodwill was one more casualty of those Vietnam years.

The first two pieces in this book—"The Multiple Crises in Our Museums" and "An Inventory of Art Museum Roles"—were written against that background. For me, at least, they had a tone that I didn't think could be recaptured if I tried to make them more timely. The same was true for many of the later pieces—particularly those from the mid-seventies. Viewed from today, that was a good time. The anger of the war years had drained largely away, public support for the arts was burgeoning, and the museum community could afford to abandon its defensive stance and focus inwardly on how museums might be made better. Occasionally, I played the role of Savonarola.

With but gentle persuasion, the Smithsonian Institution Press eventually agreed that—save for minor changes to correct some blatant errors, eliminate outright duplications, and excise what was wholly irrelevant—these pieces should be published in their original form. Whatever substantive updating was needed could be—and has been—done through a series of interspersed "afterwords." Minor clarifications of fact have been inserted into the text in brackets. Inconsistencies remain, and readers will have to reconcile these as best they can. Most are minor: Some pieces were written for print, some to be spoken; and they differ in style. Some deal only with art museums, others with museums generally; but I have tried to indicate which are which. And some reflect the different times that produced them. Along the way, I have changed also—I've gotten older—and that too may account for some changing viewpoints.

The readers of this or any book that deals with museums will find another inconsistency, though, and one not so easy to reconcile. It is an inconsistency—a contradiction, actually—implicit in the way that we think about museums. The orthodox theory of museology holds that museums have five basic purposes: to collect, preserve, study, exhibit, and interpret. However, as David M. Wilson, the director of the British Museum, pointed out in the 1982 issue of *Museum* devoted to conservation, there is an underlying contradiction between the mandate to preserve and the mandate to exhibit. Preservation serves the future at the expense of the present. Exhibitions serve the present at the expense of the future. "The curator must ensure that he passes on his collection intact and unharmed to subsequent generations," Wilson explained. "At the same time, he must amaze, stimulate and educate his public."

Compounding this contradiction is a paradox: if museums were to opt entirely for the future and preserve all of their collections as scrupulously as Pompeii was preserved for nearly seventeen hundred years under a protective blanket of Vesuvian ash, what then? Would not any particular future have the same obligation— or perhaps a heightened one—to preserve those same objects for the use of some still more distant future? And yet, unless one or another of those futures could actually *use* those objects for exhibition, interpretation, and study, to what purpose would generation after generation of museum caretakers have devoted themselves? On the other hand, if museums were to opt entirely for the present—if they recklessly exposed every last artifact in their care to the hazards of light, pollution, excessive handling, unstable environments, and incessant travel—would they not undermine the fundamental basis on which they were originally established?

How does one mediate between those conflicting obligations? The easy answer is "balance," but it tells us little. Where is the proper balance? Anything that approached the Vesuvian extreme would surely be unacceptable, but so might the risk involved in sending the collected extant works of Leonardo on a five-year fifteen-stop tour around the world. Left to themselves, I think that most museum professionals would—as I would—tilt more heavily toward the side of preservation. They are not, however, left entirely to themselves. To the extent that the conflict here is one between the present and the future, the present holds a trump card—it pays the bills. Probity is admired, but the continued accessibility of collections is what the larger public most basically demands of museums. Would the crowds that cheered so wildly for Tutankhamen respond with the same enthusiasm if asked to pay the cost of a new storage facility?

Assuming, though, that agreement could be reached about a proper balance between the obligations to preserve and exhibit collections, the chronic shortage of funds under which museums habitually operate would still be an obstacle to achieving it. With adequate resources for conservation, research in display techniques, gallery security, and better climate control, museums could more easily reconcile these conflicting demands of present and future. Without such resources, they are continually forced to make hard choices. Museums have too often failed to make clear that the only adequate level of funding would be one that supported *all* of their basic obligations, not just one or another.

A second major subject of this book is the law, both as it affects museums and as it applies to the visual arts. What must be acknowledged here is my own profound ambivalence. For thirty years I have carried on a love/hate affair with the law. Fascination with it drew me through the doors of the Columbia University School of Law in 1953. Some ten years later, a surfeit of its minutiae drove me from its practice. The pieces reprinted here reflected both those feelings.

That the rule of law is indispensable to the conduct of our lives cannot be disputed. What I would question, though, is whether there might not be some *de minimis* threshold below which its operation could be suspended without substantial loss. Less pretentiously, in a society as litigious as ours, might there not usefully be at least a few more things to which the law could say a resounding "So what!"?

As things now stand, we are defeated by our virtuosity. With enormous ingenuity we have constructed a legal framework capable of dealing with virtually every human activity regardless of how remote it might be from the law's grander and more traditional concerns. In our zeal to provide a rule for every situation, a resolution for every dispute, and a remedy for every wrong, we have extended our notion of what might be justiciable to cover everything from the propriety of sexual banter in the workplace to the relative aesthetic merits of Corot's various figure paintings. (As to the latter, see "Some Thoughts on 'Art Law'" at pp. 199–209.)

As the rules through which we govern ourselves continue to proliferate, they threaten to intertwine into a mass so dense that little short of their total overturn might permit us to clear away the excess. We seem to be caught in a dynamic of endless refinement, determined that the law find a way to make fair even the tiniest detail of our lives. Fairness for each, not the enrichment of all, has become our obsession. What may have been overlooked is that it might not always be worse to have "more" in a sometimes

unfair and arbitrary world than to have "less" in one that is dominated by perfect justice. Are we so sure, for that matter, that the
tilt of the arbitrary does not produce a certain vital energy, an
energy we would sadly lack if and when the ever more finely
detailed workings of the law bring us in the end to a state of
absolute equilibrium?

Happily, the involvement of the law with museums and with
art is not at so grandiloquent a level. It is, nonetheless, instructive
about the process—seemingly inevitable—through which legal
considerations penetrate ever more deeply into every aspect of
contemporary life. To this problem, I have no solution to offer,
but I have tried—if not always successfully—to write about it in
a balanced way.

The last few pieces in this book are about the art market. I
worked as an art dealer from 1963 to 1967, and the market has
long struck me as a species of theater. It can provide tingling
suspense, occasional comedy, remarkable characters, and the
constant prospect of a good surprise ending. It has been fun to
write about, and I hope that comes through.

Here then is a personal record of how museums, art, the law,
and the market have appeared to one witness—a changing person
in a changing time—over the span of a dozen years. If the "warts
and all" with which they come should happen to disfigure these
pieces beyond consideration as authoritative texts, I trust that
they can still stand scrutiny as credible evidence. Good order
suggests, in any case, that authority should withhold its judgment
until all of the evidence has first been presented.

Washington, D.C.
September 1982

MUSEUMS

The Multiple Crises
in Our Museums (1971)

While American museums may be largely exempt from taxes, they are in no way exempt from history. And the things we see happening in museums today—the three crises I want to talk to you about this morning—are as inseparable from the history of American institutions in this century as are the seemingly different problems that today afflict a General Motors or a Standard Oil.

I

Many years ago, Professor Adolph Berle of Columbia identified a process that would transform the American business corporation in the twentieth century. He saw the corporation as passing from the privately controlled, socially irresponsible, and voracious monster it had become by the end of the nineteenth century into a closely regulated source of production required to operate under careful public scrutiny and in the broadest public interest. Moreover, he saw this transformation as occurring with little outward change in the corporation's basic structure. Stockholders would continue as its ostensible owners, and directors and managers would retain their traditional functions.

We are in the midst of that transformation now. And it has occurred—just as Berle suggested—not through some convulsive

Copyright © 1971 by Stephen E. Weil. All rights reserved. This lecture was delivered as the keynote address at the Forty-eighth Annual Meeting of the Western Association of Art Museums (now the Art Museum Association) in Los Angeles, California, October 27, 1971. The author was then the administrator of the Whitney Museum of American Art, New York City.

change in the nature of our system but, rather, through step-by-step government regulation, by the growth in power of such countervailing forces as organized labor and—more recently—organized consumers, and by the ability of one or another disadvantaged group to arouse public concern and mobilize public pressure.

Seventy years ago, big business could do almost anything it wanted. Today, its operation is hedged by rules prescribing virtually every aspect of its conduct: whom it may employ, how its securities may be marketed, what safety standards must be met within its plant, and, sometimes, even what should be the quality of its product. And now [1971], for the third time in thirty years, wages and prices have been brought under public control.

I believe that a parallel transformation is occurring in nonprofit institutions, including our art museums. While American art museums have always been public in one sense—from their beginning they were open to the public and operated not for profit—in another sense most of them were profoundly private at their start: private in the sources of their funds, private in their control, and private even in the sense that their senior staff was drawn from a privileged social class.

Like business, museums are now in the midst of a transformation. By the end of this century, I think we will find that they have become public institutions in a far broader sense than they were seventy years ago. Is it imaginable, even now, that so great an institution as the Metropolitan Museum could remain closed on Sundays out of respect for the religious scruples of several of its trustees? And yet it did, until 1891, when—and I think this is significant—it was forced open by the New York City Council, which threatened to withdraw the then small subsidy it was giving the museum. Can you imagine the consequences if a major museum today decided to refuse admission to blacks or Jews or people with red hair on the grounds of its own private choice? In short order it would find its tax exemption gone, its state and federal subsidies withdrawn, its loan exhibitions boycotted by artists and other museums, its staff expelled from professional associations, and its building surrounded by pickets.

We are in the course of a transformation. It will not be a straight course. There will be wrong turns, false starts, and occasional halts. The shape our art museums will take is by no means clear, and many traditional relationships are going to be upset in the course of getting from one place to another. I want to talk about three specific crises that most museums face today—crises of money, power, and identity. All three, I think, have their roots in this ongoing transformation of the American museum from a quasi- to a broadly public institution—and all three, I think, must be met with understanding and some skill if we are to complete this transformation successfully, without losing something vital along the way.

II

Let's begin with the financial crisis.

In terms of operating funds, we are—for the most part—broke. That is a secret kept largely within the museum world. To much of the outside world, American museums with their magnificent holdings and palatial buildings are the very symbols of wealth and opulence. Militant groups demand that collections be sold off to provide funds for the contemporary artist; others would like to see this wealth used for other causes. That such a step would undermine one of our basic purposes is almost beside the point. The fact is that this wealth is largely illusory—there is just no market, other than museums, that could absorb our collections.

For all practical purposes, then, we are broke and must continue to be. An art museum simply cannot support itself through admissions, membership, and other activities. If it could, then surely one or more giant conglomerates would have museum subsidiaries by now, and it might be fun even to watch them being traded, merged, and publicly offered.

Unless a museum is endowed so well that it has no need for outside funds (and there are such museums: the Frick with its $40 million endowment, the Huntington Library, Winterthur, the Gardner, and some others), it *must* raise operating funds from some other source. Traditionally, of course, this source has been the trustees. But as the operating expenses of museums soar, and as other social causes make their legitimate and competing demands on the funds available for private philanthropy, trustees are simply no longer able to close the gap between expenditure and income. Just as we are a long way from the time when the

Metropolitan could be closed on Sunday, we have come a long way from the time when J. P. Morgan could look around a room and tell each of his fellow trustees at the Metropolitan what he was expected to contribute toward any proposed acquisition or prospective deficit.

This situation is not unique to museums. Similar changes have occurred across the whole spectrum of nonprofit organizations: symphony orchestras, hospitals, libraries, and universities.

Some of the reasons for these soaring expenses are common to all. And, quite appropriately, they find their roots in the very twentieth-century transformation that we first talked about. The greater public that uses museums today requires us to keep longer hours and hire larger staffs. Unionized blue-collar workers demand—and rightfully receive—wages equal to those paid by private industry on the grounds that they, of all people, should not be asked to subsidize nonprofit institutions. Professional employees—no longer drawn from an elite social class or blessed with independent incomes—expect, and are beginning to receive, salaries commensurate with their training and adequate to their needs. And public accountability, plus sheer institutional size, requires new levels of bookkeeping and internal accounting.

Other reasons for these soaring expenses are peculiar to art museums. The physical scale and weight of much contemporary art involves us in shipping, storage, and installation costs beyond anything known in the past. Demands from the public, and from inside our own staffs as well, for ever more vigorous programs of loan exhibitions drain our budgets. Soaring art values push the insurance cost of these loan exhibitions toward the prohibitive point. And finally—ironically—we have been the victims of technology. Rather than particularly increasing the productivity of museum workers, technology has worked backwards to increase the expense of museum operation: contemporary advances in temperature and humidity control, in lighting, and in conservation cannot be responsibly ignored.

And so we have these soaring expenses—caused not, I think, by extravagance or waste, but rather by the times we live in and the directions art has taken. And while trustees and private donors still meet, and will I hope continue meeting, a substantial part of these expenses, they simply cannot meet them all. Our first crisis, then, resolves itself into two questions: Who is going to pay the bills? And with what complications for us, as museum people?

For the moment, the major answers to the first question must be government—both federal and local—and business. The answers to the second question will become apparent as we go along.

I'd like to tell you something about our experiences with the New York State Council on the Arts. During the past two years, the New York legislature has appropriated some $31 million to the council, with roughly $9 million of this earmarked for the visual arts. In determining how that money was to be spent, the New York museums and the council have been engaged in a process of mutual education. We have taught the council some of the realities of museum life; the council, in turn, has taught us some of the harsh truths of public administration.

Initially, the council sought to use its museum funds to underwrite new programs. We tried to explain that this was like putting icing on a cake and that the real problem was that we didn't have enough dough to make a cake in the first place. A council-sponsored exhibition on the fourth floor of a museum wasn't going to mean much if there was no one to run an elevator up to that floor. Moreover, the very programs toward which the council gravitated were our most immediately attractive ones—those for which we were most likely to find funding from other sources. If council grants took a form that chased away other forms of support, then we would really wind up getting nothing. And further, by associating itself so directly with specific programs, the council would lay itself open to attack by those who disagreed with the content of those programs.

Lurking in everyone's mind, I think, was some fear that state support might soon be followed by state censorship. To date, that fear has proved unfounded. But I can remember a day last year when it was suggested by the president of the state museum association that we invite our state senator and assemblyman to see a current exhibition. I walked through the exhibition wondering if they would like what they saw and feeling that we had passed some historic moment if such a question even had to be asked.

I'm happy to say that we've succeeded in getting the New York State Council to understand the difficulties in their original approach and to come closer to our point of view. This year [1971] their basic grant to the Whitney, for example, has been specifically designated for building maintenance and security—the kinds of unexciting things that nobody else wants to pay for but that are the absolute prerequisites for any other programming. This seems by far the most productive way of channeling state funds into the museums.

Another issue that has caused difficulty is the existence of museum endowments. Museums compete with performing arts organizations for state funds. The great majority of performing arts groups have little or no endowment. Most of the New York museums, on the other hand, have endowments ranging from modest to substantial. Some spokesmen for performing arts have urged that the council grant no funds to museums until their resources and board-restricted endowments (if not their endowments themselves) have first been consumed by deficits. While the council has not adopted this view, the issue still emerges from time to time. We are trying to make it clear that art museums—if they are to continue to attract acquisitions—must be seen as different from performing arts groups in their need to guarantee continuity. No one is going to entrust a valuable work of art to a museum without some certainty that the museum will somehow go on from year to year, despite temporary disfavor with the public or among politicians.

Another question has arisen about smaller amounts allocated by the council for dance, music, poetry, and film programs in museums. Should these be charged against the visual arts programs, simply because they take place in museums, or should they be charged against their respective fields? Again, I'm happy to be able to say that the council has, for the moment, taken the second view—that its support of the primary functions of museums should not be diminished as museum programming extends to other art forms.

I do not want to touch too long on municipal funding. I suspect that you in the West have had more experience with this than we in New York and are far more familiar with whatever problems it may raise. But one point should be mentioned. For many years in New York there has been a pattern under which the land and buildings of one after another cultural organization have passed into public ownership, with the original organization—either by lease or otherwise—remaining to operate its privately determined program in a publicly owned, and often publicly maintained, building. This has happened to most of the components of Lincoln Center, it happened more recently with Joseph Papp's Public Theater, and it is being explored seriously by many other organizations. Such arrangements guarantee the community the continued presence of a cultural facility while unlocking the otherwise frozen funds of such an institution to permit its continued operation. At the Whitney, for example, we have $6 million invested in land and building. If we could somehow free this, and add it to our endowment, the integrity of both our collection and overall program would be assured for many years to come.

What help can we expect from the federal government in meeting our financial needs? Here we must look at two different things— tax policy and direct federal funding.

Of these, I think tax policy is still the more important. Federal grants will have to increase manyfold before they can begin to match the benefits that museums enjoy both through their tax exemption and as the recipients of tax-deductible contributions. Nowhere is the historical shift we looked at earlier more clear. For the museum in transition toward being truly public, the Tax Reform Act of 1969 raised the portion of income that might be deductibly contributed from 30 percent to 50 percent. For the museum that retained its private status, the deduction remained frozen at 20 percent. More important, for the first time such museums became subject to federal income tax—a tax of 4 percent on their net investment income. It will be only a matter of time until state taxes follow in the wake of this federal tax. I understand that this is already under consideration in California.

Tax policy is, beyond question, being used to push American museums toward being public in an expanded sense. The regulations proposed under the new tax act deal with such matters as the composition of the board, the inclusion of a fund raising officer on staff, and the zeal with which the museum seeks outside funds.

The dark side, of course, has been the choking off of the deductible contribution of art works by artists and dealers and the cloud cast over contributions that may not be for the "exempt purposes" of the museum. Hopefully, Senator Frank Church's proposed amendment to the Internal Revenue Code will cure this in part. But meanwhile, as a footnote, we have that delicious gold-lettered sign over the collection box in the lobby of the Frick: "To help maintain the standards and support the educational activities of the Frick Collection, contributions in any amount are welcome." Not because the Frick needs the money—it doesn't— but because it might help to show that the Frick, one of the most private of museums, is really public after all. What would help a great deal more would be removal of a nearby sign reserving the Frick's right to refuse admission to anyone whose style of dress does not meet the standards set by its trustees.

As for direct federal funding, the amounts thus far available through the National Endowment and under the National Museum Act are only beginning to be significant enough to make a real impact on the finances of our museums. But there is every reason to hope that these funds will increase over the next few years. Certainly, if the Museum Services Act, introduced this past June by Congressman John Brademas of Indiana and now pending before the Subcommittee on Education, is passed, federal funding will become very important—and especially important if, as may be the case, it can be used for building repairs, capital expansion, and acquisitions for which state funds are generally not available.

Business support for museums is in its infancy. It should be remembered that it was only relatively recently that corporations *could* contribute directly to the arts. The Internal Revenue Code was amended in 1936 to allow corporations a charitable deduction, and questions about the legal power of corporations to make charitable gifts have had to be sorted out state by state. While virtually every state has legislation today that permits this, questions as to corporate power to make gifts were being litigated as recently as the 1950s. Nationally chartered banks have had the power to make gifts only since 1939.

It is unrealistic to expect corporate philanthropy ever to be pure in the Maimonidean ideal of an anonymous donor. Corporate giving at any substantial level will always be geared to programs of high visibility. This is one of the reasons it is so important to steer state and federal support into less glamorous channels.

Corporate support can, of course, take many forms: corporate memberships, the underwriting of exhibitions, and gifts of technical assistance, expertise, and material. Another form of corporate support with which we have experimented successfully is a plan that the Whitney originally worked out with the Geigy

Chemical Company. In return for an annual payment based on the number and location of its employees, Geigy's employees can use their corporate identification cards to gain free admission to the museum for themselves and their families. Geigy regards the plan as one aimed at benefiting employees, rather than the museum. Questions of corporate donation do not even arise since the plan is treated as a fringe benefit for employees rather than as a contribution to the museum. We have since extended this program to several other corporations, and, together with the New York State Council and a group of other museums, we are exploring how it might be broadened further still.

During the past few years, the Business Committee for the Arts has emerged as a potentially powerful intermediary between the art and corporate communities. Recently, it launched an advertising campaign aimed at raising public consciousness of the need for financial support of arts organizations.

Buried in the Business Committee's approach, however, is the dangerous notion that greater popularity might perhaps be the key to obtaining greater business and government support. In a statement issued in connection with its current advertising campaign, the committee says:

> Businessmen and local, state and Federal governments are showing an increased awareness of the importance of the arts to the individual and society. The likelihood and level of their efforts to provide financial support of artists and arts organizations will depend in large measure on increasing evidence of public interest.

I think this misses the point entirely. If a million people a month would pay three dollars to see, for example, a Matisse exhibition, we would not need financial support. And if we deliberately set out to find out what a million people a month *would* pay three dollars to see, then we would not be museums anymore—we would be Disneyland. Performance in the arts must be measured by the quality of the product, not by the size of the market.

Should a museum make moral distinctions about the kinds of corporations from which it will accept support? And, if so, whose morality is to be used as the yardstick? I think this may prove to be an area of considerable disagreement among (and even between) trustees and staff in years to come.

III

The second crisis is over power.

The transformation we are undergoing brings with it a certain turmoil. Traditional relationships are called into question. Within the museum, the long-standing and unfettered power of trustees to determine policy is under challenge by the staff. Outside the museum, artists, special interest groups, and the general community question the right of the museum—of both trustees and staff—to operate in customary ways.

Let's look first inside the museum. Legally, of course, the ultimate responsibility for making policy belongs to the trustees. In some museums, this is tightly held; in others—and the Whitney is one—many decisions, at least on exhibitions and acquisitions, have been largely delegated to the staff. The range—to adopt a phrase from Calvin Tomkins—is from trustees who run museums to trustees who see to it that they *are* run.

This structure was directly and dramatically challenged during the ten-day strike at the Museum of Modern Art this past August [1971]. The newly certified Professional and Administrative Staff Association of the Modern demanded not only improvements in salary and job security—demands that might be expected of any union—but a role in the Modern's policy-making process as well.

And, to see the extent to which our various crises are intertwined, it should be noted that this issue arose at just that time when the Modern's operating deficits, soaring far beyond anything the trustees could meet, had resulted in a sharp cutback in its exhibition program.

In the end the staff association won what would seem a hollow victory. They will be advised in advance of policy issues on the trustees' agenda and, with the consent of the director, will have the right to present their views to the trustees or trustee committees—something presumably they could always have done if everyone agreed they could do it. But the very fact that this concept is now embedded in a collective bargaining agreement must be seen as altering the situation. The precedent has been established that this is a negotiable issue, and future agreements may well see this provision take a stronger form.

In the next few years we may possibly see the rapid growth of collective bargaining among museum professionals, with questions of museum policy included as one of the issues of such bargaining. The *New York Times* recently reported organizing activity among professional employees at the Metropolitan Museum, the Corcoran Gallery, and the Minneapolis Institute of Art. And those of you who were at the recent [1971] American Association of Museums (AAM) meeting in Denver may remember hearing about some of the organizing activities now going on in the history museums.

Again, we are dealing here with a historic shift—not simply a problem unique to museums. An article in *Harper's Magazine* for October [1971] reports the existence of collective bargaining agreements covering the faculty of some 170 American colleges and universities—agreements that in many cases touch on substantive educational questions. Further afield are the recent instances of members of the Cleveland Orchestra voting their preference for a successor to their late conductor, George Szell (their vote was ignored), and of Boston University, where a new president was, for all practical purposes, chosen by a joint student-faculty-trustee committee. Certainly, I think, we are coming into a time when concerned employees within cultural institutions will demand as a matter of right—and not merely as one of grace— to participate in making those policy decisions that vitally affect their institutions. And whereas trustees may once have been able to resist such demands on the grounds that they, the trustees, were paying the bills and ought therefore to make final decisions, contemporary history is eroding that defense.

Moreover, museum staffs may no longer hesitate to seek other legal remedies for their grievances. Within the past week [October 1971], the *New York Times* reported the settlement of a complaint filed with New York State's attorney general by some eighty employees of the Metropolitan Museum alleging discrimination against women in hiring, promotion, and salaries. One of the features of that settlement is the establishment of a forum within the museum to hear and discuss charges of sexual discrimination. The attorney general's office will retain jurisdiction to assure that the terms of this settlement are being complied with.

There are, I think, two other areas in which we can discern a shift in the role of the museum staff. One of these is its relation to fund raising. In my experience, dealings with the state councils and the National Endowment have been handled almost entirely at the staff level—and to some extent this is true of corporate support as well. Certainly, the relative position of the staff vis-à-vis the trustees becomes immeasurably stronger when it—the staff—is the chief point of contact with substantial outside funders.

The other area where we can see a change is in what I would call ecumenicism, the growing interest among museum staffs in attempting to solve common problems on a cooperative basis. We are, for example, exploring a project with the New York State Council under which a group of art museums would share warehouse and trucking facilities, establish a joint purchasing office, exchange equipment, and otherwise work together. In the San Francisco Bay Area, a similar cooperative project would establish a series of specialized restoration laboratories available for the use of all the participating museums. The Museum Computer Network, now in its fifth year, hopes to standardize the registration procedures of its member museums so that a uniform system of machine retrieval will ultimately be possible. And the Museum Stores Association may well become a vehicle for purchasing printing and other sales desk material on a cooperative basis.

Perhaps we may soon see a time when the museums of a metropolitan area can collaborate in acquisition, exhibition, and other programs to form an effective regional museum system. The spirit behind projects such as these stands, I think, in sharp contrast to that of an earlier time when each museum was the jealously guarded preserve of its own founders or trustees.

This forming of ranks among museum staffs extends right up to the directorial level. While the Association of Art Museum Directors does not in itself function as a union, there runs through the minutes of its recent meetings some suggestions of rules about the rights of directors in the face of arbitrary trustee action. And this can go past mere suggestion, as in the association's censure of the Everson Museum of Art of Syracuse, New York, for its peremptory discharge of Max Sullivan this past year.

Meanwhile, other groups outside the museum question the authority of both trustees and staff. Recent dealings between museums and artists—both individually and collectively—in New York are extraordinarily interesting in this respect.

Some artists have, for example, claimed the right to retain control over their work even after it has been purchased by or given to a museum. At one level—that of reproduction rights—this is not particularly troublesome. Since 1965, New York law has given the artist a retained right over reproduction of his work in commercially exploitable forms. This was in accord with policies that already existed in many museums.

More troublesome, though, is the artist's claim to retain rights over how and when the museum displays work that it owns. This kind of demand first came to wide attention several years ago when the sculptor Takis, together with several of his friends, kidnapped one of his works owned by the Modern from an exhibition there. He explained that he disagreed with the thesis of the exhibition insofar as it applied to him and had, accordingly, elected not to have his work shown.

There is currently circulating a proposed agreement, drafted under the auspices of a New York art dealer, Seth Seigelaub, called the Artists Reserved Right Sales Agreement. One of the clauses suggested in this agreement would permit an artist or his heirs to veto any public display—by a museum or otherwise—of a painting or sculpture sold subject to its terms. While this veto right is, supposedly, not to be exercised unreasonably, the spread of this type of restriction could virtually paralyze museums in dealing with the contemporary part of their permament collections.

Involvement by artists in museums policy gives rise to another set of problems in the case of retrospectives. It is general practice today to seek the consent of an artist and his dealer when giving a retrospective; the consequence is that all too often the retrospective takes the form of a success story rather than the cool and professional appraisal it started out to be. Recent work, in which the artist is still engaged and that the dealer has for sale, will emerge as the triumphant climax of the show—with the rest as preliminary. The curator's real evaluation of the work may well be buried in the compromises necessary to get everyone's cooperation. And in the most extreme cases, the museum may not even be able to make its own assignment of a curator or to install the exhibition itself. Where the museum should be taking a responsible and critical stance, it has been perverted into a super art gallery.

The most recent and extreme clash we've had in New York between an individual artist and a museum was in the case of the Hans Haacke exhibition that did not take place at the Guggenheim last April. While the issues and personalities involved were somewhat complex, the problem in the end centered on the artist's insistence that he had the right to show two works that neither the museum's director nor its trustees wanted to show. After the exhibition was canceled, some five weeks before its scheduled opening, much of the New York art world interpreted the underlying issue as one of censorship. The artist, it was said, had been unjustly deprived by the museum of his right to speak freely about certain political and social issues. Lost almost completely from sight in the general hubbub was another question: the legitimacy of the museum's claim that it—and not the artist—must ultimately determine what it shows.

Conflicts between museums and artists as a group can range far beyond aesthetic questions. This was the case in May of last year [1970] at the time of the Cambodian incursion and the Kent State killings. Angered by their inability to be heard in any national forum, artists in New York turned in frustration against the museums, virtually all of which were forced to close for at least one day. The Robert Morris exhibition at the Whitney was closed permanently; an exhibition at the Jewish Museum was shut for two weeks, which may have helped to push that museum out of contemporary art altogether. At a mass meeting at New York University, artists called for museum staffs to join them in an alliance against trustees or to remove the trustees and install the artists instead. Museums were advised that a correct political stance— not by trustees or staff members individually but by the museum acting as a corporate whole—would be required of them as the price of further cooperation from artists. An attempt was made to impose a private tax on all art transactions, and a so-called emergency cultural government began to fire off demands of one sort or another. Ultimately, this entire squabble spilled onto the floor of the annual meeting of the AAM held in New York several weeks later, to the consternation, I think, of those who had not watched it develop.

Happily, much of this ill will has subsided, and, for the moment at least, generally cordial relations have been re-established in New York between the museums and the art community. Meanwhile, however, other groups of artists with special interests or special problems continue to hammer at the museums, demanding a voice in policy making. When the Whitney, partially in response to discussions initiated by one of these groups, staged an exhibition of painting and sculpture by black artists this past spring, it found itself caught among various factions, one of which thought the exhibition should not be given at all, another of which thought the exhibition should be postponed until a black curator was put in charge, and a third of which wanted the exhibition to proceed as scheduled. In the end, a boycott organized by the second group was partially successful, and a number of artists withdrew just prior to the exhibition's opening. Earlier pressures from other groups succeeded in forcing the Metropolitan to withdraw the catalog of its exhibition *Harlem on my Mind*. Currently [October 1971], as the result of the tragedy at Attica Prison, a group of artists is demanding the removal of Governor Nelson Rockefeller from the board of the Museum of Modern Art.

An exhibition such as the Whitney Annual can become the occasion for widespread protest. In 1970 a group of militant women artists launched a campaign demanding that 50 percent of the sculptors represented in the annual be women. They were quickly joined by a militant black group demanding that half of those women be black, and that half the men represented in the show be black as well. Picket lines were followed by a campaign of harassment against the museum. Forged press releases were distributed; forged invitations were sent out for the opening; and, in the end, there was a near riot. Within the museum, trustees and staff dug in to take a strong position that aesthetic, and not social, standards would be used in selecting the exhibition and that the museum staff, and it alone, would do this without quotas of any kind.

But outside pressures do not come merely from the art world. From the community at large come demands that the larger museums disperse parts of their collection into decentralized neighborhood museums, that greater emphasis be given to training minority group members, and that special provision be made for the handicapped and the elderly. Some of these demands seem legitimate; others farfetched.

Most farfetched, to me, are the demands of those such as Barry Schwartz—writing in the June 1971 issue of *Ramparts*—that art museums must become whatever the community wants them to be, including (presumably) nonmuseums. Leaving aside the question of what community a museum serves—is it that contained in a twenty-mile-wide circle with the museum at its center, or a national community, or even one that lives in the past or future instead of the present?—this is ultimately a suggestion that art museums commit suicide in the name of the public interest. Here we come to an elitist sticking point. We may simply have a better idea of the value of what we are doing than the community at large or those who claim to speak in its name.

IV

Which leads us directly to our third crisis—an identity crisis.

Caught up in historical change, dependent on new sources of support, and torn by conflicting pressures from both within and without the profession—toward what shapes are museums being pulled and pushed?

It is not as if the art museum had entered this period of change with a monolithic purpose. From the start, its roles have been diverse.

When the Louvre was opened in 1793, the general public was admitted on only three days out of each ten: five were reserved for artists, and two for cleaning. Several years before, when the collection of the Belvedere in Vienna was rehung on historical principles, with paintings grouped in schools and chronologically within schools, the installation was denounced as pedantic. Museums, said its critics, should be for delight and entertainment, not instruction. In America, where no great hoards of royal treasure could serve as their base, museums were spoken of from the beginning as educational or uplifting in nature. As one speaker said at the dedication of the Metropolitan a century ago, its purpose was to "humanize, to educate and to refine a practical and laborious people." And yet, as we have seen, it was twenty years before the Metropolitan opened its doors on Sundays, the only day on which that "practical and laborious people" was not at work and could visit the museum.

At the most recent AAM convention some of these diverse strands polarized about the reiterated insistence that museums must become "people-oriented" rather than "object-oriented." Clearly, they have long been—and will continue to be—both. But, before coming to our own role in this, let us see what sorts of identities would be emphasized by the other factors in our changing situation.

Section 7 of Congressman Brademas's Museum Services Act defines a museum as follows:

> For the purposes of this Act, the term "museum" means a public or private nonprofit agency or institution organized on a permanent basis for essentially educational or aesthetic purposes, which, utilizing a professional staff, owns and utilizes tangible objects, cares for them and exhibits them to the public on a regular basis.

As you will recognize, this language is drawn from the accreditation standards of the AAM. A similar standard is used by the National Endowment. The preservation and exhibition of objects are certainly the most traditional of art museum functions. Any museum hoping to share in the $40 million initial appropriation under the Museum Services Act is going to make damn sure that they continue to be.

Contrast this with our experiences with the state art councils. I can think of no program less likely to obtain state council support for a museum than the care of its collection, cataloging, or scholarly research. And acquisitions—for which provision is made by the National Endowment—are completely outside the scope of state funds, at least in New York. What our state council is interested in is how broadly the public is being served. The numbers they want to see concern attendance and service to other organizations within the state. Allon Schoener, chief of the Visual Arts Section of the New York State Council, explains it this way:

> The kinds of questions that are going to be asked of museums are the kinds of questions that are asked of us, The New York State Arts Council, by budget examiners in Albany. . . . Who is being served by the money spent? How many people are going to expect something as a result of this money? Where is this money going to be spent? These questions really have not been placed before museum people in the past, because their financial support has come from a restricted audience that was able to maintain it.

While I think there are sound political reasons for these divergent federal and state approaches, there may be a psychological reason as well. To some extent, I think we would like to see the federal funds that will come to museums diverted from defense spending, supersonic transports, or, possibly, superfluous highways. There is a sense, on the other hand, that state funds are being diverted from already impoverished social welfare programs and that, in going toward cultural activities, they should still retain some flavor of social service.

Meanwhile, other pressures push the museum toward a more "educational" stance. For many years, "education" has been a key word in obtaining both foundation grants and odd scraps of federal money. In 1931, only 15 percent of American museums had formally designated education departments. Today that figure is well over 80 percent.

The Internal Revenue Code has also played a role in tagging museums with an educational label. Section 501(c)(3)—the basis on which our tax exemption rests—offers only seven possible purposes that an organization can pursue in order to qualify as exempt: religious, charitable, scientific, public safety, literary, prevention of cruelty to children or animals, and education. In our dealings with the Internal Revenue Service, it is—naturally— our educational face that we put forward. Interestingly, in the recent negotiations between the Museum of Modern Art and its staff association, the analogy between museum and university appeared several times in the union's demands: in its successful demand for sabbaticals for professional personnel, and in its unsuccessful demand for a salary scale based on that prevailing in the City Univesity of New York, with full curators equated with full professors, associate curators with associate professors, and so on.

What shape would artists like to see the museum assume? In the nineteenth century, the artist's major contact with the museum was in his own training. The Louvre was at that time, as Germain Bazin calls it, "the great laboratory where modern art was developed."

Today's artist-in-training, as often as not, learns the art of the past through slides and color reproductions. The museum, for him, has other purposes: it can be a showcase for new work— especially works such as earth works, conceptual works, and process art that may not be suitable for a commercial gallery. But more importantly, he views the museum in its role as discoverer and connoisseur, an institution that can stamp its imprimatur on his work and short-cut his way to fame and even, possibly, fortune. [This theme is treated at somewhat greater length in "An Inventory of Art Museum Roles," pp. 30–55.] Several years ago Lawrence Alloway pointed out that museums and art galleries had largely switched roles in this regard. The galleries, he said, now dealt with the safe and established while it was the museums that went hunting for undiscovered talent.

The pressures to emphasize the museum's role as discoverer and connoisseur do not come from the artists alone. There are also donors to the museum seeking guidance or confirmation about what is new and what is good, as well as pressures from our curatorial staffs. Harold Rosenberg has pointed out the phenomenon of the curator who views the museum not merely as the recorder or repository of art history but also as its author. There is no great harm in this except when we fail to tell the general public we ostensibly serve that we genuinely think that some of what we show are masterpieces we hold in trust for them—and that other things are, for the moment, simply things we find interesting, with the question of masterpiece to remain open for a long time.

And finally, among the forces contending to determine our identity are those who think that art museums should not be art museums at all, that they are relics of an outworn past, and that the funds and energy necessary to maintain them could better be applied to other ends.

V

So, there you have them—three crises that spring out of this time of transition in which we find ourselves. We are, along with other institutions of every kind, caught up in history and for the most part have little choice but to bump along with it as best we can.

The financial crisis will be with us for a long time. Even if government or a good fairy turned up tomorrow to meet all our current operating expenses, I know of hardly a single museum that could not—with perfect legitimacy—immediately add another 25 or 50 percent a year to what it is spending now: money for maintaining its collection, for acquisitions, for better security, for longer hours, and for staff salaries.

As for the struggle to control museums, this too will go on for a long time. Trustees, staff, artists, and the community will all clamor for a role in making policy. In the end they may all share that power together.

But what we, as museum people, can do something about—a great deal about—is determining, with greater clarity than we have in the past, what it is that *we* want art museums to be. We are on our way toward becoming more truly public institutions. Hopefully, there will come a time when our finances are stabilized and the struggle for power will have been resolved. Having passed through this difficult time, with what identity do we want to arrive at the other side? From the many uses the community has and will want to make of museums, what purposes do we want to disentangle and identify as our own?

There is, of course, no single answer. Art museums have throughout their history embraced a multiplicity of purposes. And the situation of each museum will be different. University museums may choose a different emphasis than municipal museums. Some of our museums are in communities where the job of dealing with contemporary art is adequately handled by local galleries and dealers. Others are not and must do more of this themselves. Some can work together with other local institutions to permit a degree of specialization in exhibitions and collections. Others will have to cover a broader range by themselves.

But one thing must, I think, be common to all our answers. It is a simple thing—but often lost sight of in the midst of all our other problems. And that is a basic, irreducible commitment to the importance and vitality of works of art, to the excitement of their creation, and to the experience of seeing them. That is the heart of what we are about: not museums as vehicles for immediate social or political change, not museums as sponges to absorb the public's newfound leisure, not museums to cosmeticize our society's failures—but museums as places where there is a stubborn insistence on the importance of the visual arts as a human activity; places where we preserve as best we can the creativity of the past and encourage as best we can the extension of that creativity into the future; places in short, where we celebrate the discoveries, delights, and deep awareness that can come uniquely through the visual.

There will be times when this will seem a monastic vocation. This may be such a time. Substantial and responsible elements in the community feel that our buildings would be better used for day-care centers, that the wealth locked into our collections could better be applied to job training, and that the enormous energy required to run our museums would better be directed toward issues of peace and social equality.

Let's have day-care centers, job training, and, above all, peace and social equality. As a country, we can afford them. And let's also have art centers where people can learn the satisfaction of creative work, and neighborhood museums under neighborhood control where problems of immediate relevance can be dealt with. Let's create open situations in which every artist can show his work. Without diluting our own purposes, we can help to create these other institutions. But not at the expense of our art museums and not at the expense of our commitment to the importance of art. If the great world around us does not share that commitment, then we must insure that our museums survive until some new renaissance when it does—and we must proselytize as well, to speed that renaissance on its way.

Our job, then, is to bring the art museum through this time of flux without losing our balance. The trick—no easy one—will be to find ways to make the museum both responsive to the various constituencies that it serves and, at the same time, authoritarian—even autocratic—in its approach to art. If we can avoid being apologetic, if we can project some clear vision of why we think there ought to be art museums and what they ought to be—then we, as museum people, can play a major role in determining the identity they will finally assume. Financial problems will remain; the power struggle will go on. But, at the very least, we will have established a position for ourselves—a position that, if pursued with sufficient conviction, may in the end prevail. Good luck to us all.

Afterword

Reading this again some dozen years later, it seems all too clear that I was no more exempt from the millenarian passions of 1971 than museums are exempt from history. The *Zeit* had more of a *Geist* than I then suspected, but maybe every *Zeit* does.

The millennium, in fact, did not arrive. There were repeated efforts—by Senator Church and others—to restore to artists their pre-1970 fair-market-value charitable deduction for gifts to museums, but none of these succeeded. They continue, nonetheless, and not without hope. The Museum Services Act (establishing the Institute of Museum Services) *was* ultimately adopted, but not until 1976. The annual appropriation to the institute, though, has never exceeded $12.2 million, far less than the $40 million (the equivalent today of nearly $100 million) we so confidently, if innocently, expected. Ecumenicism *has* made progress—consider, for example, the movement toward shared collections (see "Custody Without Title," pp. 151–59) or such innovations as the intrastate art transport service provided to museums by the Gallery Association of New York State—but at nowhere near the pace that then seemed possible. And the art reference library of the Frick still maintains a dress code—coats and ties for the gentlemen and skirts for the ladies.

If there was no millennium, though, neither was there a cataclysm. No broad movement toward state taxation of net investment income ever developed, and the federal tax—applicable in any case to only a small group of privately controlled museums—was ultimately cut back from 4 percent to 2 percent. The argument that endowed institutions such as museums ought to get a lesser share of public funding never took hold. On the contrary, the *encouragement* of endowment building—for museums as well as other cultural organizations—became an official part of federal arts policy in 1976, when the Congress authorized the Arts and Humanities Endowments to establish their respective challenge-grant programs. Nor did museums become engulfed in arguments over the morality of support from particular corporate sources. The question, if anything, was scarcely addressed.

What, then, of our three crises? To a great extent, the latter two—those of power and identity—would seem for the moment to have abated if not been entirely resolved. The sense that trustees (or, for that matter, staff) ought not to exercise unfettered control over collections and other resources held in public trust is no less strong today than it was in 1971. The intervening years, though, saw a remarkable development: the growth and increasing substitution of legal rather than political constraints over what may previously have been perceived as an arbitrary power. (This is discussed at length in "Breaches of Trust, Remedies, and Standards in the American Private Art Museum," pp. 160–88.) While this development has not been particular to museums—it has occurred across the entire nonprofit sector—its application to museums has been immeasurably aided by the role of museum professional organizations in promulgating and disseminating standards of conduct for trustees and staff alike.

While contemporary artists may still launch periodic assaults aimed at changing the exhibition or collecting policies of one or another local institution—the Corcoran Gallery in Washington was under such an attack as recently as 1982—the relationship between museums and artists in general seems far less contentious than it was in 1971. One contributing factor may have been the extraordinary growth in the number of so-called alternative spaces—often artist-controlled—that offer broadly expanded opportunities for emerging painters, sculptors, and others to have their work shown outside the traditional museum and commercial gallery systems. Encouraged by public funding (and often assisted by the museums themselves), such "alternative spaces" have also given artists a greater scope for the kinds of immediate political and social expression that are so difficult to accommodate within the more complex organizational structures of most museums.

The unionization of museum staffs has continued, but only slowly. The focus of union demands, however, has shifted largely from policy to economic issues, and I know of no instance in which, as a result of such demands, a museum board has surrendered any of its traditional management prerogatives. Clearer now, though, than it was in 1971 is that the National Labor Relations Board (NLRB) will consider a museum (or one, at least, with gross annual revenues of more than $1 million) to fall just as squarely within the framework of federal labor law as it would any other industrial or commercial employer of comparable size.

Nothing could better symbolize the tenacity of the NLRB in retaining this jurisdiction than the 1975 case of the Frick Art Museum in Pittsburgh, a modest institution whose shop was described as offering for sale "three postcards, two art booklets and a color photograph [sic] of the Madonna and Child" and for 1973 reported a total of $368.85 in sales. The NLRB nonetheless held that the operation of the museum—because of its large endowment income, much of which was dispensed to other charitable organizations—had a "significant impact on interstate commerce" and that the museum itself fell squarely under the National Labor

Relations Act. In 1981, the Field Museum of Natural History in Chicago—faced with several (ultimately unsuccessful) union organizing drives—argued (as had others previously) that museums were not the type of employer that the Congress had envisioned in adopting this act. The argument failed again, and the issue seems closed.

Concerning the identity of their institutions, the past decade has been one filled with consciousness-raising for those who work in American museums. For a number of reasons—among them, to prepare "case statements" for prospective donors, to formulate long-term financial plans for submission to various federal funding sources, and to establish collections management policies for their own internal use—they have been required as never before to examine and articulate the goals of their organizations. Coupled with this has been the spreading use of zero-based and similar budget devices that have required ordering priorities among these goals. The results have been salutary. In marked contrast to a period when they may have shared the doubts of their critics that museums any longer served a useful purpose, American museum professionals today have a keener sense than ever of the goals, objectives, and values of their institutions. Correspondingly, they are also more keenly aware than anyone else of how distant their institutions still remain from ideal.

This heightened awareness has been reinforced by an explosive growth in professional training. Undergraduate and graduate level programs intended to prepare students for museum careers proliferated throughout the seventies. Specialized midcareer training, virtually unknown to the field in 1971, was offered through a number of organizations. Most notable among these were the Art Museum Association (formerly the Western Association of Art Museums), which in conjunction with the University of California established the Museum Management Institute in Berkeley, and the Museums Collaborative, which set up a series of courses at Arden House and other locations in cooperation with Columbia University. Concurrently there has been substantial expansion of both general museum literature and publications that address such specialized topics as registration, accounting, museum-related law, trusteeship, personnel policy, and conservation. Through their publishing programs, the AAM and American Association for State and Local History have both contributed enormously to the further professionalization of museums and their staffs. With this professionalization, many of the doubts in which the crisis of identity was initially rooted would seem to have dissolved.

Which leaves us with the last of our three crises—money. Simply to consider the enormous capital expansion that is currently planned for American museums might suggest that this crisis too has been resolved. Across the country, major additions (and even whole new museums) are being built or planned in New York, Washington, Richmond, Atlanta, Dallas, Los Angeles, and a host of smaller communities. Ironically, though, the capital funds needed to build such projects have generally proven easier to raise than the additional operating funds they will later require. Indeed, annual operating funds were just what we suddenly found in such short supply in 1971.

And that crisis (if it ever went away) is with us again. Museums still, and for the foreseeable future will, lack the operating funds they require for the proper discharge of their public obligations. The question today is the same as then: with the annual operating expenses of American museums now in excess of $1 billion, and with no possibility that any combination of current endowment income, earned income, and trustee contributions can nearly cover this cost, who is going to pay the bills?

The answer offered then was "government . . . and business," and for much of the seventies, it seemed like a good answer. At every level of government, and particularly the federal, there was a steady escalation in the nominal funds made available to museums. Moreover, both the federal government (through the Institute of Museum Services) and New York, the state with the largest appropriation for the arts, had by the mid-seventies specified that a portion of their support be directed toward basic operating expenses—the critical need of museums—rather than programmatic add-ons. Corporate support, meanwhile, showed a steady growth both in the share of corporate charity directed toward cultural institutions (and museums particularly) and in the sophistication with which funds were distributed. While overall corporate giving remained at a relatively fixed percentage of corporate profits, profits at least were growing and corporate giving with them.

Nonetheless, there were difficulties. Wholly unanticipated was the savage inflation of the seventies. As government and corporate support increased, expenses by the end of the decade increased even faster. Weak financial markets pushed the ratio of museum endowments to annual operating budgets down to lower and lower levels. Individual giving, still the largest single source of contributed income, showed signs of long-term weakness. Meanwhile, the possibility that massively increased government support might be needed raised new fears of government control. (See the review of *The Endangered Sector,* pp. 97–100.)

In the early eighties it became clear that "government . . . and business" might not be the answer after all, or might only be a partial answer at best. The steady escalation in federal funds available to museums began first to stall and then threatened to move in reverse. Among the other things from which museums turned out not to be exempt was a national budget crunch. Meanwhile, the corporate sector—much of it caught in a cyclic downturn of its own—made clear that it could not both sustain its own past level of giving *and* fill the gap caused by receding public funds. Museums, it seemed—to the extent they could not get by on internally generated income—would have to look more heavily than ever to individual donors.

Here, though, museums face a situation very different from that of 1971. Tumultuous as that time may have been, one of its few certainties was the perpetuity of a sharply progressive federal income tax system that offered substantial incentives for charitable giving. Such certainty no longer exists. Out of widespread discontent with the present system of taxation, ideas that once seemed only "fringe"—that some or all of the present income tax might be replaced by a value added tax, or that a "flat" tax with few or no deductions might be substituted for the current progressive tax—are now working their way toward the center.

Much of what we suppose about the relationship of tax policy to charitable giving is good-faith guesswork. Some suppose that people who have more after-tax dollars will be more generous than ever, and others suppose that the more a charitable gift might cost in real out-of-pocket dollars the less likely it is that someone will make such a gift. Thus, we can only guess at what the impact of one or another of these proposed changes might be. Museums, though, must be ready for the worst case. They have no alternative but to think through (and not simply guess) how they will support themselves if a radically changed system of taxation should drastically reduce their success in soliciting individual contributions. Even within the present system, it is still unclear what changes in charitable giving may be anticipated as the rate reductions (and, ultimately, indexing) provided by the Economic Recovery Tax Act of 1981 fall into place over the next few years.

Certainly, to the degree that the future may not look like the past and that individual contributions may not be available as a fallback, new funding strategies will be necessary. The options, though, are limited. Basically they must involve some combination of earned income, endowment income, and cost control. These seem to me the areas in which prudent museum managers must concentrate their efforts in the coming years. With issues of power and identity no longer so pressing, the critical question that remains is how American museums might move toward a financial independence that would reduce their need to rely on government and/or business and/or individual donors to meet their basic operating expenses. Their future may well depend on how well they can answer that question.

An Inventory of
Art Museum Roles
(1972)

The Museum and the
Object-ness of Art

Art museums have come under increasing attack during the past few years. They have, it is said, become irrelevant. They are dusty storehouses of the past, musty relics of an outworn elitism concerned with objects and not with people.

Let's accept that for a moment. Let's clear the paintings and other objects out of our museums. Let's use the buildings for creative people-centered programs. Let's provide day-care centers, draft counseling, and the latest in multimedia equipment.

Now, what are we to do with the paintings? Even the harshest critics of art museums would, I think, agree to a few basic things. The paintings should be stored, and stored in a safe place where they can be properly protected. There should be an appropriate staff, trained to take care of them. There should be restoration facilities available in case of deterioration or damage. There should be some means by which those who still wish to see them may do so. And, possibly, there might even be some amenities—perhaps a library, a smoking lounge, or a coffee shop—for their convenience.

You might, if you wish, call this newly established facility a Public Access Central Art Repository. But it sure as hell looks, smells, and sounds like an art museum.

The art museum is, first and foremost, a consequence of the

Copyright © 1972 by Stephen E. Weil. All rights reserved. This lecture was originally given at Cooper Union, in New York City, in February 1972. The author was then the administrator of the Whitney Museum of American Art, New York City.

"object-ness" of art. Its principal features are derived from this object-ness, and, given general agreement that the visual arts are an important part of our common heritage, then the emergence of the museum over the past two hundred years must be seen as almost inevitable.

We neither have nor need comparable institutions for music or literature or theater. Original manuscripts may be of use to scholars and valuable as memorabilia, but the continued existence or nonexistence of a handwritten script for *Hamlet* is not essential to the public availability of *Hamlet. Hamlet* is fully embodied in its infinitely reproducible printed form, not in any object.

This is not true of a painting. In a painting there is an absolute coincidence of intellectual concept and material manifestation. Reproductions and slides are only shadows of the original; they do not bear the same relation to a painting that a printed book does to its manuscript. To remain fully part of our heritage, the painting itself must be both preserved and kept publicly accessible. This requires a place. The museum—in its most fundamental role—is that place where objects are preserved for the public to see.

Paintings are objects: objects belong to someone; they are property. Again, there is no parallel with other artistic forms. There are, of course, property *rights* in music, literature, or theater. These may be protected by copyright for a certain period, but sooner or later—as the price of such protection—their essential qualities must enter the public domain. A collector may own a second quarto of *Hamlet*, but no one owns the text—it belongs to everyone.

Copyright is relevant to *reproductions* of paintings, but it has no bearing on the object itself. The only way that a painting can "belong" to everyone—whether pursuant to Lenin's dictum that "art belongs to the people" or in consonance with our own legal concept of public domain—is by vesting its ownership in a governmental or other public institution. A second fundamental role of museums is to exercise ownership over the objects that constitute our patrimony.

Art works, as objects, are uniquely vulnerable to neglect, alteration, and destruction. A poem cannot be vandalized; a painting can. A symphony cannot be ruined by harsh sunlight or sudden shifts in temperature and humidity; a painting can. If someone wants to rewrite *Hamlet*, with improvements—fine; the original will still exist unsavaged. But nowhere can anything be done if the private owner of a Rembrandt decides to scrape parts of it down and substitute passages by Peter Max.

There is, then, a substantial public interest that the institutions in which the ownership of our art works is vested do not have the unqualified right—as would a private owner—to neglect, alter, or destroy them. Such institutions should be designed and maintained to minimize external damage, they should be staffed by specialists in areas that range from crowd control to conservation, they should undertake a trust not to tamper with the things in their possession, and they should be sufficiently bureaucratized to limit the danger of irrational individual decisions.

The institution that meets those needs is the museum.

The Museum as Recreation

For much of the public, the museum is not that awesome. For them it is primarily recreational: a place you go for relaxation and a good time, like a Neil Simon play, only cheaper. "Going to the museum" is an activity different from "Looking at paintings." Matrons do it on weekday afternoons, young couples do it on Saturday afternoon, families do it on arriving with their children in a foreign city, and singles do it looking for other singles.

Museums, which often must meet a substantial portion of their budgets from admission fees—or, in the case of municipal museums, must justify public funding by demonstrating broad public use—are painfully aware that this part of their audience must be kept entertained and interested. How this is done varies from museum to museum. Some schedule special exhibitions, intended for a wider public; Norman Rockwell will be playing ten American museums over the next two years. Others rely on pleasantly furnished restaurants and lounges. And still others look to membership programs featuring glamorous openings, fancy dress balls, and group excursions to Europe.

Curiously, when the original charter of the Metropolitan Museum was drafted in 1870, it provided as one of the museum's chief purposes the furnishing of "popular instruction and recreation." In 1908 the Metropolitan—having achieved a dignity beyond anything its founders envisioned—quietly deleted this reference to recreation as frivolous. But today, there are only a handful of museums as financially independent as the Morgan Library or the Frick that can afford to pursue their artistic programs without regard to the recreational demands of a general public.

The Museum as
Temple of Contemplation

For another part of the public, and occasionally for editorial writers, the museum is a "Temple of Contemplation." In this view, the museum is not so much a place to see things as a place where you go to be immersed in beauty and—by osmosis—to be trans-fixed and exalted. Works of art are reduced to random stimuli.

This attitude may first have sprung from the Greek meaning of *museum*—literally, a "Temple of the Muses." Or it may relate to the piety that underlay the founding of American museums in the nineteenth century. As Orpheus calmed the waves, so would the power of art provide moral uplift for the masses who came to visit.

Regardless of its origins, the general air of solemnity that still pervades museums is deliberately encouraged, and for the most practical of reasons. Museums have generally found that a rela-tively serious atmosphere in the galleries reduces the dangers of vandalism or accidental damage. Life-denying or constricted as this may seem, it is certainly preferable to putting a separate uniformed guard by each painting—an economic impossibility in any case—or imprisoning everything in heavy lucite boxes as some California collectors have done.

A second reason for encouraging this "museum atmosphere" comes from the peculiar conditions under which art is seen. Un-like literature, which is ideally enjoyed in isolation—or music, theater, movies, and dance, in which a form of isolation is sim-ulated by darkening the space in which the audience sits—paint-ings in museums are mostly seen in the midst of a bustling crowd. The closest the museum can come to the isolation of other art forms is by reducing the level of this bustle—the speed of move-ment and the volume of sound—as far as possible. Solemnity is a tool for this purpose.

Consider, for a moment, the matter of smoking in museums. Generally, it is not permitted. Ostensibly, this is because the smoke might damage paintings or a lit cigarette might brush against a canvas or another person. In fact, paintings do hang constantly and with little perceptible damage in smoke-filled studios, private homes, and galleries, and museums often permit smoking during members' openings and other special events. The reason we don't permit smoking in museums, I suspect, is to reinforce the solemnity of museum behavior—we don't permit smoking at funerals either. Unlike Andrew Mellon, who reportedly discouraged *both* smoking and drinking in those parts of his house where his religious paintings were hung, most of us really don't think smoking is disrespectful to art.

On occasions of national mourning—such as after the assassinations of the sixties—the tensions among perceived museum roles become particularly evident. Those who view museums as primarily recreational think that they should be closed for the day; those who view them as "Temples of Contemplation" insist that, like churches, they should be kept open extra hours.

The Museum and Education

Of all the roles museums play, it is in their educational role that they most frequently appear in public. The word *education* reverberates throughout museum literature—it is included in practically all museum charters, it is the principal category under which the Internal Revenue Code classifies museums as tax-exempt, and it is the password that must be used in applying for foundation grants. Here I am speaking not of formal educational programs—something that more than 80 percent of American art museums have today—but rather of the notion that the museum is itself, by its very existence, per se educational.

In the earliest European museums, education was intended as much for the artist as for the general public. This was not the result of enlightenment. Just the contrary: the artist was considered a propagandist for the state, and his improved education would enable him better to serve the state. When the Louvre opened in 1793 only artists were admitted on five days out of each ten. Three days were for the general public, and—there being no

satisfactory way to light the museum at night—two were needed
for cleaning and maintenance.

The consequences of this were unexpected. The museum did
not make artists better civil servants. Instead, it turned out to be
as explosive a factor for the development of nineteenth-century
painting as the invention of color halftone printing has been for
art in the twentieth century. Before the establishment of museums, painters were virtually cut off from the art of earlier eras.
What little they knew of former times came from black-and-white
woodcuts or engravings. Now, for the first time, there was an
authority to look to beyond the Academy. The past existed to be
used. The evolution of painting was freed from master-to-pupil
progression, and the Louvre became, as Germain Bazin calls it,
"the great laboratory where modern art was developed."

American museums, on the other hand, envisioned their educational role very differently. It was, as we have seen, the moral
uplift of the masses, and not the education of the artist, that was
central to their concern. At the opening of the Metropolitan in
1870, Joseph Choate described its purpose as "to humanize, to
educate and to refine a practical and laborious people." It was
not clear then—nor is it today—quite how this was to be done:
by wall labels, by catalogs, by lectures, or by sheer propinquity?
A century's talk of education in the museums seems to have made
little difference: our visual illiteracy rate is still shockingly high,
and ugliness is embraced on every side.

It should be evident by now that museums alone cannot provide
a general visual education. Those who would most benefit from
it are least likely to come to the museum or, if they do come,
least likely to come under circumstances conducive to any learning
experience. If all the talk of education in the museums is to be
anything more than obligatory rhetoric, museums must find ways
to get beyond their own walls and work with other institutions in
the society. It is a hopeful sign for the healthy future of museums
that they are doing just that in many major cities across the country.

The Museum as Journalist

Lawrence Alloway has observed that the art world once had a
hierarchy as neat as professional baseball's: dealers were the scouts,

galleries were the farm teams, and museums were the major leagues. An artist's work did not reach the museums until he was well along in life, or sometimes past it.

In New York, this has been turned upside down. Galleries are now the ones that most often play it safe and deal with art that has already been established. The museums, meanwhile, go out beating the studios looking for new and exotic talents. If the public is responsive, then the galleries move in.

This reversal of roles may be due in part to the manner in which some contemporary artists work; process art, earth works, conceptual art, and works of enormous scale are difficult—or even impossible—for galleries to deal with commercially. In assuming the responsibility to show these, museums meet a real need.

Beyond this, though, there is a general expectation in both the community and within many museums that one of the most important of museum roles is to report "what's new." Many important New York museum exhibitions of the sixties—exhibitions such as *The Responsive Eye* at the Museum of Modern Art in 1965 and *Primary Structures* at the Jewish Museum in 1966—were cast in this mold. And failure to play this role can draw criticism; this past December [1971], for example, Hilton Kramer of the *New York Times* took the New York museums to task for not telling the public enough about the resurgence of representational painting over the past few years.

Why museums have assumed a role that might more logically belong to the art magazines or the galleries is not quite clear. It may stem from defensiveness engendered when the museums are attacked as too concerned with the past. Or it may reflect a desire by younger curators to establish quick reputations, show their peers that they are "with it," and lay claim to an instant place in art history. Henry Geldzahler, for example, has complained that the complex and thickly programmed schedules of the New York museums, which often commit space for up to three years in advance, prevent them from "surveying developments as they occur." The assumptions are that developments are constantly occurring and that museums must discover, define, report, and evaluate them.

This leaves, of course, a nasty question: which comes first, the developments or the museum's discovery of them? For example, an announcement that the Museum of Modern Art would, in three years, stage a major exhibition of flower paintings executed on black velvet in acrylic would not be without feedback in the art community. Alerted that such a movement is important enough to precipitate a major museum show, there would be artists across the country who, looking into their souls, discover there a long-suppressed desire to paint acrylic flowers on black velvet. Museums, at such moments, no longer reflect art history; they take a large hand in making it.

The Museum as Connoisseur

The most general of all assumptions about the museum is that it plays the role of connoisseur. When we speak of a work as a "museum piece," we mean that it has achieved a certain standard of excellence. And when Cézanne said that he wanted to make impressionism "something solid and durable like the art of museums," something of the same was involved.

The museum plays no other role that is so controversial. To a degree, it is not even a role that American museums initially sought. When the Metropolitan was first organized, its founders believed that the great treasures of the past would never be available; they intended that the museum's collection be instructive and comprehensive, rather than sublime. Almost immediately, though, an upsurge of economic and political problems in Europe combined with the growing wealth of the United States to lure important art works to America; before anyone quite realized it, the Metropolitan was in the connoisseurship business, identifying and acquiring masterpieces.

Only recently, many of our museums were filled with plaster casts of classical and Renaissance sculpture. These were intended for the instruction of a large public that, it was assumed, would never have a chance to see the originals. These casts have mostly been sentenced to the storerooms—not, I think, because of the greater ease of public travel but rather from a growing attitude that it is debasing for museums to show mere copies. Copies lack the requisite sublimity—that "fragment of the true cross" element—that connoisseurship demands of museums.

The public assumption that art shown by museums is by definition "great art" raises a particular problem in dealing with contemporary painting and sculpture. Here, all judgments must be tentative; no one can say with certainty what things will prove to have been original or influential or have lasting value and what things will turn out to have been ephemeral. Of much of the work that they show, museums would often like simply to say, "here, this interested us—we're putting it up because we thought you might be interested too."

But museum practice has generally not permitted this. Within the same building we simultaneously show important works of the past and the latest in contemporary art, all labeled in the same way, all presented in the same deadpan fashion, and all—to the public mind—judged by the museums to be equally significant. What the museum is presenting as journalism is interpreted by the public as connoisseurship; failing to understand why the museum considers these new things to be masterpieces, the public may go away confused, frustrated, or just plain angry.

Connoisseurship also comes into conflict with the museum's educational role. If a museum determines to buy the work of a particular artist, which work should it be—what the museum thinks of as his "best," or what it thinks most "typical"? Connoisseurship points toward the "best," education toward the most "typical." Or, if the Metropolitan *had* to spend $5.5 million—the price of its new [1971] Velázquez—on acquisitions, might there not have been 55 less sublime objects at $100,000 each that—from an educational point of view—would have enriched the collection immeasurably more? When a retrospective is assembled, should it include only the finest of the artist's works, those that demonstrate his talent and justify the exhibition; or should weaker paintings— which illuminate his career and document his development—be included as well?

For the artist, the museum's role as connoisseur creates a different problem. If the public equates inclusion of his work in a museum with his stature as an artist, then it may be of critical importance to him—in terms of his subculture, if not his livelihood—to have his work shown in and bought by museums. Yet he may feel—and often rightly—that museum people, no matter how knowledgeable they are about the past, are in no real position to judge new work and especially his. He senses that they have control over his career, and he resents this. At the same time, he is dependent on them for sympathy and understanding. Is it any wonder that the relationship between museum and artist in New York sometimes resembles that of a stern father to a rebellious son?

There have been various suggestions about how this problem might be met. At the most recent Corcoran Biennial in Washington, the museum picked half the artists, and they, in turn, picked the remaining half. This past December [1971], the Guggenheim Museum opened an exhibition selected (from among their own works) and installed by a group of ten artists who had approached the museum to suggest such a project. Larry Bell, with other West Coast artists, has proposed a plan under which, through the use of a computer, some of the work shown in museums would be chosen by the consensus of hundreds or possibly thousands of artists.

All of these, I think, miss the point. The problem is not that museums have power as taste makers—if that power were delegated to someone else, it would still remain power, and the same resentments would ultimately surface. The problem lies rather in the uncritical association of museums with connoisseurship. Its solution might lie in reducing the high pressure and elevated rhetoric that now surround so much museum activity. Greater candor by museums about what they think of the work they show would be a step in this direction.

The Museum as a Symbol of Power

This sense that museums are powerful is not confined to the artist. For the general public, too, museums are symbolic of power, the power of great wealth and of a social elite.

In Europe, this symbolism is bound up in the museum's history. European art museums are the immediate descendants of royal or ecclesiastical collections and the remote descendants of classical treasure hoards. Starting in the late eighteenth century, political revolution or the threat of it converted these collections to public use. Still, these collections, as well as the former palaces in which many of them are housed, retain some flavor of their aristocratic past. We tiptoe through them—these were the things that once belonged to kings; now they belong to everyone, or at least to the state, but a whiff of royalty lingers on.

The American experience is different. Here, our major museums were largely founded before there were collections to fill them. These new museums were not created in response to political events but rather, like public schools and libraries, were connected with post–Civil War ideas of general education and self-improvement. From the start, control of the new museums—at least at the trustee level—fell into the hands of a social elite. Virtually no public funds were available, and if museums were to operate they had to involve themselves with those who could pay the bills.

The public still thinks of American museums as dominated by wealthy trustees. And the wealthy trustees still exist, but their dominance—organizational, aesthetic, and financial—varies from museum to museum. Almost everywhere, it is under attack: museum directors have banded together to protest arbitrary discharges, professional staffs have begun to unionize, and artists and other groups within the community have started demanding a role in decision making. Most important, at both the federal and state levels, government is showing an increasing willingness to meet directly some of the enormous expenses that museums incur—expenses that have in any case soared beyond what individual trustees may be reasonably expected to carry. When trustees can no longer pay the piper, they may no longer call all the tunes.

Another element in the aura of wealth that surrounds American museums is the enormous prices for which art works are sold. The best-known fact about art in America is that it is very expensive. Popular journalism delights in reporting new records. The discovery of five new paintings by Rembrandt might never make the front page of the *New York Times*; the sale of one for five million dollars surely would—and just as surely, some part of the public would be drawn to see all that money hanging on the wall.

Considered one painting at a time, the value of the works hanging in our great museums would be enough to feed and house the poor for a very long time. Why should museums be allowed to be so rich? This wealth, alas, is largely illusory. If a major museum collection were offered for sale tomorrow, there would simply be no market to absorb it at newsworthy prices. As we will see later, these prices exist only *because* of the paintings that are safely locked up in museums. In terms of real, spendable money, museums—glittering symbols of wealth and prestige as they may be—are remarkably poor.

The Museum as a
Center for Scholarship

Museum people like to think of the museum as a center for scholarship. In part this arises from the analogy they draw between museums and universities—as in the demands by the staff association at the Museum of Modern Art that curators be granted sabbatical leaves and receive salaries commensurate with those of City University of New York faculty members. And today more than ever, museum people have academic credentials comparable to those of university art historians, a very different situation from that at the turn of the century, when museums were staffed largely by gentlemen amateurs.

Museums do publish an impressive volume of exhibition catalogs, although the texts—particularly in museums of contemporary art—generally run more toward the interpretive than the studious. And many serve in their local communities to identify paintings that the public brings in and to help students through term papers. But, generally, except at the largest museums (and in university museums) very little real scholarship gets done. Most museums are far too thinly staffed to afford this luxury. Moreover, funds for scholarly activities are among the most difficult to raise. Organizations such as the New York State Council on the Arts prefer to channel their money into programs with a community flavor; corporate donors lean toward large exhibitions of high visibility; foundations favor education. At most smaller and medium-sized art museums, scholarship is an undernourished step-child.

This has had one curious side effect: an intensification of museum activity in colleges and universities over the past ten or fifteen years, as evidenced, for instance, in the growth of the New York University Collection, the expansion of museum activities at Yale, the opening of the new [1970] museum at Berkeley, and the proposed Newberger Museum at the State University in Purchase [opened 1974]. It may be that scholars, unable to find a congenial place in the older museums, have simply decided to have their own—with a higher salary scale and three months' summer vacation.

The Museum as Bureaucracy

During the Metropolitan Museum's centennial celebration, I passed a teacher talking to some children on the main steps. She had just told them the Museum was one hundred years old, and they seemed suitably impressed.

What she did not explain was *what* it was that was one hundred years old. It wasn't the building or any of the people in it—they were all younger. It wasn't the paintings—they were largely older, although most of them had been in the Museum for substantially less than a century. The thing that was one hundred years old— the thing that was being celebrated with such pomp—was the museum's bureaucratic structure.

Museums, like any other organizations, cannot devote their full energies to carrying out programs. Some substantial part must be reserved for their internal regulation and ensurance of their continuity.

Continuity is far more critical to an art museum than it is to, say, a ballet company or a publishing house. A choreographer or novelist might not hesitate to entrust his work to an organization simply because there is no guarantee it will still be there in ten or twenty years. But no one is going to entrust valuable works of art to a museum without some reasonable certainty that the museum will continue—year after year—to look after them.

By contrast with the people with whom they most frequently deal—artists, who represent the ultimate in individuality, and dealers and collectors, who run them a close second—the museum's bureaucracy seems singularly elephantine. Yet it is essential. Some rules are necessary to run any organization past a certain size. Others have been created to protect the staff—and especially the curatorial staff—against the pressures and temptations to which they would be subject from artists, dealers, and collectors if they had the power to make aesthetic decisions independently, without acting through committees. And finally, as we saw earlier, this bureaucracy functions to protect the works in museums against the kind of irreversible individual decisions to which they—as objects—are particularly vulnerable.

At its best, the museum bureaucracy can still be frustrating to deal with, but it is, at least, generally invisible. When it stops working smoothly—when the staff goes on strike, for example— then it becomes highly visible indeed and can disrupt the museum in every aspect of its being.

The Museum and the Migration of Objects

Before the growth of art museums, important paintings floated from one collection to another on the tides of history. Raphael's *St. George and the Dragon*—now in the National Gallery in Washington—belonged at one time or another to the Duke of Urbino, several kings of England, a long string of French collectors, Catherine the Great of Russia, and Andrew Mellon. Dynastic upheaval, the mortality of collectors, or simple looting sent masterpieces toward whatever center of power had most recently emerged.

In general, museums are bringing this migration to a halt. They cull the most important works from the market, sometimes by purchase but more frequently as the beneficiaries of a system of estate taxation that makes it prohibitively expensive to pass great paintings down through a family by inheritance. And while a museum may occasionally sell a group of important works—as the Soviet government sold twenty-one paintings from the Hermitage to Andrew Mellon for $7 million in 1931 (paintings that are today in the National Gallery in Washington)—museum collections are generally stable.

This concentration of important works in museum collections has had tremendous consequences for the art market. Prices for the last works of old masters remaining in private hands have been driven up by scarcity to stratospheric levels, pulling all other prices with them. More importantly, the vacuum caused by the permanent unavailability of older paintings has been filled by the works of successive generations of contemporary painters. If all the works by Rembrandt, or even by Renoir—paintings, drawings, prints, everything—safely sequestered in American museums were today to come back on the market, the impact on the Noland or de Kooning markets might be devastating. Deprived of one thing to collect, collectors turn to another.

It is ironic that one of the most important figures in the growth of American art museums was the dealer Joseph Duveen. Fearful that his most important clients—men such as Henry Huntington, Andrew Mellon, and Henry Frick—would not outlive him, and that the maintenance of his market would force him to buy back from their estates the ever more expensive paintings he had sold them, Duveen successfully urged that they leave their collections to public museums, or even found new ones if necessary. The Huntington Library, the National Gallery, and the Frick Collection are monuments to his persuasiveness.

The Museum as a Terminal
in a National Museum System

American art museums, unlike those of France or other European countries, are not constituent parts of a formally organized national museum system. Nevertheless, our museums do, to a surprising degree, constitute a system of their own.

Consider the loan exhibition, a format first used in Manchester, England, in 1857 and popular ever since. Loan exhibitions are probably the most frequent occasions of individual public visits to a museum. Many of the paintings will have been borrowed from other museums, and this could not be done without the broad experience museums have developed over many years in dealing with each other on such matters as reciprocal loans, shipping, insurance, and conservation. Through the medium of the loan exhibition, the people of one community gain access to works from other museums throughout the country. The local museum is the point of contact.

A more recent development is the traveling loan exhibition. If a major exhibition from the Cleveland Museum or Los Angeles County Museum travels to New York, no one expects it to be shown at the Chase Manhattan Bank, the Colosseum, or on two floors of the Waldorf Astoria. When a museum exhibition travels, it travels to other museums. A community without a museum has no access to the system. Communities build museums, sometimes without owning anything to go in them, in order to have something to plug into the system.

What is most striking is the total decentralization of this system. As we have seen, the control of each museum may, at the trustee level, be in the hands of a small group of wealthy or powerful people. But there are hundreds of art museums and, thus, hundreds of these groups. This has a healthy side—no one group, nor even any practical combination of groups, can control the system. There is room for a variety of viewpoints and offsetting eccentricities instead of the single "official" view that a centralized system might produce.

On the other hand, this decentralization results in enormous duplication of function and adds substantially to the cost of American museum operations. This last point is becoming more clearly understood, and today there is some movement toward administrative ecumenicism, i.e., finding ways in which museums can work more efficiently together in administrative areas while continuing to remain independent with respect to their exhibitions and acquisitions. [Some cooperative projects under consideration are discussed in "The Multiple Crises in Our Museums," pp. 3–29.]

A little artistic ecumenicism might even be in order. Objects that exist in multiple form—sculpture or prints made in editions—are a problem for our decentralized system. What are we to make of an identical print by Rauschenberg or Johns being collected simultaneously by the Metropolitan Museum *and* the Museum of Modern Art *and* the Whitney? Of what service is this to the public? Is it merely a reflex action? (If it's good, collect it.) Or a psychological drive toward wholeness? (The collection just would not be complete without it.) Or an ego trip? (My collection is as good as yours—with museums still carrying on the tradition of rival princes competing in splendor.) None of these seems sufficient justification for the expense and effort involved in collecting identical material in the museums of a single city.

Our decentralized museum system parallels, to some extent, the system by which the federal and state governments provide museums with financial aid. While we often hear that the federal government contributes only about ten or fifteen cents per capita per year to support the arts—as contrasted with amounts as high as two dollars per capita in some parts of Europe—that figure only reflects direct aid. Indirect aid, through the medium of the charitable deduction, runs considerably higher. The charitable deduction in turn, is a device by which the allocation of aid among qualified organizations—in this case, museums—is determined by individual taxpayers and not by any central authority.

While there are flaws in this—chiefly that the system most benefits affluent taxpayers and gives them the largest voice in how indirect aid will be channeled—the charitable deduction device nevertheless assures that our museum system will not become monolithic. And, unless you relish the thought of Richard Nixon as curator-in-chief of the nation's museums, I think that is to the good.

The Museum as
an Agent of Social Change

During the past few years, there have been increasing demands that art museums act in social areas outside their traditional functions.

I am not referring to the pressures brought by black or women's groups for a greater participation in existing museum programs. These are not attempts to change *what* museums do; they arise, rather, out of criticism of *how* things have been done in the past. Such pressures have, beyond question, succeeded in massively raising the collective consciousness of museum people in their dealings with women artists and minority groups.

Very different are demands that the museum engage in political action, especially in connection with the war in Indochina. This demand is made not only with respect to individual staff members, many of whom may have participated in the peace movement, but also with respect to the museum as a corporate whole. It is a troubling one.

Museum staffs are united by a common interest in art, not by a common political stance. While curatorial and administrative personnel may tend to be liberal in their politics, in many museums they are outnumbered by guards, porters, and other blue-collar workers who are often conservative. Who, then, is to speak for the museum? The division of duties within the museum—together with their specialized training—may give curators the right to speak *ex cathedra* on matters of art. But they have no more right than any other member of the staff to speak for the museum on nonartistic matters.

What, then, of trustees? There is another problem. A trustee, no matter how convinced of a political cause, may legitimately hesitate to support it in the name of the museum—not only because he may seriously endanger the museum's tax status, which requires the avoidance of any political position, but also because he *is*, literally, a trustee and not a proprietor. The museum is not like his own business, to do with as he wishes; he is only a transient supervisor of what is essentially a public property. Museums, by the very nature of their organization, may simply not be useful tools for political purposes—or at least not useful enough to justify disabling them for any other purpose.

Social change, however, embraces an area larger than political action, and there are other ways in which the museum may prove more effective. These mostly revolve about an emerging redefinition of the museum's relationship to the community.

There is a parallel in the situation of the hospital as Michael Crichton described it in *Five Patients*. In the past, the hospital was a place you went if you were sick. But unless you went, you were outside the orbit of its concern—the hospital's role was essentially passive. In hospitals today, there is a growing concept of outreach—a sense that the hospital is not merely a place that treats the sick inside its walls but that it is also the center of a health system serving a community far larger than its bed or clinic patients or even those already sick.

Something similar is stirring both within the museums and in the demands made on them from outside. Should museums use their expertise to improve the teaching of art or art appreciation in the schools? Should collections be dispersed into decentralized neighborhood or branch museums? What responsibilities do museums have to provide career training to minority group members? What is the museum's relation to the environment? A host of questions will have to be answered in the coming years. But, clearly, museums—if they are to ask for continued public support—will have to become more than mere fortresses in which art works are passively stored; the community will require that they be resources whose collections and expertise are actively available to all. Much remains to be learned about how this can best be done.

The Museum as
Representative of the Artist

Some contemporary artists see the museum as their agent—a sort of super art gallery whose function it is to present their case before the public. This is a relatively recent role for museums. It comes, I think, from the "difficult" nature of contemporary art and the feeling that it needs a champion to do public battle for its acceptance. Neither the Museum of Modern Art nor the Guggenheim, for example, was established to meet any broadly felt public need; they were, rather, founded to "sell" the public on certain then recent developments in art: the work of Picasso, Braque, and Matisse at the Modern; of Kandinsky and other non-objective painters at the Guggenheim.

Museum people find this a sympathetic role: it is flattering to be thought so discriminating and powerful; in representing the artist they participate, to a degree, in his magic; and, assuming that he *does* go on to become a Picasso or a Kandinsky, they will be entitled to a share of the glory.

There are, however, some difficulties with this role. How does the museum reconcile its obligations to the public—for whom it is ostensibly working, and who is being asked to pay its bills—with its role as agent? Ideally, there should be no conflict of interest; in practice, there often is.

Consider a one-man exhibition. We saw earlier that this could involve a conflict between the museum's roles as educator and connoisseur. Protection of the artist's interest complicates the situation still further. A retrospective should—in terms of public expectations—be a cool, professional appraisal of an artist's career, a candid disclosure of his strengths and weaknesses, the visual equivalent of a critical article. If, as may happen in the case of an older artist, his best work was done some years earlier, that too should be made clear.

But the living, still-active artist, whose cooperation may well be necessary if the exhibition is to be mounted at all, may see this differently. He would prefer to be shown only by his strongest work. But he will also want the exhibition to end on a crescendo, with his most recent work—what he is doing *now*—appearing as its triumphant climax. No working artist wants to be shown as a has-been.

What purports to be an exercise in criticism may, in practice, wind up as puffery. On the side of the angels, perhaps, but puffery just the same. How to reconcile their sympathy for the artist with their roles as connoisseurs, educators, and honest journalists is a dilemma museums have not yet solved.

The Museum as Patron

Another role in which artists sometimes envision the museum is that of patron. If the museum, as collector, is successor to the great Renaissance princes, should it not—with all its apparent power and wealth—succeed them as a patron of the arts as well?

Museums do, in fact, sometimes act as patrons by purchasing the work of younger artists. In this, their motives may be mixed: they want to encourage the artist, but also acquire his work while prices are still relatively low. But full-scale patronage—outright financial grants, or the sponsorship of activities that do not generate for the collection objects of a value commensurate with their cost—is another matter. Most museums look upon this as an improper diversion of their already slender resources.

Beyond that, though, for the museum to play patron is to add another negative element to its already difficult relationship with the artists. To have a patron is to be patronized. While the Renaissance artist, freshly risen from the status of craftsman and living in a far different society, may have accepted this condition without resentment, the artist today will not. Patronage, even if financially possible, is an unrewarding role that most museums are reluctant to play.

The Museum and the
Cult of the Artist

Goethe, who witnessed the first flourishings of the art museum in Europe, saw it as a temple in which the public paid tribute to the genius of the artist.

In Western museums, it is most often the individual artist— and not the collective accomplishment of an entire people—that is enshrined. In this, the museum reflects a liberal ideal of the nineteenth-century world in which it matured. It is part of an open society in which talented individuals will have an opportunity to develop their abilities to the fullest and receive the honors they are due.

The image of the artist also reflects a liberal ideal: that of the model citizen. He is the man whose energies are employed for creative, not destructive, ends; he is self-disciplined; his accomplishments do not require him to manipulate or exploit others; he is aware of tradition but not its slave; and by working outside of an organized structure, he takes full responsibility for what he produces.

We honor him for this in our museums. But more, something still deeper, is involved. From the Renaissance, the artist has also emerged as hero, complete with all the trappings the myth of the hero requires. His typical biography is that of a man who, having passed through the double underworld of his own suffering and public scorn, triumphantly returns to the upper world—to society—bearing the secret that enables him to transform the basest of materials into something precious. Museums honor the artist as alchemist.

Imagine three objects displayed side by side in an art museum: a curiously shaped piece of driftwood, a carved wooden sculpture of identical scale and form, and a second sculpture also identical in scale and form but cast in pure gold. The first interests us only briefly; it belongs in a natural history museum. The third will most likely be repellent; its inherent value as pure gold overwhelms whatever artifice has gone into its making—it comes across as jewelry. It is the middle object, something that takes its value from the transformation an artist has worked, that holds our interest.

If this is so, then art museums may be as much about artists as they are about art. And the more mythic the life of the artist, the greater will be the public response.

Van Gogh packs them in every time.

The Museum as Monastery

No museum can play all these different roles at once. To try to be everything is to wind up being nothing. Each museum must choose which roles to emphasize, and this choice, in turn, may depend on the museum's own resources, the changing needs of the community, the particular interests of the museum's staff and trustees, and the level and type of activity in other museums of the area.

But there is, I think, one last role that every art museum must play. It is that of monastery: of the museum as a community of people committed to the truth that the visual is a separate, vital, and important part of human experience.

No other institution in our society plays this role—it is unique to art museums. In all that the museum does, the preservation and extension of the visual tradition must be the common element that gives coherence to its other roles.

Museums are not irrelevent to the better life we seek for everyone. To see well is to live richly, and the museum can be a school for seeing, a place where seeing is celebrated. In this role, its other functions are reconciled. Education, journalism, connoisseurship, service to the artists, and the caretaking of objects—all, in the end, have a common purpose: the propagation of our faith that the visual offers delights, discoveries, and forms of awareness that are available in no other way.

A day may come when visual literacy is universal and the art museum, as we know it, is no longer necessary. Then it may shed some of its other roles and slip back into being merely a caretaker for objects, a storehouse of historical data. Until then, however, it has other important work to do.

Afterword

This text, printed here for the first time, was originally prepared for a lecture that Dore Ashton invited me to give in the Great Hall of Cooper Union in February 1972. It was a miserable night—New York City winter at its damp sloppiest—and the audience was scant and chilly. Some people had wandered in, or so it seemed, only to escape the cold.

In retrospect, I'm no longer sorry that so few people heard this. Some passages now strike me as simplistic—among them the cursory discussion of scholarship and several of the references to trustees. Elsewhere, it seems shrill. In two particulars, though, I find it troubling in more fundamental ways. One of these relates to the final paragraph. The other concerns the references both in the final paragraph and elsewhere to "visual literacy" and some presumed (and perhaps wholly concocted) opposite, "visual illiteracy."

To begin with the end: In their casual denigration of the museum's custodial role—"merely a caretaker for objects, a storehouse of historical data"—I find the last few sentences inexplicable. Possibly I meant what I said—but I find that hard to believe. Perhaps they were meant as an ironic pendant to the earlier bitter-tinged allusion to a Public Access Central Art Repository. If so, however, I have no recollection of crafting something so artful. What is more likely, I think, is that the entire closing section of the text was another defensive response to the antimuseum agitations that still racked New York. Ashton had asked me to describe what museums did and how I thought their roles were perceived by the public. Instead, I suspect, I set out to do a selling job, to persuade an (imagined) audience that—regardless of whatever it might otherwise have heard—museums, deep down, were truly lovable.

What, though, could I offer that might be persuasive? Cooper Union in that dark season of 1971–72 scarcely seemed the most opportune place in which to proclaim my conviction that museums ought to be valued primarily because they focused (by preserving their collections) on their obligations to the future and only secondarily because they could (through their exhibition and education programs) enrich the present. The present, just then, was noisily insistent, and the future in any case seemed faintly contingent. Hardly better would have been to speak of the past—and of the museum's duty to keep intact the material evidence of that past. The past was in bad odor, and there was considerable talk around that it should perhaps be overturned. The only thing still left to "sell" was the utility of museums to the present. The most persuasive peroration I could give would be one that focused on all of the virtuous and wonderful things that museums could be doing for everybody *right now, at this moment, immediately, and no waiting!!!* And that's what I think I did.

For whatever reason, the priorities were inverted. It has long seemed to me clear—and it should have been clear to me even then—that collecting and preserving are and must remain the foundation for all of the museum's other activities. The custodial role is central; the rest—no matter how important—is still peripheral. (Occasionally, in midnight fantasies, I test my commitment to this proposition. As the Napoleonic commander in chief of the Metropolitan Museum of Art, I am faced with a shortage of operating funds so severe that I may have to shut my galleries entirely for weeks or months or even years. Should I sell an object from my collection—just one, and just this once—to keep them open? At midnight, anyway, I am steadfast, brave, and resistant to every pressure. "*Jamais,*" I answer. "Never. Neither my grandest painting by Rembrandt, nor my humblest and most redundant scarab.") To whatever extent the public would not readily accept this position, then to that same extent have museums thus far failed in clearly communicating their basic importance.

Such an insistence on the primacy of their custodial role need not require that museums be either dull or rigid. With the care of collections maintained as a pedal point, there is still ample scope for improvisation both in their exhibitions and in their public programming of every kind. And other generations will improvise in other ways. Adele Silver puts this nicely in *The Art Museum as Educator*:

> museums are inventions of men, not inevitable, eternal, ideal, nor divine. They exist for the things we put in them, and they change as each generation chooses how to see and use those things.

"Those things," though, must continue to be there—and continue to be preserved as best we know how—before each succeeding generation can choose for itself "how to see and use" them. Museums preserve more than the evidence of the past. Properly conceived, and basically optimistic, they also preserve the options of the future.

Turning to my reference to "visual literacy" and "illiteracy," to some extent this was simply a poor choice of words. What I really meant was something like "sensitivity" and "insensitivity." Thus amended, the relevant passages might amount to nothing more than a comforting (albeit slightly defensive) syllogism: the world (or America or Duluth) would be a better place if people were more sensitive; the art museum can make people more sensitive;

ergo, the art museum can make the world (or America or Duluth) a better place.

I suspect, though, that also involved was an assumption about museum education that I today would question. Implicit in the context—"our visual illiteracy rate is still shockingly high and ugliness is embraced on every side"—was a different syllogism: the world (or America or Poughkeepsie) would be a better place if people understood what "beauty" is; the art museum is possessed of a unique understanding of what "beauty" is; ergo, by teaching people what beauty is, the art museum has a unique potential to make the world (or America or Poughkeepsie) a better place.

For this to be so—and for the art museum to find one of its justifications in such logic—the middle term of this syllogism would have to be proven. Is the art museum, in fact, about "beauty" at all? Might not its subject better be defined as the interplay of tradition, mastery, and innovation in a particular (and relatively restricted) realm of human activity? Does the expertise of the museum extend to this activity as it has been carried on in every time and place, or is it an expertise concentrated along what art historians might perceive as the major lines of development? Are the values, tastes, and standards that inform the museum broadly based, or are they essentially those of the individuals—trustees *and* staff—responsible for its establishment and operation?

The middle term may not hold. The art museum may not be possessed of "a unique understanding of what 'beauty' is" because there may be no universal criterion through which any such understanding might be had. The "beauty" understood by any one museum might be no more than a tiny fragment split off from the mass of this world's possible beauties. There is nothing wrong with this, but it makes a hash of what I suggested that blustery evening at Cooper Union—that a basic mission of the art museum, and one for which it is uniquely qualified, is to hasten the day when "visual literacy is universal."

If museums themselves are not universally literate, then a universal literacy based on museum tastes and standards would be a diminution and not an enhancement of the world as we know it. To imagine that museums might impose their tastes and standards as the norm—that these could be made the test by which visual literacy was to be measured—is a hegemonic fantasy un-worthy of public support.

There are many things that an art museum can teach. "Sensi-tivity" is one. "Literacy," learning to master the language of the museum, is certainly another. To make such "literacy" central, though, would be to cut away from the museum all of those who might choose (or have no choice but) to speak in another tongue. Viewed from this perspective, the basic educational role of the museum should not be to inculcate—to make every last visitor adopt the museum's "beauty" as his own. It should, instead, be to stimulate—to demonstrate how the museum's involvement with its own values might serve as a model from which others, who need not necessarily share those values, can learn to involve them-selves more deeply with values of their own.

Toward Greater
Museum Integrity
("The Snodgrass Sermon")
(1974)

O ne of the old comedians used to start
by saying, "A funny thing happened
to me on the way to the theater." Since we are all museum people,
I'll start by saying, "I read a funny label on the way to the meeting."
It was at the Metropolitan, about two years ago. Next to a little
landscape by Asher B. Durand—a thoroughly insignificant painting—was the following:

> The Metropolitan is uniquely fortunate in its holdings of large gal-
> lery-scale landscapes by Hudson River painters, and those of Asher
> B. Durand are especially imposing. However, like his colleagues, Dur-
> and painted the overwhelming majority of his pictures in small format
> so that they could hang comfortably in the normal-sized parlors of his
> patrons. As the Metropolitan plans the addition to the American Wing
> which will encompass all the American arts of the eighteenth and
> nineteenth centuries, we intend to set aside appropriate pictures to
> hang in period vignettes and rooms that will provide the Museum
> visitor with an accurate idea of what people at the time put on their
> walls. Durand's *River Scene*, a glowing vista down a country lane
> toward a stand of oaks and beyond, to the Hudson River, is an excellent
> representative picture for such a purpose, as well as for lending to
> other museums. The painting has been cleaned since the Museum
> received it, and it proves to be a very attractive picture, which is the
> primary reason we are fortunate to add it to the collection.

Translation: "This is a dog. Somebody gave it to us, and we're
stuck with it. We have to show it at least once, but for God's sake,

*Copyright © 1974 by Stephen E. Weil. All rights reserved. This lecture was delivered
at the Western Association of Art Museums/San Diego Gallery of Fine Arts Regional
Seminar held in San Diego on February 22, 1974. The author was then the administrator of the Whitney Museum of American Art, New York City.*

don't think this is why Asher B. Durand was a good painter, and don't think that *we* think that this is up to the general quality of what the Metropolitan should be showing."

Later this year the National Endowment for the Arts will be publishing a survey called *Museums U.S.A.* that includes a breakdown of some 1,821 American museums by types: there are 340 straight art museums, 186 art-history, 164 art-history-science, and 55 art-science. That is a total of 745 museums which are art museums in one sense or another. If you figure that each has an average of 200 objects on exhibit at any time, that means there are, at any given moment, at least 150,000 objects being shown in art museums throughout the United States. Very clearly, these are not all masterpieces, and there is no reason they need to be.

I think we all know the different reasons why something might wind up on our walls. It may be a minor work in a major exhibition; it may be the best we are able to get at a particular time; we may hang it because it is typical; it may have come as a gift from the president of the board. There are all sorts of reasons to hang these things, and there is no harm in showing them.

But there is, I think, a great deal of harm in permitting the public to misinterpret what we are showing and why we are showing it. And to understand that, I think you must turn and look at how the public sees museums, especially art museums. In every field, whether it is law or medicine or prostitution, things look different from inside and out. We who work in art museums know that they serve a great many functions. Perhaps the most important—their root function—is the preservation of an honest record of human accomplishment and human aspiration, as translated into the tangible objects that we show. But to the general public, I think, connoisseurship is what museums are about. There are very important implications to this. In the visual arts, as in music and literature, public taste is formed by recourse to concrete examples and not by the application of abstract theory. And when the public does form its taste, what are the examples it looks to? Certainly not what it sees in Aunt Matilda's living room or at a Greenwich Village art show or a local church fair. *The public forms its taste on the basis of what it sees in museums.* To the public, *museum* is not merely a noun, a place; it is also an adjective, meaning "quality," meaning "the best." When the public describes something as "a real museum piece," I think it is referring to that object the way Matthew Arnold referred to certain things as "touchstones," specimens of the highest quality.

The questions, then, are: What are our responsibilities when, as we constantly do, we show specimens of less than the highest quality? How do we deal with the public with regard to these? Let's have a fantasy of what it might be like. Let's say that you have in your museum a perfectly pleasant, small, but not particularly distinguished portrait by Renoir. Consider that, following the example of the Metropolitan, you might label it as follows:

> A typical small-scale work by one of the foremost of the French impressionist painters. Although somewhat weaker in its modeling than the portrait now hanging at the local University Gallery, its fluent brush work and fresh juxtaposition of colors clearly indicate the strengths on which the artist's reputation is based. This painting was one of the first by Renoir to be privately owned west of the Mississippi and was given to the Museum by R.J. Snodgrass, the grandson of the original owner and vice-president of the Museum from 1963 to 1970. When sufficient funds and a suitable opportunity are available, the Museum hopes to acquire a finer example of Renoir's work.

Why don't we do this? Ego? "My museum is better than your museum." Defensiveness? "Everything is splendid." Or is it because of Mr. Snodgrass and all the potential Snodgrasses who might stop giving us paintings if we don't say nice things about them, or at least keep our mouths shut if we can't say something nice? We, who are constantly being caught between the Snodgrasses and the public, generally opt for Snodgrass and console ourselves that the public has got to learn to see for itself.

Let's look at this from another angle and talk about exhibition catalogs, which are very peculiar documents. Imagine a person coming to a museum to see a retrospective. He looks at it with a great deal of care, takes the catalog home, reads the essay, and says "Oh wow! That's not at all what I thought when I saw those paintings hanging there today." How often does it occur to him that the curator who wrote the catalog may not think so either? The curator had *never seen those paintings together* when he wrote that catalog essay. If he is a conscientious curator and his museum has travel funds, maybe he at least got to see the paintings individually. In other cases, he may only have seen all the photographs together, all 8 by 10 inches, with no idea of how the scale of one painting would work with another. He is simply guessing at how the show is going to look. In a way, even, the show is to find out how the paintings *will* work when they are all brought together. When Bill Agee was a curator at the Whitney, I used to wander into his office late in the afternoon and say, "Bill, how is such and such a show coming? What's it going to look like?" Bill would say, "How the hell do I know what it's going to look like? We'll get it up on the walls and find out."

What can we do about this? Two things, both of which are impractical. One, we could assemble an exhibition and put it up six months before it opens to its public. That's out of the question. Or we could publish the catalog six months after the exhibition closes. Let's fantasize again. What kind of publication could we put out after an exhibition is over? It could have installation photographs plus the usual reproductions. It could have selected reviews and articles based on the exhibition. Above all, it could have an essay by the curator drawn from his experience of seeing the work all together for six or seven weeks, and being able to really look at it and think about it. It might be a pretty good document, and who would object? The answer is: just about everybody. Everybody would become the Snodgrass you'd have to worry about. Your publication people would tell you immediately that they couldn't sell a catalog under those circumstances; they could only sell it while the show was on. If it's a retrospective for a living artist, he would want no part of it either. There would be too much risk. You might get all the paintings up and discover that you didn't like the way they looked together, and he sure as hell might not want an honest essay written after that. The lenders to the show wouldn't like it. They would want the catalog out, with their names in it, while the show was still current and topical. And you might even run into resistance from critics who would like to see the catalog before they started writing, so they could use it as a target at which to shoot. So we do what we do all the time. We please everybody, all the Snodgrasses, everyone except the people we are supposed to be serving—the public. For them we have a souvenir booklet, and what we finally think of the show, they will never know.

There are some other peculiarities to catalogs. When the public buys a catalog with forty-eight black-and-white illustrations and six color ones, what does it think about those six paintings reproduced in color? Probably that they are the most important works in the exhibition. What does a museum professional think when he sees such a catalog? He wonders whether the museum got somebody to subsidize those six color plates, which, after all, is better than no color plates. Again, it may be fine, but it certainly isn't candid.

The catalog of an artist's exhibition in many cases is the only monograph about the artist that most people will ever buy or see. Given that, there's another issue: are catalogs even what we should really be publishing, or should there be something different? Might there not be a cognate publication that parallels the exhibition and does in the form of a book what the exhibition does in a museum form? John Coplans did that very beautifully at Pasadena for the Andy Warhol show a few years ago. We have done it several times at the Whitney; we did it for our Olmsted exhibition in 1972, and again this year [1974] for our folk art exhibition. When you are dealing with the public, strict adherence to the catalog format—an illustrated annotated checklist with an essay in front and some scholarly apparatus in the back—can lead to some pretty bizarre things.

Take, for exmple, the Géricault exhibition at the Los Angeles County Museum in 1971. The painting that haunted that exhibition, and the cornerstone of Géricault's reputation, was, of course, *The Raft of the Medusa*. In the catalog, Professor Lorenz Eitner first mentioned *The Raft of the Medusa* in the second sentence of the introduction and talked about it continually. Ultimately, he said, "It remains one of the very few works in modern art which raises an actual event to the level of grand style and timeless significance." Shown in the exhibition, and illustrated in the catalog, were at least a dozen sketches associated with *The Raft of the Medusa*. But what if you, as a member of the public, wanted to see *The Raft of the Medusa* itself? No way; absolutely no way. That it was not in the exhibition, because the Louvre would not lend it, was understandable. But that it was not illustrated in the catalog! It may have been a rule of the County Museum, "If you won't lend us your painting, we aren't going to make it famous by printing it in our catalog." It might even be a good rule. Or the decision could even have been scholarly purity. But what kind of public service leaving it out of the catalog was supposed to be, God only knows!

Let me give just a few more examples of this kind of thing. I was in a large midwestern art museum a few weeks ago with somebody who was quite knowledgeable about paintings but not about museums. In one of the impressionist galleries, there is a particular spot that is clearly the most prominent place in the room: a panel, running from floor to ceiling. You see it—a very long view of it—when you come in. On it was a Degas sketch that was, I thought, one of the weakest things in the gallery. There were marvelous paintings on both the side walls, with just this sketch hanging on the panel. The woman I was with looked puzzled and said, "I just don't understand why that's hanging there." I said, "I'll bet you anything that it's the only thing in the room from a living donor." It was. It was there to please the donor, and the public had no way to interpret that. They just had to believe that the museum thought it was the finest painting in the room. That again is the Snodgrass problem: trying to please somebody, not necessarily at the expense of the public, but also without letting the public know what it's all about.

Take another example. When you get involved with a retrospective for a living artist, you are generally going to need his cooperation to do the show. You may need the cooperation of his dealer as well. And then you start to get into trouble because, from the artist's point of view, there is no question as to what is most important in his work: it is what he has just painted. Artists are no more prone than boxers or insurance salesmen or politicians to see themselves as being past their prime. From the dealer's end, it comes out the same way. What he has got the most of to sell is the newest work, and that is what he wants the exhibition to push. So the artist and the dealer may begin to lean on you. There is pressure to have the exhibition become one great sweeping crescendo that bursts into an exultant finale, a socko finish with the work of the last year or two as the exhibition's climax. That may be O.K., if it reflects reality, but a lot of the time it doesn't. There are artists who have peaked at forty and have been imitating themselves ever since. The public comes to see a show that, in the number and scale of the paintings chosen from different periods and in the way it is hung, tells a story far different from the one the curator might have liked to tell. The issue is the same: service to the public versus service to the Snodgrasses, whom we genuinely need to build our collections, finance our programs, and lend us their paintings. And again, we console ourselves and say, "Well, it was better than not having done the show at all."

We can all think of more examples: when we elect to show the Snodgrass private collection instead of some other because we expect something from Snodgrass; when we do shows drawn from the collections of our membership, and the only theme connecting the paintings is that members of the museum own them; when we fail to write candidly about things in catalogs because we don't want to offend the lender; when we mount an exhibition because a curator has insisted over a period of years that he or she wants that show and the museum feels the curator should be rewarded but never tells the public that it is an individual and not an institutional choice.

If we acknowledge all of these as problems, what can museums do about them? The answer, I think, is nothing, because museums, as such, cannot do *anything*.

We have, I think, fallen too much into the habit of ascribing moral or sentimental attributes to organizations, as if they were people. In a diary entry for January 1, 1928, Dean Christian Gauss of Princeton noted his astonishment at encountering a poster that wished him a happy new year from the local railroad. "Railroads," he wrote, "used to be railroads and wished you nothing." One can imagine the good dean saying to himself, "My God, what a remarkable thing, that the ———— Railroad even knew I would walk down here today. I wonder how they went about it. Did they call a board meeting, and did somebody say, 'Let's wish Dean Gauss a happy new year and put it on a poster'? Or did the brakemen get together and decide that a poster was the best way to do it? Or do the stockholders have to be polled before the railroad can wish someone a happy new year?" In such a gentle vein, he might have gone on to muse about the change from individual sensibility to a new kind of synthetic corporate sensibility.

We had a less humorous example of this in New York several years ago at the Whitney. During the height of the peace movement, there was great pressure from the artists in New York for the Whitney to take a position against the war. In the ensuing turmoil, people began to think and ask: How *does* a museum take a position against the war? Does it mean that a majority of the people on the payroll feel that way? We did a poll of our staff, which is about 65 or 75 percent blue collar, and discovered that a majority were not against the war. We went back to some of the people who were pressuring us, and they said, "We don't mean the whole staff; we mean just the people who really count." We said, "That isn't the museum." They said, "Oh sure, when we say the museum, that is what we mean." We said, "Well, what about the board? Should we poll the board?" "No, that isn't the museum either." It turned out that there wasn't any place you could point to and say that the museum was against the war or that the museum was for the war.

The Renoir label we were fantasizing about before is, in a way, just such an impossibility. Again, a museum can't have an opinion about a painting; curators in the museum can, and if there ever were such a label, I would think it ought be signed, with the implication that this is the opinion of someone who is going to stand up and defend it. A museum can no more wish someone a happy new year or oppose a war or judge a painting than a museum can have a hangover or fall in love. The only people who *can* act are we, the museum professionals. Are we the ones to blame, then, when museums fall short of meeting public responsibility? Oddly enough, I think the answer for now is no. We are not to blame; or, at least, not yet.

In his play *The Great God Brown,* Eugene O'Neill wrote, "Man is born broken; he lives by mending." And I think the same is true of museums. Museums were not born into innocence; they have not been corrupted by Snodgrass and by time. I think it is just the opposite. Museums, like man in O'Neill's quotation, were born broken. They were born undefined and incomplete, founded from a variety of motives, and—certainly until the last 25 or 30 years—supervised as often as not by people who lacked both professional training and the clear sense we have today of the extent to which the museum is a public institution. I think it is just now that the museum movement in the United States is coming into maturity, that museums are in the process of mending and redefining themselves. We *can* do something, because this is not a case of Paradise Lost; it is a case of Paradise not yet attained. And I don't think the time has ever been more ripe or conditions more favorable for attaining it.

Let's see some of the things that we have going for us now. To begin with, we have our professional associations. We have meetings such as this [the Western Association of Art Museums's first regional seminar at the Fine Arts Gallery of San Diego] and those sponsored by the American Association of Museums (AAM), together with workshops and seminars where professionals can get together to find out about each other's problems and how they deal with them. We have the accreditation program of the AAM, which is another important step in establishing professional standards. We have, from the Smithsonian Institution, which is certainly the largest factor in the American museum world, an excellent series of workshops developed by its Office of Museum Programs; these are open without charge to any museum professional. Then, there is the extraordinarily important document—"Professional Practices in Art Museums"—published by the Association of Art Museum Directors (AAMD) in 1972; it is a real charter for museum staffs contrasting the responsibilities that are properly in their province with those belonging to their trustees. Also important is the code of ethics that the AAMD first published in the sixties and reformulated in the early seventies, dealing with conflict of interest questions affecting trustees, directors, and curators.

At another level we have the Tax Reform Act of 1969 with its very clear preference that museums be publicly rather than privately funded. We also have in the act a continuation of the notion that a museum must serve exclusively educational purposes; it is not to be there to meet the needs and wishes of the Snodgrasses around it; it is there as an educational institution. Further, we have today a post-Watergate atmosphere, and a desire on people's part to see institutions run for their proper purposes and not perverted to some other kind of use. I think that most important of all, though, is the public financial support that began in the sixties and the growth of funding through the state arts councils, the National Endowment for the Arts, the National Endowment for the Humanities, and the National Museum Act. These are important not only because they are a source of funds but also because these funds normally come into the museum at the staff, rather than the trustee, level. In so doing, they tend to reinforce the position of the staff and give it a greater importance than before in the power structure of the museum. Beyond that, I think it must be clear that something happens when the public is not only the people we serve but also the source of our support. Our failure to serve it honestly becomes more than ethically questionable. It becomes downright stupid. The public is paying the bills.

So there is a trend here that we can ride if we want. There is natural support we can find in a community of fellow museum professionals. There are tools available to fortify ethical positions that we would like to take. In the older and largely private museums on the East Coast, there has been a clear pattern of how museums evolve over several generations into those that are more truly public. We have seen this at our own museum, the Whitney, and you can see it at the Guggenheim as well, and even in so absurd a situation as that at the Barnes Foundation, where the public interest gradually forced it open. Museums as a species can evolve in the same way that individual museums have, toward a greater sense of being public institutions.

I recall an incident at a meeting last year, when a number of us were discussing some means by which museums might generate additional income out of their own operations. Once again we had a Snodgrass there. This time he was a museum efficiency expert. In the middle of the meeting, he said, "You know, you guys are all nuts! You're not exploiting your print curators." We all said, "How?" He said, "Look, if your print curator is supposed to be able to identify the best new prints as they are published, why do you buy just one? What you should be doing is buying three or four. Then you take one, put it in the permanent collection, push it for the next ten years, just keep it up on the walls, keep everybody knowing it's a good image and about ten years from now you can sell the others and be sitting pretty." Everybody at the meeting just exploded with shock, and when the noise finally died down, the two phrases that kept coming through were "destroy credibility" and "destroy integrity with the public."

And *integrity*, I think, is the key word in all of this as far as our dealings with the public are concerned. One of the Roman poets wrote, "Integrity is praised, but starves." I wonder if this has to be; I wonder if integrity might not thrive. Might not a clear, projected, unimpeachable integrity—a wholeness of purpose on our part—be the very thing that would bring us the cooperation and support we so badly need? And might it not be the lack of such integrity—a sense the public has that we sometimes play too many games with too many Snodgrasses—that stands in the way of our getting such support today?

The question is not one of being anti-Snodgrass, for if it were not for the Snodgrasses, we might not even be here. But, by the same token, if it were not for the museums, the Snodgrasses might never have been inspired to make or collect art or want to be immortalized in museums. Snodgrassism is not something that is good or evil. It is just a fact that is there. How important a fact it is depends on the way things are at any time—because things can change, can be changed, are being changed now. So the question, I think, is one of pushing our own evolution. To the extent that we succeed, those we are so fearful of offending—all of the Snodgrasses, whether they be lenders or donors or artists or experts or whatever—may be prouder than ever to be associated with us.

Man is born broken; he lives by mending. Museums did not spring full blown into the world. They exist as they are made to exist. They cannot transform themselves. There is no "they." There is just us. We can make of them what we will. Let's get together and make that something good.

Afterword

In earlier days, it seemed to me that some of the more lamentable practices to be found in art museums might be curbed through a combination of greater professionalization and a heightened consciousness of the museum's role as a public institution. In retrospect, though, I wonder whether there was not (and still remains) a third factor that I wholly failed to understand: the consequences of living, as most American museums do, in a state of chronic mendicity.

To be perpetually involved in soliciting is an enormous drain on the energies of trustees and staff alike. Beyond this, it can skew the conclusions of nominating and search committees, deflect the judgments of connoisseurship, and produce the dislocation in values that follows when, for example, development officers (née fund raisers) are paid higher salaries than curators. What museums need to examine, though, is whether the constant need to be pleasing—solicitation's inevitable corollary—might also tend to erode their integrity.

Consider, as one instance, the matter of gifts. In accepting objects for our collections, how often have we been motivated solely by a desire for the proffered object—it was just or nearly what we would buy ourselves if we only had the money—and how often have we yielded to the temptation to accommodate the donor? There are few museums, I suspect, where desire alone has unfailingly prevailed. We must, after all, be practical. Beggars, if they cannot be choosers, might at least be pleasers—and institutions such as museums, which are so overwhelmingly dependent on others for their continuing operation as well as for the growth of their collections, may reach the point, if care is not used, of being all too pleasing indeed.

It is perfectly evident, for example, that some museums (in every discipline) have in recent years permitted themselves to be used as the terminal points in tax-abuse schemes based on the artificially high valuation of charitable gifts. The defense offered for this involvement has been the traditional rubric, "Valuation is the donor's business and none of ours." As a rationale, this is threadbare. To the extent that the public comes to perceive any museum as entangled with someone's private gain rather than the general good, then the positive perception of all museums is to some degree weakened. To the extent that administrative or legislative confidence in the workability of the full fair-market value charitable deduction is undermined, museums may jeopardize their chances ever to get gifts of the objects they really want to be given. Such concerns, contrary to the rubric, are very much our business.

Worse still are those several reported instances in which, at a donor's behest, receipts or deeds of gift have been backdated in an effort to get more favorable tax treatment. While those responsible may not have pondered it deeply, such conduct—light years past any question of integrity—may well violate a federal criminal law. The odor may be no more than that of pandering, but the underlying crime involves complicity in the preparation of a false tax return.

We mistake the situation if we consider the maintenance of

integrity to be an accomplishment for which we will be applauded or even a basis on which we can justify an appeal for greater public support. It must, rather, be seen as no more than a minimum expectation, a threshold to be met as a matter of course. Conversely, though, we must understand that any failure of integrity can damage every museum. (See "No Museum Is an Island" at pp. 103–13.) To the extent that we must rely on public funds, our continuing access could well be constricted or even blocked when there is no longer confidence that what we do is done with the disinterestedness essential to our status as public institutions.

Meanwhile, if it *is* the case that our position as mendicants only serves to exacerbate the Snodgrass problem, then we must be all the more careful. There is a natural instinct to cater to those who support our operations and enrich our collections, but we cannot let this tempt us into straying from our primary responsibility to serve the public. We ought also to consider how much more easily this temptation could be resisted if our dependence could be reduced. The establishment of financial independence would not merely release our energies for more appropriate museological purposes. It might also remove a substantial impediment in our progress toward greater integrity.

MGR: A Conspectus
of Museum Management
(1982)

I n a 1975 *Harvard Business Review* article, Henry Mintzberg observed that the tasks a typical manager performs on a daily basis are characterized chiefly by their "brevity, variety and discontinuity."[1] His observation appears valid for museums. To those in senior management positions, nothing could be more evident (and sometimes more frustrating) than their constant diversion from what they may suppose to be the classic tasks of management—planning, organizing, coordinating, and controlling—in order to deal with a kaleidoscopic array of seemingly unrelated matters in need of urgent attention. What about a curator's request for additional travel funds? Should Gallery 302 be shut to the public so that the floor can be fixed? Will the museum honor its agreement to send an exhibition to an East European country with which diplomatic relations may momentarily be severed? Would the funding application for a forthcoming exhibition be better addressed to the National Endowment for the Arts or the National Endowment for the Humanities?

A corresponding situation prevails in the study of museum management. The complaint most frequently heard from management students concerns the apparent lack of connection among the topics that typically constitute their course of study. What sense, they ask, is to be made of a day spent jumping quickly from the mysteries of accrual-basis accounting to the implications of McGregor's assumptions *X* and *Y* to the intricacies of bylaws and governance? What has long-range planning to do with situ-

Copyright © 1982 by Stephen E. Weil. Reprinted from Museum News, *vol. 60, no. 6 (July/August 1982).*

ational leadership? How do either of these relate to professional standards?

MGR was originally developed for the Museum Management Institute in order to show more clearly the underlying continuity among the varied tasks that together constitute the museum manager's daily work. It is *not* a system of management. It is, rather, a provisional effort to describe how the concerns with which every manager must regularly deal relate to one another and to the overall purposes of the museum. While it is based primarily on the governance structure of the private voluntary museum—the organizational form of more than half of American museums—it can be adapted as well to state, county, and municipal museums and to museums that are subunits of some larger entity such as a university or cultural complex.

MGR is an acronym: *M* for *Methods,* *G* for *Goals,* and *R* for *Resources.* For reasons that will become evident, the *G* for *Goals* is given the central position. The premise of MGR is that management consists fundamentally of the methodical or other employment of institutional resources toward the achievement of institutional goals.

Under MGR a clear distinction is made among methods, goals, and resources. A corresponding distinction is made among tasks that are primarily method related, goal related, and resource related. These tasks, in turn, are broadly defined as planning, implementing, evaluating, and documenting. While the focus of any given task may be on one or another method, goal, or resource, the nature of these tasks is seen as relatively constant. The traditional distinction between policy and implementation (i.e., the board makes policy; the director and staff implement policy) is not recognized. Policy is envisioned, rather, as one of several methods for employing resources, and policy making is perceived as an activity that is pervasive throughout the museum.

While the following analysis will focus primarily on the work of senior management, it must be understood that management in its larger sense embraces the sum of every activity performed within the museum and, accordingly, that the board and every member of the staff are to a degree engaged in management. The difference between a museum director and a frontline supervisor lies not so much in the nature of the tasks they perform (planning, implementing, evaluating, documenting) as in the focus of the tasks for which they have immediate responsibility and the scope of the resources under their control.

Institutional Goals
and Goal-Related Tasks

By definition the general goals of any museum must be those of museums generally. As Joseph Veach Noble has explained, these are to collect, preserve, study, interpret, and exhibit.[2]

In every museum these general goals are coupled with particular goals that specify what it is that is to be collected, preserved, studied, interpreted, and exhibited (maritime artifacts, Oriental art objects, local history memorabilia) as well, in most cases, as the purpose or purposes for which this work is to be done. A museum's particular goals will customarily be set forth in its charter or other founding document. These goals are the "givens" of the organization in the pursuit of which substantial resources will already have been assembled and invested. As such, they lie beyond the purview of management and will only rarely be changed. The pursuit of any other goal is improper.

The board of trustees is charged by law with the overall management of the museum. While its authority is ostensibly complete, the highest level of choice it will ordinarily exercise is to set priorities among the organization's permitted goals and (as in the case of a museum with several types of collections) within such goals. What is to be emphasized, to what degree, and for how long? Should resources be diverted from a series of scholarly publications to begin an outreach program? Should a large, unexpected, and unrestricted bequest be used to furnish a new conservation laboratory or to endow an acquisitions fund? If there is a shortfall in income, what program areas should be scaled back or eliminated? How much of a new wing should be devoted to galleries and how much to classrooms? While senior staff may play an advocacy role in setting priorities among the museum's permitted goals, this task is essentially one to be performed by the board. Typically, it will do so through its adoption of near-term budgets and long-range plans.

The management tasks of the director and senior staff begin at the level below this. The director's authority to perform such tasks is derived from the board through delegation. Paramount among these tasks is the translation of the museum's priority-ordered general and particular goals into public programs. Put otherwise, the principal goal-related task of senior management is to convert the institution's skeletal and essentially abstract goals into a concrete and visible form. In this regard it should be noted that both the display and conservation of the museum's permanent collection are considered under MGR to be programs to exactly the same extent as would the presentation of a special loan exhibition or the preparation of a catalog.

The translation of goals into programs is an ongoing management task and cannot be fully accomplished within the lifetime of an institution. The most important of museum goals are basically unattainable. Short of the end of time, there is no point at which the goal of preserving any object will have finally been met. No collection of contemporary art, history, or science can ever be brought to completion. In this respect museums differ substantially from other nonprofit organizations dedicated to the achievement of such theoretically attainable goals as the eradication of a particular disease or the commemoration of a specific event.

In the performance of its ongoing goal-related tasks, senior staff will typically separate its program initiatives into a series of discrete components ("objectives") that—together with some further delegation of the authority originally derived from the board—can be assigned to subordinate staff members. At each intermediate level, this process (including the identification of sub-objectives and a further delegation of authority) may be replicated within the narrower compass of these assigned objectives. The sum of accomplished objectives and subobjectives will constitute the actual program of the museum.

Under MGR, goal-related tasks are distinguished from resource- and method-related tasks by the directness with which they relate to the museum's public programs. Thus, to plan or write a collections handbook would be classified as a primarily goal-related task. Selecting a printer for such a handbook would be classified as primarily resource related. The design or implementation of a procurement system through which the museum might regularly purchase its printing would be classified as primarily method related.

Institutional Resources and
Resource-Related Tasks

The only purposes for which museum resources may be legit-imately expended are those that demonstrably relate either to its governance or directly or indirectly to its goal-related programs. Any other expenditure—whether of a staff member's time, a sum of money, or the use of a gallery—constitutes a waste of resources for which the board may be held accountable.

For the purposes of MGR, the resources that museums employ toward the achievement of their institutional goals are considered as falling into seven clusters. Chief among these, because it is implicit in the definition of the museum, is:

● *Collections:* included here are not only accessioned objects but also any object that may be currently or potentially available for study or exhibition through loan, gift, excavation rights, or oth-erwise.

Of the remaining six clusters—all of which (unlike collections) are common to virtually every enterprise—there are three which include resources that are more or less tangible. These, and some of the principal resources within each, are:

● *Human Resources:* trustees, paid staff, volunteer staff, inde-pendent contractors, consultants, donors, members, vendors.

● *Fiscal Resources:* cash, accounts receivable, prepaid expenses, pledges, future interests, investments in securities, and similar assets that can be quantified monetarily.

● *Tangible Noncollection Resources:* land, plant, equipment, tools, supplies, inventory.

The remaining three clusters include resources that, while not so tangible, are no less vital. These are:

● *Information:* included here is everything from collections rec-ords, photographs, films, tapes, and correspondence files to the operating manuals for power tools and a set of telephone books. Also included is the full range of scholarly publications available from both internal and external sources as well as such products of documentation (a basic management task) as the museum's fiscal and personnel records, its plumbing and wiring plans, and the minutes of meetings. Codes of professional conduct and the museum's established operating procedures, while arguably each so distinctive as to constitute a resource of another kind, are also considered forms of information.

● *High Public Regard:* the totality of positive ways in which the museum is perceived by its various publics, both internal (trustees, staff, volunteers, members) and external (visitors, vendors, collectors, museum professionals, the community, the press, funding sources, local government).

● *Time:* notwithstanding some anomaly in considering time as a resource, it functions as such in the case of planning ("To accomplish X, we will need A people, B dollars, and C time"). Moreover, it shares with other resources the quality of being convertible. Thus, the lack of time to complete a specific project in a routine way might be made up by expending dollars (a fiscal resource) for additional help (a human resource). Conversely, the cost of carrying out a specific project might be reduced by deferring the date of its proposed completion and thus, in effect, converting some period of time into dollars.

Tasks that are primarily resource related may be divided roughly into those that are performed within the framework of an established method and those for which no method has been prescribed. As a rule, the more routinely that such tasks must be performed, the greater the likelihood that management will have established a method—that is, a "routine"—to regulate their performance. The more infrequently a task must be performed or the more unanticipated the circumstances that might occasion the task, the less likely it is that any methodical framework will have been provided for its accomplishment.

Most often the level of the museum at which a resource-related task is to be performed will be inversely related to the extent to which a method for its performance has been established. Thus, in a museum charging admission there would commonly be a well-established routine by which the day's proceeds are held in safekeeping overnight and deposited the following morning. Except in unusual circumstances, the daily performance of these tasks would be the immediate responsibility of subordinate staff members. By contrast, the discovery in the museum's lobby of a steamer trunk filled with gold bullion and a note reading "In gratitude for so many years of pleasure" would inaugurate a series of resource-related tasks that would necessarily involve senior staff and most likely the board of trustees.

Because the resources employed by museums have such widely varying properties, the techniques appropriate for managing them must be equally varied. A malfunctioning typewriter and a depressed and unproductive staff cannot be "fixed" in the same way, and the criteria for choosing an endowment investment will not be the same as those for selecting an object to be accessioned. Nonetheless, the underlying nature of these resource-related tasks tends to be the same. Once more, they are broadly defined as planning, implementing, evaluating, and documenting.

Methods and Method-Related Tasks

The effective manager does not make many decisions. He solves generic problems through policy.

—PETER DRUCKER[3]

The term *Methods*, as used in MGR, embraces the entire range of policies, procedures, practices, systems, arrangements, and routines that may be established, negotiated, or permitted to develop for the regular and systematic performance of resource- and goal-related tasks. Management's method-related tasks are planning, implementing, evaluating, and documenting such policies, procedures, practices, systems, arrangements, and routines.

As Drucker suggests, a principal function of an established policy is to relieve management from the necessity of having constantly to determine how a recurring task is to be performed. To this extent methods operate to conserve management time— a museum resource. The establishment of methods may also be indicated for certain nonrecurring tasks—e.g., the evacuation of the museum in case of fire or the treatment of a stricken visitor— when the brief time available in which to perform the task may preclude making a "good" decision and when the harm to be anticipated in the absence of such a decision might be very great.

Given the variety of resources employed by museums and the corresponding variety of the techniques that must be used to deal with them, it follows that an equally varied range of methods is also required. A collections management policy will be no more helpful in determining how to pay employees required to work on holidays than will the adoption of an accrual-basis accounting system assure that an adequate supply of spare light bulbs is kept on hand. Each cluster of resources will require a different and appropriate series of methods for the routine performance of its relevant tasks. A methodical approach to such goal-related tasks as budgeting and long-range planning may require still further methods.

The magnitude of management's task in providing methods for dealing with all of a museum's varied resources may be suggested by listing some of those that might be established with respect to paid staff. In some cases these may be unilaterally prescribed by the board and/or senior management. In others they may have to be reached through negotiation with a collective bargaining agent acting on behalf of the staff.

• A system of delegation (generally reflected in a table of organization) pursuant to which a share of the authority vested by law in the board and originally delegated to the director may be subdivided among those subordinates who will be charged with immediate (but not ultimate) responsibility for the exercise of such authority. Integral to such an arrangement will be a variety of controls as well as procedures for evaluating and documenting the operation of the system.

• Personnel procedures prescribing the manner in which employees are recruited, interviewed, and hired; how records are kept of their salaries, benefits, and attendance; the documents to be completed on their voluntary or involuntary termination and the records to be retained after such termination.

• A salary and fringe benefits program.

• A payroll and withholding system.

• A comprehensive set of personnel practices covering such matters as hours of work, overtime, leave policy (including holidays, vacations, sick leave, leaves of absence, jury, voting, and military leave), disciplinary and grievance procedures, probationary employment, employee discounts, travel reimbursement, and training opportunities.

• A system of job descriptions, performance review, and evaluation.

● An equal opportunity policy that may also provide for affirmative action and upward mobility programs.

● A compilation of health and safety procedures.

● A code of ethics covering such matters as outside employment, private collecting, conflict of interest, dual compensation, and the use of privileged information.

● An internal communications system employing such devices as telephones, meetings, memoranda, minutes, newsletters, and bulletin boards.

The list is by no means complete, and paid staff is only one element in the cluster of human resources that a museum employs toward the accomplishment of its institutional goals. Other methods will be needed to conduct the affairs of the board, to assure that the gifts of donors are promptly and properly acknowledged, and to be certain that museum members receive renewal notices as their memberships expire. Beyond the human resources cluster, the method-related tasks of management require that regular ways be established to do everything from keeping the museum's financial records and maintaining its climate controls to recording its collection and carrying out the trash. In each case, what is involved is again planning, implementing, evaluating, and documenting.

Potential Uses of MGR

How might this schema be useful to museum managers and students of management?

First, MGR could be helpful in avoiding certain confusions endemic to museums. Under MGR, for example, it would appear evident that a museum cannot have as its goal "to operate in the black" or "to break even." Money is a resource, not a goal. While fiscal probity is a necessary precondition to a museum's survival, it is no measure of its success toward achieving its actual general and particular museological goals. A museum may operate with a constantly balanced budget and still, by its failure to generate programs commensurate with its goals, be an inadequate museum.

Staff morale and museum collections stand in the same condition. Staff is a museum resource, not its purpose for being. A demoralized staff can make it difficult if not impossible for a museum to work effectively toward its goals, but high staff morale would no more indicate a museum's success than would a constantly balanced budget. Collections, too, are a resource, and the measure of museum management lies not in what the institution has historically acquired but in the current programmatic use to which the collection is put.

Methods, too, may be confused with goals. The resulting proposition would be that a well-administered museum was a well-managed museum. Administration, however, is no more than the sum of the methods established to employ institutional resources. It is a way of facilitating the work of the museum—a "how"—but it is in no sense the "why" for which such resources have been assembled. Sound administration can make a major contribution to the success of a museum. Again, though, it is ultimately by its programs, not by its administration, that a museum must be judged.

Two further uses of MGR might be to test the "fit" between a proposed activity and a museum's general and particular goals and to generate such questions as may be necessary to assure that all of the implications of undertaking such an activity have been considered.

The high regard of its various publics is among a museum's most important resources, and this question of "fit" is important in maintaining this regard. It is not sufficient that these publics understand the museum's underlying goals. It is just as important that, as the museum's programs evolve, all of its publics have a clear understanding of how each of its successive activities relates to these goals. The inability of the museum to demonstrate to its publics (including trustees and staff) that there *is* such a relationship can only raise suspicions that the museum's management is pursuing a proposed activity for reasons that are capricious, of personal rather than institutional advantage, and/or part of some undisclosed agenda. The damaging effects of such suspicions can spread beyond the proposed activity to reflect negatively on the museum as a whole.

If, however, a proposed activity can be demonstrated to have the requisite "fit," then the questions generated by MGR might be useful in forecasting how the activity would affect the museum's various resource clusters. The questions are those that an experienced museum manager would instinctively ask:

- What people will be involved?
- What funds will be required, and what offsetting funds might be generated?
- What space will be needed? What supplies and equipment?
- What additional information may be required?
- Will the activity itself produce information of value?
- How will the activity affect the perception of the museum by each of its publics?
- What time periods will be needed for planning and implementation?
- How will the activity be evaluated, by whom, and when?
- What documentation will be necessary?
- Will any new procedures or routines have to be established?
- Which of the resources required will have to be newly obtained and which can be diverted from some prior use?
- For those to be newly obtained, what sources will be looked to?
- For those to be diverted from some prior use, what will this diversion cost the museum's present activities? How does this cost measure against the benefits to be anticipated from the proposed activity?

MGR may also be used as a tool for analyzing a museum's overall management. As such, it would provoke a different series of questions:

- Have the museums's general and particular goals been clearly articulated?
- To what degree are these goals understood by the museum's various publics?
- Are the museum's public programs demonstrably consistent with such goals?
- Have these programs been designed to make optimum use of the museum's available resources?
- To what extent is senior staff engaged in goal-related and method-

related tasks? To what extent is it burdened with the performance of routine resource-related tasks that could better be delegated to subordinates? Conversely, has its energy been misdirected into the establishment and maintenance of a methodical framework larger and more complex than the museum's circumstances in fact require?

● How are energies of the board apportioned among goal-, resource-, and method-related tasks?

● At what organizational levels are planning and evaluation the predominant activities? At what level is the focus on implementation and documentation?

These uses aside, MGR could be a crutch for managerial sanity. As a map on which less experienced museum managers might plot the relationship between institutional goals and the seemingly disconnected concerns that bulk so large in their working days, it might help to relieve an intermittent sense of disorientation and discontinuity. Equally, it might be of help to students who need to learn that managing a museum is, in the end, not merely having the skill to handle a particular resource—knowing how to motivate an employee, organize a capital campaign, use time efficiently, or select the right word processor. Museum management is, rather, an art that requires the orchestration of all these skills, and more, in support of a museum's basic purpose: to perform an essential public service. MGR might make this clear.

NOTES

1. Henry Mintzberg, "The Manager's Job: Folklore and Fact," *Harvard Business Review* 53, no. 4 (July/August 1975): 49.
2. Joseph Veach Noble, "Museum Manifesto," *Museum News* 48, no. 8 (April 1970): 16–20.
3. Quoted in John J. Tarrant, *Drucker: The Man Who Invented the Corporate Society* (New York, 1980), p. 258.

The Filer Commission Report: Is It Good for Museums? (1976)

The Commission on Private Philanthropy and Public Needs (more often
referred to as the Filer Commission, after its chairman, John H.
Filer) was established in November 1973, at the initiative of John
D. Rockefeller III and with the encouragement of high-ranking
members of Congress and the Department of the Treasury. Its
objectives, as outlined by the commission, were:

- to study the role of both private philanthropic giving in the
United States and that area through which giving is principally
channeled, the voluntary "third" sector of American society; and
- to make recommendations to the voluntary sector, to Congress,
and to the American public concerning ways in which the sector
and the practice of private giving could be strengthened and made
more effective.

The commission's work has increased by a quantum leap our
understanding of charitable donors and donees, the tax incentive
and other mechanisms which link them, and the social context in
which philanthropy occurs. Its findings and recommendations
have been published in a final report, *Giving in America: Toward
a Stronger Voluntary Sector.* Though brief, the report is the dis-
tillation of more than eighty studies conducted under the commission's sponsorship and reflects as well the expert testimony
of more than one hundred consultants and advisors.

Elsewhere, the report will be discussed in the broad terms that

*Copyright © 1976 by the American Association of Museums. Reprinted from Mu-
seum News, vol. 54, no. 5 (May/June 1976), by permission of the American Association of Museums.*

Recommendations of the Filer Commission

Broadening the Base of Philanthropy

1. That to increase inducements for charitable giving, all taxpayers who take the standard deduction should also be permitted to deduct charitable contributions as an additional, itemized deduction.

2. That an additional inducement to charitable giving should be provided to low- and middle-income taxpayers. Toward this end, the Commission proposes that a "double deduction" be instituted for families with incomes of less than $15,000 a year; they would be allowed to deduct twice what they give in computing their income taxes. For those families with incomes between $15,000 and $30,000, the Commission proposes a deduction of 150 percent of their giving.

3. That income deducted for charitable giving should be excluded from any minimum tax provision.

4. That the appreciated property allowance within the charitable deduction be basically retained but amended to eliminate any possibility of personal financial gain through tax-deductible charitable giving.

5. That the charitable bequest deduction be retained in its present form.

6. That corporations set as a minimum goal, to be reached no later than 1980, the giving to charitable purposes of 2 percent of pretax net income. Moreover, the Commission believes that the national commission proposed in this report should consider as a priority concern additional measures to stimulate corporate giving.

Improving the Philanthropic Process

7. That all larger tax-exempt charitable organizations except churches and church affiliates be required to prepare and make readily available detailed annual reports on their finances, programs and priorities.

8. That larger grant-making organizations be required to hold annual public meetings to discuss their programs, priorities and contributions.

9. That the present 4 percent "audit" tax on private foundations be repealed and replaced by a fee on all private foundations based on the total actual costs of auditing them.

10. That the Internal Revenue Service continue to be the principal agency responsible for the oversight of tax-exempt organizations.

11. That the duplication of legal responsibility for proper expenditure of foundation grants, now imposed on both foundations and recipients, be eliminated and that recipient organizations be made primarily responsible for their expenditures.

12. That tax-exempt organizations, particularly funding organizations, recognize an obligation to be responsive to changing viewpoints and emerging needs and that they take steps such as broadening their boards and staffs to insure that they are responsive.

13. That a new category of "independent" foundation be established by law. Such organizations would enjoy the tax benefits of public charities in return for diminished influence on the foundation's board by the foundation's benefactor or by his or her family or business associates.

14. That all tax-exempt organizations be required by law to maintain "arms-length" business relationships with profit-making organizations or activities in which any member of the organization's staff, any board member or any major contributor has a substantial financial interest, either directly or through his or her family.

15. That to discourage unnecessary accumulation of income, a flat payout rate of 5 percent of principal be fixed by Congress for private foundations and a lower rate for other endowed tax-exempt organizations.

16. That a system of federal regulation be established for interstate charitable solicitations and that intrastate solicitations be more effectively regulated by state governments.

17. That as a federal enforcement tool against abuses by tax-exempt organizations, and to protect these organizations themselves, sanctions appropriate to the abuses should be enacted as well as forms of administrative or judicial review of the principal existing sanction—revocation of an organization's exempt status.

18. That nonprofit organizations, other than foundations, be allowed the same freedoms to attempt to influence legislation as are business corporations and trade associations, and that toward this end Congress remove the current limitation on such activity by charitable groups eligible to receive tax-deductible gifts.

A Permanent Commission

19. That a permanent national commission on the nonprofit sector be established by Congress.

its importance clearly warrants. Museums should follow these discussions with interest; whatever impact the commission's report may have on the quality of American life generally must, at least incidentally, also affect both museums and those who work for them. Nevertheless, while fully acknowledging the deliberate parochialism of the question, it is necessary to ask of the report: "Is it good for museums?" The answer, insofar as the commission's specific proposals are concerned, appears to lie somewhere between "not very" and "not at all."

Carrots and Sticks

Concluding the report are nineteen recommendations which, as viewed from the nonprofit sector, can be considered of two types: carrots and sticks. Nourishing as some of the carrots may be for *other* nonprofit organizations, they promise little added sustenance for museums. Some of the sticks, on the other hand, could prove painful for everyone.

There is no reason to believe that the commission bore any animus toward museums. To the contrary, museums (or more precisely the categories of "civic and cultural," "cultural institutions," "arts and humanities," and "other" in which they are variously classified) are referred to positively when they are referred to at all.

The fact is that museums are not a significant segment of the universe the report seeks to embrace—an estimated *six million* private nonprofit organizations. By any conventional statistical measure, they are dwarfed by the giant educational, religious, medical, and welfare organizations that tower above the nonprofit landscape. When measured by number of organizations, aggregate operating budgets, annual contributions, or number of employees, museums account for less than 1 percent of the total. Not even the accumulated wealth represented by their collections, endowments, and physical plants is of major consequence when compared to the combined holdings of American universities, churches, and hospitals. The significance of museums must thus be measured by other means. Given the commission's broad mandate, it is not surprising that museums were not treated with greater particularity.

If museums cannot complain of hostility on the commission's part, neither should they have any quarrel with the assumptions that underlie its recommendations. These are set forth in the first part of the report—an eloquent summary of the case that public needs may be best met by a mix of private and government initiatives. There is, said the commission,

> the deeply rooted American conviction that no single institutional structure should exercise a monopoly on filling public needs, that reliance on government alone to fill such needs . . . risks making human values subservient to institutional ones, individual and community purposes subordinate to bureaucratic conveniences and authoritarian dictates.

The commission's argument goes deeper. The value of private nonprofit organizations is not simply as a hedge against monolithic government. By their very nature, they can experiment and act with a speed and flexibility seldom practical for public agencies. Because of their smaller scale, nonprofit organizations may provide vehicles for individual expression and influence at levels not possible in the "giant and impersonal institutions of business and government." Most importantly, unlike government, they can "support causes and interests that may be swept aside by majoritarian priorities and prejudices."

Those who cherish the qualities that set the American museum system apart from the state-dominated organizations of many other countries can only applaud the commission's analysis. Its recommendations, on the other hand, should cause them serious concern.

The Low-Fat Carrot

Private nonprofit organizations can remain private only as long as they have reliable sources of funds, other than those flowing from various levels of government for special project support or as direct operating grants. The commission first addressed itself to these private funds.

Over the past decade—in the face of inflation estimated by the commission to have increased the costs of goods and services for nonprofit organizations faster than for the economy as a whole—overall philanthropic giving, measured as a percentage of aggregate personal income or of gross national product, has shown evidence of slipping.

To reverse this trend, the commission's principal recommendations would establish additional tax incentives to stimulate increased tax-deductible contributions by families earning up to $30,000 annually and by taxpayers—largely in the low- and middle-income brackets—who claim standard rather than itemized deductions on their federal tax returns. The commission estimated that these changes initially might generate as much as $11.7 billion in additional annual giving, with an estimated corresponding loss in annual tax revenues of $9.1 billion.

If museums were to share proportionately in this additional giving, they would have little cause for concern. In all likelihood, however, they would not share proportionately at all. Tables published by the commission reveal that the largest share of giving by low-bracket taxpayers has gone to religious organizations and to such federated drives as the United Fund and various community chests. The percentage of individual giving directed to all other kinds of nonprofit organizations—from colleges and hospitals to "culture," with its array of symphony orchestras, ballet companies, theaters, and museums—becomes substantial only in the higher income brackets. The figures for 1972 appear below:

Adjusted Gross Income	% of Giving to other than Religious Organizations and Federated Drives
Under $10,000	17%
$10,000 to $20,000	19%
$20,000 to $50,000	33%
$50,000 to $200,000	57%
$200,000 and over	84%

Why should museums be concerned if the additional giving stimulated by new tax incentives were primarily to benefit other organizations? The answer lies in the estimated $9.1 billion loss in annual tax revenues. Nothing in Washington's present climate suggests that Congress would surrender such a sum without seeking to offset it elsewhere. The commission acknowledged this, but its analysis does not seem to have been carried far enough. "It should be borne in mind," says the report in referring to these reduced government revenues, ". . . that the net budgetary impact would be less than the tax loss projected, since the charitable contributions stimulated would to some extent reduce the need for governmental expenditure in the areas to which the new giving would go.''

How could this happen so neatly? In families with adjusted gross incomes of less than $20,000, more than two-thirds of charitable giving goes to religious organizations. Since these nonprofit organizations receive virtually no government support, in their case there would be nothing to reduce. The only alternatives would be to reduce spending in other areas or to increase tax rates generally. In either case, museums might stand to lose as much or more as they might gain initially under the commission's recommendations.

The present scheme of charitable deductions has served museums resonably well. Giving for "civic and cultural" purposes—one of the classifications in which museums are included—is the single area which, as a percentage of total giving, has increased steadily over the past thirty-five years. It constituted less than 1 percent of all philanthropy in 1940, but approached 10 percent in 1974. Unless museums are prepared to shift their fund-raising focus toward lower-income taxpayers or to become more deeply involved in community-wide fund-raising drives—both issues too complex to discuss here—they should be hesitant to endorse any sweeping changes in the present method of calculating charitable deductions.

Only sixteen of the commission's twenty-eight members—57 percent—concurred fully with the first two recommendations. In general, dissenting members took the position that the existing system of progressive income tax rates itself makes the charitable deduction inequitable and that the recommended changes would simply increase this inequity. A number of dissenting commissioners preferred a system of charitable tax credits. None of the dissenters addressed the particular situation of cultural institutions.

Of the remaining carrots, the most noteworthy for museums concerns the donation of appreciated property. While recommending that the present form of this deduction "basically [be] retained," the commission suggested (without specific details) some adjustment "to eliminate the possibility of personal financial gain through tax-deductible charitable giving." Such an adjustment might be felt most particularly by art museums that solicit contributions of highly appreciated objects. These institutions have already lost a major source of donations through the elimination of fair-market-value deductions by artists under the Tax Reform Act of 1969.

As for corporate giving—increasingly important as a potential source of private support for museums—the commission was unable to agree on any firm recommendation which would stimulate corporate support above the 1-percent-of-net-income level at which it has hovered in recent years. Seven dissenting commissioners favored one form of legislation or another that would impose a tax penalty on corporations failing to make at least some charitable gifts. The majority settled for what several dissenters characterized as an exhortation that corporations try to do better in the future and, *mirabile dictu*, recommended that the problem be studied further!

Some Pointed Sticks

The proposed *quid pro quo* for these not very promising recommendations would be an increased level of public regulation. While the commission's recommendations are offered not in such bald terms but rather under the heading of "improving the philanthropic process"—an effect they might undoubtedly have in some cases—the question remains, how appropriate are these recommendations for museums? As for some, the abuses sought to be remedied are not abuses characteristic of museums. As for others, there is doubtful practicality in applying a single remedy across the entire spectrum of nonprofit organizations.

One recommendation, for example, would extend to all endowed, private nonprofit organizations—museums included—a scaled-down version of the payout rules first applied to private foundations under the Tax Reform Act of 1969. The minimum percentage suggested by the commission would be "less than 5 percent." Such a payout requirement, said the commission, "should be satisfied by the use of funds for direct conduct of the organization's activities, including . . . the acquisition of art objects by museums and so forth."

While virtually every endowed museum now classified as a

public charity could meet a less-than-5-percent payout requirement with laughable ease, there is no reason why these institutions—not even suspect of unnecessary or excessive accumula-
tions of income—should be burdened with additional record
keeping, reporting, and supervision. Moreover, once such a law
were on the books, it would not take such great effort for another
Congress in another time and mood to substitute a higher payout
requirement—one that museums might not find so benign as "less
than 5 percent."

Two other recommendations, if adopted, could subject museums to increased reporting requirements and additional layers
of supervision. One would require the federal regulation of interstate charitable solicitations. The commission suggested that

> a special office be established in the Internal Revenue Service or
> in some other federal agency or regulatory body, such as the Federal
> Trade Commission, to oversee charity solicitation and take action against
> improper, misleading or excessively costly fund raisings. This special
> office might be supplemented by and guided by an accrediting or-
> ganization, which would review the finances of and certify all exempt
> organizations whose solicitation practices are found to merit approval.

Aside from whatever problems might be involved in accrediting
and reaccrediting so vast a number of organizations, the question
recurs: why should this be applied to museums? Museums do
not include among their vices "improper, misleading or exces-
sively costly fund raisings." They do include among their virtues
an ongoing and self-imposed system of accreditation.

The other recommendation would establish a permanent national commission on the nonprofit sector. This proposal con-
templates, among other things, that a registry of nonprofit organizations be maintained and that "a modest charge on all
charitable organizations should be considered" to help defray the
commission's expenses.

Dissenting from this recommendation, one member of the Filer
Commission wrote: "All such a national commission would do is
increase the administrative costs of nonprofit organizations, thus
reducing the funds available for their beneficiaries. Far from aiding
these institutions, the national commission will be another financial drain and another administrative burden."

Of the recommendations that might be considered sticks, there is one other to which museums should give special attention: "All larger tax-exempt charitable organizations . . . [would] be required to prepare and make readily available detailed annual reports on their finances, programs and priorities." Palatable as this may seem at first, it takes on a different flavor when coupled with the commission's explanatory text.

"Larger tax-exempt charitable organizations" are not simply the American Red Cross, the American Cancer Society, and the like. The commission defines them as organizations with annual budgets of more than $100,000. Based on the figures collected by the National Endowment for the Arts in Museums USA, this requirement would have applied to at least 650 museums in 1971–72; that figure would certainly be higher today. "Prepare and make readily available" would not simply require that still another report be filed with appropriate state and federal agencies; it would also require that museums make such reports "directly and swiftly available, at or below cost, to any person or organization upon request."

Most ominous, however, is the commission's suggestion as to the form of such reports. Without finally committing itself, the commission appears to have flirted with prescribing a single accounting form for use by every nonprofit organization in the United States. In the end, it hedged by suggesting that, at the minimum, uniform accounting measures be required of all comparable organizations. Those who participated in preparing the museum accounting guidelines recently published by the Association of Science-Technology Centers can testify to the enormous problems that this might entail. Even if comparable embraced no larger a class of organizations than museums, the variety of American museums is such that no common mold has yet been developed into which all of their financial reporting can be neatly fitted.

Without external prodding museums have taken the initiative in formulating general guidelines that will, at the least, bring their financial reporting into conformity with generally accepted accounting principles. In time, the experience of applying these guidelines may permit them to move even closer to some ideal of financial comparability. The interruption of this process through the sudden imposition of specific and uniform accounting measures by some outside authority is not a sanguine prospect.

Early in its report, the Filer Commission made an impassioned argument for strengthening the third sector so that government would not "exercise a monopoly on filling public needs." It is ironic that so many of its recommendations would entangle nonprofit organizations with government more deeply than ever before.

Some Conclusions

In his preface to *Giving in America*, the chairman refers to his commission's subject as "a dimly known region of American life." It is abundantly clear from the commission's report that this region is far too large and diverse to be encompassed by a single set of rules. The needs, virtues, and vices of the Metropolitan Museum of Art are not the same as those of the Calendar Reform Foundation or the Boy Scouts of America.

Museums must insist on their particularity. As modest elements in the nonprofit world, they cannot assume that larger segments of that world should or will protect their interests. They must be prepared to stand on their own, to speak out when necessary, and to insist on the importance of what they do.

It will not be enough merely to clarify their interests. Underlying the commission's recommendations is the rising public demand that nonprofit organizations adopt higher standards of accountability than heretofore. If museums are not prepared to develop these standards from within their community, there will be little defense against their imposition from outside. Here the commission's recommendations may well serve as a warning.

Finally, while insisting on their particularity, museums would do well to consider searching out areas in which they might make common cause with other nonprofit organizations. A stimulus here can be found in the opinion of those commissioners who dissented from the recommendation that Congress establish a permanent national commission. "The priority need for strengthening the nonprofit sector," wrote one commissioner, "is not an expansion of government, as proposed in this report, but a strengthening of the nonprofit sector's capacity to initiate and implement joint action."

Although it is doubtful that Congress will move quickly to consider or adopt its major recommendations, the Filer Commission report is sure to be widely discussed in the coming years and may, in whole or in part, have persuasive impact. Those who are concerned about the future of museums should study *Giving in America* with care.

Afterword

Since the publication of *Giving in America* in 1975, a number of the steps that the Filer Commission recommended to broaden the base of philanthropy and improve the philanthropic process have been implemented through federal tax legislation. That the tax laws should have been the vehicle for such changes is wholly in accord with the commission's own Recommendation 10—that the Internal Revenue Service continue to have the chief federal oversight responsibility for tax-exempt organizations.

Recommendation 1—that nonitemizers be permitted to deduct their charitable contributions—was adopted as part of the Economic Recovery Tax Act of 1981 (ERTA), which amended Section 170 of the Internal Revenue Code by providing a "direct charitable deduction" to be phased in during the years 1982 through 1985. During this introductory period, the maximum amount of charitable contributions that a nonitemizing taxpayer can deduct is a percentage of his actual contributions—subject, for the first three years, to a fixed dollar ceiling on the amount that may be included in making the required computation. In tabular form, it would appear thus:

Year	Applicable Percentage	Ceiling	Maximum Deduction Permitted
1982	25%	$100	$25
1983	25%	$100	$25
1984	25%	$300	$75
1985	50%	None	No limit

In 1986, this new provision will be fully in place and an individual taxpayer claiming the standard deduction may, in addition, deduct (subject to the code's *other* limitations) his charitable contributions in full. While the provision for a "direct charitable deduction" is now scheduled to expire in 1987, a strenuous effort will undoubtedly be made to extend it further.

The commission's Recommendation 15—urging a flat 5 percent minimum payout requirement for private foundations and a lesser one for other endowed tax-exempt organizations—was also implemented in part by ERTA, but in an oddly inverted way. At the time of the commission's report, the minimum payout requirement for a private foundation was (grossly simplified) the greater of its adjusted net income or an amount equal to 6 percent of the fair market value of its net assets. The commission noted that the 6 percent figure was "higher, by a significant degree, than the yield that can be anticipated from a balanced investment portfolio." Thus, for many foundations it was this 6 percent alternative—rather than their actual income—that determined their required minimum payout. To meet this figure, they had to invade their capital. The Congress provided partial relief in the Tax Reform Act of 1976 by reducing the 6 percent figure —the so-called minimum investment return—to 5 percent.

With the great interest rate and inflation surge of the late seventies and early eighties, the situation reversed itself. The adjusted net income of foundations began to exceed 5 percent, and, because of the formula, they were now required to pay out all of this increased income even though some of it reflected inflation and not a genuine return on their assets. Whereas they had been previously forced to invade capital, the new situation caused the nominal dollar value of their capital to be maintained while its true purchasing power plummeted. With ERTA, the Congress stepped in again. This time it eliminated the formula entirely and dropped adjusted net income as a test. Henceforth, the minimum payout requirement was to be the flat 5 percent that the Filer Commission had recommended six years earlier. The irony is that the commission's recommendation had been aimed at a figure somewhat *above* the probable income of most private foundations. By the time its recommendation was adopted in wholly different circumstances, the minimum payout prescribed was probably just the reverse. The second part of the commission's Recommendation 15—that there also be a minimum payout formula for such endowed tax-exempt organizations as museums or universities—has received little or no consideration.

Among the several Internal Revenue Code provisions that the commission recommended *not* be changed was the one that permitted a deduction for charitable bequests in the computation of estate taxes. Recommendation 5 urged that this deduction be retained. ERTA did this, but it otherwise so radically "liberalized" the code's estate tax provisions that the value of this deduction will become increasingly superfluous as the revised provisions are phased in over the next few years. For many affluent individuals, the alternatives at death had previously been either to have their wealth go largely to the government or to bequeath it themselves to a charitable beneficiary. As the commission urged, the deduction for the charitable bequest has been retained. The incentive to use it, though, will be sharply reduced.

As for Recommendation 6—that corporations set a minimum charitable contribution goal of 2 percent of pretax net income—it may be thought that the provision in ERTA increasing the maximum charitable deduction permitted for corporations from 5 percent to 10 percent of their taxable income might have some relevance. To begin with, though, this is only a "ceiling." As seven members of the commission argued back in 1975, what might really be required if such a goal is to be met is a mandatory "floor." Secondly, this provision cannot be considered out of context. If the accelerated depreciation and other changes that ERTA made in the way that corporations compute their taxable incomes are taken into account, then the increase from 5 percent to 10 percent is not as great as it might at first appear. The current level of corporate charitable giving, in any case, still hovers near 1 percent, and exhortation—as several commission members complained in 1975—remains the principle public strategy for trying to increase it further. Some months following ERTA's passage, for example, Congressman Robert Garcia of New York introduced a concurrent resolution that would have expressed the sense of the Congress to be that corporations benefiting under ERTA should help offset reductions in federal domestic programs by increasing their charitable contributions. Such a statement by the Congress would be an exhortation on a grand and welcome scale indeed—but still no more than an exhortation.

Two other matters about which the commission made recommendations were addressed in earlier revenue changes. Recommendation 9 called for repeal of the 4 percent "audit" tax on private foundations and its replacement by a fee to be based on the actual cost of audit. The Congress met the commission half way. In the Revenue Act of 1978, it retained this tax but reduced it to 2 percent.

Recommendation 18—concerning the limitations on lobbying by tax-exempt organizations—was dealt with two years earlier in the Tax Reform Act of 1976. Inserted into Section 501 was a new subsection that allows public charities to elect the special status of "lobbying organizations." As such, within certain dollar limits—20 percent of the first $500,000 of expenditures and a declining percentage above that, with a top limit, in any case, of $1 million—they are permitted to expend their resources in an effort to influence legislation. They may do this either by communicating directly with the members or staff of a legislative body or, to a more limited degree, by attempting "to affect the opinions of the general public"—so-called grassroots lobbying. For service organizations such as the AAM, this change has had a significant impact.

In several other areas, the Filer Commission's recommendations have made progress through other than legislative means. Underlying Recommendation 7—dealing with the availability of detailed annual reports on finances, programs, and priorities—was the commission's flirtation with the establishment of uniform accounting standards. As discussed in "If Men Were Angels . . ." (see pp. 114–32; Recommendation 16, which proposes the regulation of charitable solicitation, is also discussed there), such accounting standards have now been developed and may shortly be fastened into place. The agency for enforcement would not, however, be any governmental entity but, rather, the American Institute of Certified Public Accountants. Whether the imposition of such standards would lead, in turn, to a requirement for wider distribution of financial information—brought through such standards for the first time, in theory at least, into comparability—is an open question.

Recommendation 14 deals, essentially, with the problem of conflicts of interest. As pointed out in "Breaches of Trust, Remedies, and Standards in the American Private Art Museum" and its afterword (see pp. 160–88), this is a problem that has traditionally been addressed at the state level and through the offices of the various state attorneys general. The commission's call for new laws to control conflicts of interest and related problems may well have been premature. Much law exists already; the problem to date has largely been a failure to enforce it. Recent events suggest that this situation may now be changing.

Review of
The Endangered Sector
by Waldemar A. Nielsen (1981)

The Endangered Sector.
By Waldemar A. Nielsen.

*Published by Columbia University Press,
1979. 279 pp.*

I n *The Endangered Sector* we are served
a generous portion of gloom topped with
just a dollop of hope. Waldemar Nielsen's subject is the so-called
third sector—that aggregate of private nonprofit organizations
(estimates of their number run well into the millions) that includes
many of the institutions most vital to the quality of our national
life.

The organizations of the third sector vary enormously in scale
and purpose. They range from our great private universities and
hospitals through a broad variety of religious, cultural, and social
welfare organizations, down to such neighborhood groups as
parent-teacher and block associations. Among them are roughly
one-half of all our museums. Despite their diversity, Nielsen sees
these organizations as bound by a common concern. In contrast
to government and business—the first two sectors of American
society—they operate "in that large sphere of life which does not
center on power or authority or on the production and acquisition
of material goods and money. They embody the countervalues
and complementary beliefs of our competitive, capitalistic, ma-
terialistic, egalitarian culture."

Nielsen questions how long the third sector can survive. His
fears are twofold. On one side is the danger of insolvency. In the
face of a steadily increasing demand for services, nonprofit organizations must cope with not only a cruelly persistent inflation
rate but also a shrinking base of contributed income. By whatever

*Copyright © 1981 by the American Association of Museums. Reprinted from Mu-
seum News, vol. 59, no. 4 (January/February 1981), by permission of the American
Association of Museums.*

measure used—charitable contributions as a percentage of adjusted gross income, of personal income, or of GNP—the years since World War II have been characterized by a distinct and significant decline in overall charitable giving.

It is the second danger, though, that Nielsen finds the more insidious. To offset the erosion of private support, the third sector has increasingly turned toward government for help. And while government, on every level, has been responsive, the long-term consequences of such governmental support appear inescapable: bureaucratization—already well upon us, as witness the web of regulations in which we all have become increasingly enmeshed—and a serious risk that the funding process itself may become politicized. Beyond these, though, he sees a larger hazard still: that there may come a time when the ratio of governmental to private support becomes so great that the organizations of the third sector will become "mere compliant adjuncts of the state." No longer capable of maintaining their autonomy or embodying a range of "countervalues and complementary beliefs," they would—regardless of whether or how long some outward form of independence might be sustained—have lost their fundamental reason to lead a separate existence. We would face the graying of America.

What, then, does Nielsen recommend? While several of his suggestions envision specific federal initiatives—among these would be increased tax incentives to encourage greater private giving and the establishment of one or more committees within the Congress and the executive branch to focus specifically on the needs and potentialities of the third sector—he sees the burden of preserving what is most valuable in our private nonprofit organizations as falling largely on those organizations themselves. If their current drift toward extinction is to be arrested, it can only be through their own effort to define and establish an acceptable relationship with the other elements of American society—and particularly with government. If it is no longer a practical goal to free themselves entirely from dependence—the time for that (if it ever existed) is long past—they can at least work toward finding the means "to coexist with dignity and integrity despite an essentially inferior and vulnerable position."

Implicit in Nielsen's program is the need for the third sector to organize itself in broader ways than heretofore and to carry its case into the political arena. As major issues of public policy are decided, "it must become more mobilized and more politicized in order to bring the force of its constituencies to bear." What gives him hope—if no more than a dollop—is his sense that we are as a nation arriving at an important moment of self-examination. He sees the traditional liberal/conservative dichotomy about the relative roles of the public and private sectors as dissolving and an effort underway—across the entire political spectrum—to find new formulas for distributing power and responsibility among government, business, and philanthropy.

If this is so, then the moment is critical; we may not have such an opportunity again. If the structure of American life is to be rearticulated, the third sector must move promptly to define the nature and conditions of its role and to establish positions from which it can negotiate. Equally imperative is that it come to terms with what will undoubtedly be demanded as the price for retaining its autonomy: increased accountability, a heightened responsiveness to the needs of constituents, and a continuing movement toward professional management. (Evidence that private nonprofit organizations are eager to find more focused ways to work together toward those goals can be found in the establishment in March 1980 of the Washington-based organization Independent Sector, whose membership embraces groups as varied as the American Hospital Association, Opera America, and the United Negro College Fund. Not surprisingly, Nielsen serves on its board of directors. Significantly, the American Association of Museums was one of its charter members.)

Why should museums be concerned? After all, museums and the arts generally have been singularly successful in maintaining their level of private contributions. In comparison with hospitals, universities, and research centers, the percentage of support they receive from government is relatively low—Nielsen estimates it overall at not more than 15 to 20 percent of their income—and the bureaucracies with which they customarily deal have so far proved relatively clement.

Such optimism, though, would ignore how recently cultural organizations have arrived at the public trough. It is only since the mid-sixties that most of the major funding programs for the arts have come into being, and it was only in the seventies that they began to receive appropriations of any significance. Our private museums are but a little way down what Nielsen calls "the slippery road of government subvention." We would do well to heed the distress signals of those travelers who started out before us.

Finally, it may be fantasy to believe that the future of museums can be divorced from that of the third sector. While we have claims to be special, so has everyone else. If there are to be profound changes in the patterns of American society, those changes will likely emerge along broad fronts. There will be little opportunity to tailor them nicely to the specific needs of particular types of institutions. In Benjamin Franklin's words, "We must all hang together, or assuredly we shall all hang separately." Waldemar Nielsen has done a great service by giving us perspective on a crisis that may shortly be upon us and by pointing the way toward what may be the best resolution for which we can hope. His book is strongly recommended to anyone responsible for the well-being of a museum.

MUSEUMS
AND THE LAW

No Museum
Is an Island (1980, 1981)

Casting about for some image through which we might better understand the evolution of the American museum community, I find myself with the fancy that we might well have come into being as an archipelago. Imagine such a genesis. Across a broad expanse there appeared—in the course of the last century or so—first a few, then hundreds, then ultimately thousands of islands. Some were large; most were small. Some were devoted to art; others to science, to natural history, or to history. Common to all, though, was their special quality of islandhood: their separateness, their independence—"every work of art is owned entirely by the trustees," the then director of the Metropolitan Museum of Art could tell the press as recently as 1973—and their sense of insulation, one from another and all from the world.

We knew, of course, that nearby—but not so close as to be relevant—there were such other archipelagoes as the university islands, the hospital chain, and a string of libraries. And we knew, too, that beyond the horizon there was the great world itself. From there came periodic rumblings and an occasional flash of lightning. Notwithstanding these omens, ours was a remote and a reasonably comfortable world.

Picturesque as such an image might be, we have come to learn—sometimes the hard way—that it is also misleading. We are not

Copyright © 1981 by the American Association of Museums. This paper was originally delivered as the keynote address at the American Law Insitute–American Bar Association Course of Study on Legal Problems of Museum Administration held in Washington, D.C., in March 1980 and appeared as an article in Museum News, vol. 60, no. 3 (January/February 1981).

separate, and we are not apart. The events that convulse the world outside are all too promptly echoed in our own. The storms that lash our neighboring archipelagoes will, as often as not, blow sooner or later in our direction. And, above all, the problems that may from time to time break out on one or another of our islands are all too likely to spread quickly to the others nearby. Considered in terms of how immediately we are linked to the world outside, considered in terms of our own interdependence, *no* museum is an island. We are all truly, in John Donne's phrase, "a part of the main."

To begin with that world outside: When the Ayatollah Khomeini overthrew the Shah early in 1979, that far-off event was quickly reflected in the problems faced by American museums that were then holding objects on loan from museums in Iran. At the Herbert F. Johnson Museum at Cornell, the dilemma was initially ethical. Should an important painting by Willem de Kooning be returned to the Tehran Museum of Contemporary Art when there were reasonable grounds to believe that, for the moment at least, it would neither be properly received nor properly cared for? On the other hand—in the face of a demand for the painting's return—what grounds had the museum for breaching the terms of its loan agreement?

When the hostages were seized at the American Embassy, the situation compounded. From one side, creditors of the Iranian government attempted to attach the painting, notwithstanding that such an attachment might be barred under Section 228 of New York's General Business Law. From the other came President Carter's freeze on Iranian assets, a freeze that was arguably beyond the scope of Section 228. The painting today [1980] remains in the museum's custody.

Similar problems arose at the Guggenheim Museum and at the National Gallery. At the National Gallery—without the protection of New York's antiseizure statute and with the comparable federal statute not in this case applicable—any uncertainty about how best to proceed was quickly resolved. On December 19, 1979, acting on the application of a group of American insurance companies asserting claims against the Islamic Government of Iran, the United States District Court for the District of Columbia issued a writ of attachment covering five sculptures by Jean Dubuffet and another painting by de Kooning then on loan from the museum in Tehran. Those works, too, still remain in custody.

When Russian troops entered Afghanistan, an early casualty was the exhibition of treasures from the Hermitage Museum in Leningrad, scheduled to open at the National Gallery in May 1980. When the International Communications Agency declined to give the certification necessary to protect the exhibition against judicial seizure, plans for the exhibition fell apart. The Control Data Corporation, which had agreed to sponsor the exhibition and had reportedly invested nearly one million dollars in its preparation, was left holding the bag. The five museums slated to show the exhibition were left scurrying about to reconstruct their schedules.

Iran and Afghanistan were major events, and their impact was felt first in some of our larger museums. What of museums generally? What might be their links to the world? Here we must look not so much to these violent convulsions as to those deeper concerns, those currents of change that, to return once more to our island image, flow constantly toward our erstwhile archipelago from beyond the horizon. Over the past decade, such concerns have revolved principally about the claims of one or another disadvantaged groups—minorities, women, the handicapped, or the aged—and have related largely to employment, promotion, physical access, and program access. These claims are far from satisfied and will surely continue.

To what additional concerns—the economy aside—might we look ahead? Let me suggest a few:

Energy: Having won our argument to exempt museum storage and exhibition spaces from the Standby Emergency Building Temperature Restrictions for existing structures, we now find that we must do battle all over again. The Energy Performance Standards for New Buildings that the Department of Energy has proposed are patently inadequate for maintaining proper climate controls in museums, libraries, and other buildings used to house and preserve collections. If this battle is to be won, it will have to be won by museums acting as a community and in concert with others—it cannot be fought island-by-island.

Taxation: There has been much discussion lately about the use of value-added taxes or an additional gasoline tax as a possible and partial substitute for the income tax. Under this approach, which may well be a good one, we would shift some of the burden of taxation from the production side to the consumption side of the economy. But what of museums? We pay no income taxes. What will be our offset for the higher prices that such consumption taxes would produce? And what might be the consequence for us if a diminished income tax concurrently diminished the importance of the charitable deduction? If fundamental changes are to be made, it is vital that those responsible for making them understand our needs. Here, again, it is not just museums that must act in concert but the entire nonprofit sector. We cannot be islands. We cannot even be an archipelago.

Artist's Rights: Last January 1, the California Art Preservation Act took effect. Under it, every museum in that state will, for the first time anywhere in the United States, be legally accountable to the artist who created it for intentional damage to—or for gross negligence in the course of conserving, restoring, or framing— any work of art in its collection. If the artist is dead, the museum will nevertheless continue to be liable to his heirs for another fifty years. [For a full discussion of this act, see "The 'Moral Right' Comes to California," pp. 226–39.] Similar moral right legislation is expected to pass in Washington State and may well spread nationwide. Still murky are such questions as how damages are to be assessed, what sort of additional insurance (if any) might be required, and what additional records might be desirable to keep.

Meanwhile, taking advantage perhaps of the changes in climate wrought by the Copyright Revision Act of 1976, such foreign licensing organizations as France's SPADEM have been emboldened to take an increasingly aggressive attitude toward American museums exhibiting the work of twentieth-century European artists.

Repatriation: This may, perhaps, be the most complex and delicate of the issues we will be called on to consider in the next few years. The pressure to do so will come from several directions. Meeting in Nairobi in 1976, the General Conference of UNESCO agreed to the establishment of an intergovernmental committee that would be "entrusted with the task of seeking ways and means of facilitating bilateral negotiations for the restitution or return of cultural property to the countries having lost them as a result of colonial or foreign occupation."

In 1978, this committee was formally voted into being with the original reference to cultural property lost as a result of "colonial or foreign occupation" enlarged to include also property lost as a result of "illicit appropriation." Twenty nations, including four from the Western Hemisphere (Bolivia, Cuba, Mexico, and Peru), have been elected to membership. While the committee's function is advisory only, its deliberations will be carefully watched. Inevitably, they will play some role in molding the public's attitudes toward questions of repatriation, and ultimately toward us.

Meanwhile, closer to home, we must be sensitive to the American Indian Religious Freedom Act. Signed by President Carter in August 1978, the act declares it the policy of the United States to protect and preserve for American Indians their right to practice traditional religions. Specifically included was the right to use and possess sacred objects. Many such objects are, of course, in our museums, and a fundamental difficulty lies in the tension between what a tribe may consider "sacred property" and what a museum may think of as its own legally held property.

In a task force report prepared under the supervision of the secretary of the interior and submitted to Congress in August 1979, this point was touched upon both gently and with some vigor. Gently, the task force observed:

> Equally elaborate concepts of personal property have developed in both Native American and western legal traditions. The problems presented by the presence of Native American sacred objects in museums will be resolved only through careful determination of what constitutes essential fairness in these conflicts between culturally distinct systems.

More vigorous was the second of four administrative actions that the task force recommended with respect to federal museums. Such museums, it said,

> should return to the tribe of origin objects in the museum's possession, as to which unconsenting third parties assert no ownership interest, that were used or valued for religious purposes at the time of their loss from an American Indian tribe or Native American community, and were alienated from that community contrary to standards for disposition of such objects then prevailing in that community,

provided that the successor modern tribe or community requests them as needed for current religious practice.

While this is no more than a recommendation, and while it applies to only a limited range of institutions, can we doubt that such a recommendation may weigh heavily in our decisions over the coming years? In one case already, a private museum—the Denver Art Museum—acting after passage of the 1978 act but before the task force report was issued, last spring restored possession of a Zuni war god to the tribe from whose custody it had disappeared nearly eighty years earlier. Other instances, cited with approval in the task force's report, involved the Heard Museum in Phoenix and the Wheelwright Museum in Santa Fe.

If we turn next to such cognate institutions as the hospitals and universities that we once thought of as neighboring, but nevertheless distinct, archipelagoes, what storms can we discern that might ultimately move in our direction? Two recent cases, both concerning colleges, could surely shake the faith of any among us who still believe that our governing boards—those tribal councils traditionally thought to be the ultimate rulers of our island kingdoms—may not sometimes themselves be called promptly to account to some higher authority still.

Zechner v. Alexander, decided in May 1979 by a local branch of the Pennsylvania Orphans Court, involved the trustees of Wilson College, a small women's college in Chambersburg, Pennsylvania. Faced with declining enrollment, the trustees had determined that their wisest course lay in closing the college at the end of the current academic year. The remaining assets would be transferred to a foundation where they might continue to be used to foster liberal education for women. A group of alumnae, together with a dissenting trustee, a number of students, several members of the faculty, and some prior donors to the college, commenced a suit to enjoin its closing. The court granted the relief requested and ordered the college to remain open.

Beyond this, it ordered the president of the college removed from the board, charging her with "gross abuses of discretion and authority." It also removed a second trustee for reasons that seem particularly striking. This second trustee was the president of Bryn Mawr College. She had presumably been elected to the board for her professional expertise as an educator. The court found her participation in the decision to close Wilson College to be an impermissible conflict of interest, concluding apparently that Bryn Mawr and Wilson were competing for the same students and that, by shutting down Wilson, Bryn Mawr would emerge the winner. It also criticized her for failing to exercise her special knowledge and expertise by not taking a more vigorous role in upgrading Wilson College's student recruitment program.

For the trustees generally—both those ousted and those who remained on the board—there was a potentially painful footnote. Apart from the sum of $7,500, which the court allowed the college to pay, the remaining costs of the trial had to be borne by the trustees themselves. Fortunately, someone had thought to buy insurance.

Meanwhile, a similar drama was being enacted at the Mannes College of Music in New York City. In the spring of 1979, faced with seemingly insuperable financial difficulties, the acting president of the college discharged a number of faculty members, dismantled a substantial part of the curriculum, and, with the approval of his board, undertook negotiations to merge the college with the Manhattan School of Music. Several faculty members as well as two trustees who had voted against the decision to seek a merger petitioned the Board of Regents of New York State to remove the majority of the trustees and to appoint replacements. Following a hearing, a committee of the regents reported—with respect to the general administration of the college, although not necessarily the proposed merger—that it was their "reluctant but unanimous and inescapable conclusion that the Mannes College board of trustees has, during the past year, demonstrated with respect to certain critical matters a collective neglect of duty which is appalling."

Nine trustees—including the two who had initially joined in the petition to the board of regents—were ousted. That they had ultimately sought to correct the situation did not, the regents committee found, alter the fact that they had been just as remiss as their fellow board members in neglecting their duties as trustees.

When Judge Gesell handed down his decision in the Sibley Hospital case in 1974, it was quickly sensed that it might be as applicable to museums as it was to hospitals. Writing in *Museum News* at this time, Kyran McGrath said:

This opinion serves notice on all nonprofit institutions that their financial operations are becoming increasingly subject to public scrutiny, and that their trustees are expected to shoulder the responsibility of the institution's strict accountability to the public.

While these recent decisions may not have the same immediacy or direct relevance to museums, they nonetheless suggest that the trend toward increased public scrutiny of private nonprofit institutions—a trend we have long observed, and from which we can by no means consider ourselves exempt—has not abated. And it can be expected to accelerate wherever and whenever museums have or are perceived to have engaged in questionable practices. Neither Afghanistan, nor American Indians, nor a Sibley Hospital or Wilson College can so quickly undermine our sense of being separate, of being each secure on our own island, as can the swiftness, the almost certain contagion, with which the problems—real or perceived—within one museum may spread to those around it.

Consider the current situations in Illinois and in New York State. In Illinois, we still don't know what consequences we will have to face from the difficulties besetting the George F. Harding Museum in Chicago. The Harding Museum was founded in 1930 and assumed its present corporate form in 1946. In 1965, the museum closed its building on the South Side of Chicago and placed the bulk of its collection in storage.

In October 1976 the attorney general of Illinois filed a complaint against the museum and five of its directors alleging, among other things, that their failure to make the museum's collection generally accessible to the public was in violation of the museum's intended purposes. Beyond that, he charged that the manner in which the collection was stored threatened it with irreparable harm; that the museum, through intentional and reckless mismanagement, had been operated for the years 1972 through 1974 at deficits ranging from $200,000 to $300,000 annually; that—notwithstanding such deficits—four of the defendants, as officers of the board, had awarded themselves salaries totaling $95,000 for each of those years; and that such deficits were being met or were to be met by the sale of objects from the collection. A final set of allegations concerned the use of the museum's assets for investments in real estate and charged the president of the board with self-dealing.

While the Harding Museum is under an order restraining further sales from its collection, the case itself has yet to come to a trial on the merits, and these are thus far allegations only. Their fallout on the other museums of Illinois has nonetheless been considerable. Following the wide publicity given these original charges, the Illinois legislature launched a broad investigation into the operation of museums generally to determine whether some revision might not be needed in the laws to which they were subject. An investigating commission was established, investigators hired, interviews scheduled, documents demanded, and questionnaires distributed.

At the Chicago Historical Society, the director and the comptroller were each required to spend forty hours or more responding to the commissioner's inquiries. The director of the Field Museum of Natural History characterized the investigation as expensive not only in terms of legal fees and senior staff and trustee time, but also in terms of the climate of mistrust and suspicion it engendered. Writing to the cochairman of the Legislative Investigating Commission on May 22, 1978, Laurence Chalmers, the president of the Art Institute of Chicago, noted that the museum had by that date already devoted several hundreds of hours of staff time to answering the commission's inquiries. "If the experience at the Art Institute is multiplied by the number of museums in the state," he concluded, "many thousands of hours will have to be devoted to compliance, hours that must necessarily be taken away from our primary purpose of providing programs and activities for the general public."

The legislature is yet to act, and *Harding* is yet to come to trial. [The case of the Harding Museum, as well as the disposals from the Brooklyn Museum referred to below, are discussed in more detail in "Breaches of Trust, Remedies, and Standards in the American Private Art Museum," pp. 160–88.]

In New York, we can see how other allegations, some less serious than those involved in the Harding case, may nonetheless set in motion a similar process. Throughout the seventies, questions have surfaced about the propriety of certain deaccession transactions in various New York City museums. The most serious of these concerned the Museum of the American Indian and resulted in the 1975 removal, by the state attorney general, of the museum's director and a majority of its trustees. Dispositions by the Metropolitan Museum of Art, the Museum of American Folk Art, and the Brooklyn Museum have also been subject to public inquiry, and there is still pending a suit instituted by the attorney general that arises from some transactions at Brooklyn.

There is a distinct possibility that the questions these trans-actions raise may ultimately lead to legislation that will affect all of the seven hundred museums and historical societies estimated by the State Education Department to be active in New York. In 1973 a bill requiring that the details of all acquisitions and dis-positions be reported to the commissioner of education was in-troduced in Albany. While it was not passed, its successors con-tinue to appear—most recently in the still pending Leichter-Grannis bill, which would require that museums make detailed records of all acquisitions and dispositions accessible to the public.

This process—a question raised with respect to one museum that leads toward the regulation of many more—is by no means limited to deaccessioning. In New York again, there have been questions about the so-called Sackler enclave at the Metropoli-tan—something many of us might view as a prudent investment of museum resources made in the hope of attracting an extraor-dinary gift. This has triggered still another investigation by the attorney general, this time of the relationship between museums and donors in general. One possible outcome, according to the attorney general's office, may be the issuance of comprehensive guidelines to "determine the proper limits in museum-donor re-lations." Once more, some seven hundred institutions may be affected.

As even these brief examples must surely make clear, there is today an interconnectedness among museums that can quickly transform the problem of any into the problem of all. As that interconnectedness grows, so too must our common interest in forestalling the problems of any. There is little we can do for the problems that the world at large makes for us. But there is much we can do about the problems we make for each other.

Critical here is the task of establishing defensible standards for ourselves before they are established for us. Over the past decade, beginning with the establishment of AAM's accreditation program in 1970, we have made substantial progress. Important too has been our progress in developing collections management policies, the extraordinary degree to which we have strengthened museum service organizations at every level, and the AAM membership's adoption in 1978 of the report of its Committee on Ethics.

Equally critical, but far more difficult, will be the question of how far we will be prepared to go in enforcing the standards we establish. When these standards are violated, will we be forthcoming about it; will we act instead of react; will we cooperate with the competent authorities in seeking to right whatever is wrong? Or will we fall back on collegiality, mumble that it's a shame, drag our collective feet, and hope that the damage can be confined? Worse yet, will we still be seduced by some song of the islands and convince ourselves that it doesn't concern us at all?

We may by now know that we are—if ever we were—no longer islands, that we are all a part of the main. But notwithstanding our good beginning, we have not yet finished the task of formulating such comprehensive standards that we can say with confidence to that world out there—to that ever-growing group that asserts that it has standing to question what we do—*yes, there is a proper way to run a museum. And yes, that is how we do it.*

Meanwhile—looking both to the world outside, where there is little we can do to affect the course of events, and to our own world, where we can be our most effective—we must learn more about where the principal dangers lie, where we are most prone to make mistakes, and how we can best take appropriate measures to minimize or eliminate these. We must learn not how to resist questions but how to anticipate them or, failing that, how to answer them credibly. In a legal context, what we must learn to practice is preventive law.

"If Men Were Angels . . ." (1976, 1977)

If you were with us at the third annual Museum Law Conference in Washington in 1975, you may recall the charming—if apocryphal—story about Moses that was contributed by Ben Mintz, an associate solicitor from the Department of Labor.

With the onrushing Egyptian army pressing the Israelites against the edge of the Red Sea, Moses entered into conversations with the Lord to determine what, if anything, the latter might be able to do in the way of providing a miracle. After they had reviewed several alternatives, the Lord—with a great clap of thunder—snapped his celestial fingers and said: "I think I've got it. What I could do," he said, "is part the Red Sea. That way you and the Children of Israel would be able to escape across on dry land."

"That's terrific," said Moses, very impressed. "Can we start on it now?"

"Not so fast," spoke the Lord. "There *is* one catch."

"Oh?" said Moses.

"Yes," said the Lord, a little sadly. "Until you file an environmental impact statement, I can't lay a hand on the damn thing!"

That even miracles may require paperwork does not seem particularly bizarre to those of us responsible for the day-to-day running of museums. We are living in a time when the requirements of the law seem to be coagulating around us, when even the simplest of projects may, somewhere between its inception and

Copyright© 1977 by the American Association of Museums, Reprinted from Museum News, vol. 56, no. 1 (September/October 1977), by permission of the American Association of Museums. This paper was originally delivered at the 1976 joint meeting in Phoenix of the Western Regional Conference of the American Association of Museums and the Western Association of Art Museums.

its completion, bog down in a swamp of wholly unexpected complexity; when Congress and the legislatures seem bent on enmeshing the most trivial of daily activities in a spreading web of regulation; and when the courts are expanding their jurisdiction to entertain novel complaints that probe increasingly deeper into organizational practices that we once considered to be of private rather than public concern.

The texture of American life is thickening. It should not surprise us that museums are entangled in this thickening. No matter how special we may feel, we are an inextricable part of the American community, and its future will be ours. As its life becomes more complex, so will ours. No Lord is lurking in the wings to part this Red Sea for us; no Michelangelo-esque Moses is waiting to rise from his pedestal and sweep us up in his arms—trustees, directors, curators, and educators alike—proclaiming: "These are my people. They are better; they are different. Let them go."

The job of those of use who are responsible for the running of museums is not to resent, regret, or even necessarily resist the changes that are occuring. In whatever manner, as private citizens, we may regard these changes and elect to respond to them, as museum people our first job is to understand them. Unless we do understand the way in which these changes are generated, the areas in which they are most likely to occur, and the directions that they are apt to take, we will be hard pressed to develop the capabilities that we will require if museums are to continue to flourish, much less to survive, in the increasingly complex environment in which they will find themselves.

How have these changes been generated? Do they arise from a plot, and, if so, is there a villain—someone, or a class of some-ones, whom we can blame for such growing complexities?

Some would, I fear, answer: "Sure, there is. It's the lawyers." This is not a new accusation. Lawyers were being blamed for the intricacies of life long before the first museum was even a tiny gleam in some curiosity cabinet's glass eye.

Others will point to that legendary monster, the bureaucracy. Here, in their view, is an ogre indeed. Swollen with self-importance and belching forth great clouds of obfuscation, it lumbers across the landscape spreading not merely death and destruction but, more terrible even, an endless flow of findings, conclusions, rules, and regulations.

Others still will want to pin blame on Congress and the legislatures. These, they would say, have degenerated into a series
of concentric circuses. They have become arenas over which, at
best, our representatives perform acrobatic feats of high-wire legislation aimed at nothing more than dazzling the crowd below.

No one can deny that lawyers may sometimes complicate things,
that bureaucrats are sometimes officious, and that legislatures may
occasionally be seduced by their own virtuosity at lawmaking. Nor
will anyone deny that the application of new rules sometimes
results in those instances of extreme absurdity in which the news-
papers take such delight. Nevertheless, on behalf of my brother
and sister lawyers and bureaucrats—and for our legislative cous-
ins—I must plead not guilty.

I do not think that we, any more than any other segment of
the community, are to blame for the accelerating complexity of
American life. Nor, for that matter, do I think even that "blame"
is the appropriate term. "Blame" implies fault, that something has
gone wrong, that a condition that was good has been succeeded
by a condition that is bad.

What we are dealing with, in this thickening texture of American
life, is not anything that is necessarily either good or bad. What
it *is* is different. And the responsibility for that difference—its
cause, not its blame—lies with all of us and with the very best in
all of us.

We speak of the "revolution of rising expectations" as if it
concerned only microwave ovens in the Third World or radio-
operated garage doors in Watts. But the expectations that have
risen since World War II are far broader than these. They are our
own expectations that this might truly be a society that is at once
just and compassionate, a society in which merit may count for
more than privilege and in which those who are entrusted with
power may be held accountable to those over whom such power
is exercised.

As we pursue these larger goals, we find that they cannot be
attained by one great whooshing leap of good will. We find, rather,
that they must be approached by a series of smaller changes that
will, more often than not, find reflection in the web of legislative,
administrative, and judge-made laws within which all of us—including museums—must operate. These changes often seem petty,
frustrating, and to no worthwhile purpose. And too often, also,

we let this pettiness blind us to their function as the necessary nuts and bolts of those larger systems through which we hope to see our larger expectations fulfilled.

In a country as vast, diverse, and highly populated as ours, the institutionalization of goodwill must carry an enormous—and inescapable—consequence in complexity. Let me demonstrate with an example from close to home. In June 1976 the membership of the American Association of Museums unanimously adopted a new constitution that will, in the view of those of us involved in its preparation, vastly increase the association's responsiveness in meeting the needs of its members. Among the changes that were most thoroughly discussed was an increase in regional representation on the AAM Council. Instead of a single appointed delegate, as previously, each of the AAM's six regions will, as of the close of the 1977 meeting in Seattle, be represented by three elected councilors.

There was, I think, universal agreement that such a change was desirable. There was not, however, immediate universal understanding that the price of such a change—a price well worth paying—was an enormous increase in the complexity of the rules by which the association would have to be run.

For example, since each AAM member was, in addition to voting for five councilors-at-large, to be entitled to vote directly for three regional councilors, what were we to do about a member—and it turned out that there were quite a few—who belonged to two regions? Could such a member vote for six regional councilors? Worse, in the unlikely event that there were museum employees both wealthy and zealous enough to join all six regions, could they each have 18 votes? Could some clique of wealthy and diabolically clever New England registrars move in and take over all of the regional councilorships? Would this subvert the intent of providing regional representation in the first instance?

To resolve this, a new concept had to be introduced into the AAM Constitution: that of an official address. A member would be entitled to vote only for the regional councilors representing the geographic region in which his or her official address was located. In the borderline case of a member who lived in one region but whose museum was in another—as happens, for example, at the Connecticut–New York border—it would be up to the member to determine which address to use for voting purposes. Simple? No. There still remained the problem of foreign members whose official addresses were not within any of the six defined geographic regions of the association. In order that these members not be disenfranchised, another few rules were necessary.

Or take the case of an elected regional councilor, who, midway through a three-year elected term, accepted a new position and moved from Arizona to New Mexico. Under the old constitution, this was no problem. The Western Regional Conference could simple substitute a new delegate. With an *elected* regional councilor, the case seemed different. Whose rights were to be treated as superior—those of the council member or those of the region? Opting for the latter, it was necessary to devise a further set of rules that would both terminate the council membership of our hypothetically mobile colleague *and* provide the mechanism for an interim replacement to maintain regional representation at full strength pending the next regular election when the balance, if any, of the unexpired term could be filled.

So basically simple a task as improving the governance of an association with fewer than 10,000 members required, as an underpinning, the addition of several dozen such "notwithstandings," "except thats," and "provided howevers." Those who have been at work drafting governing documents for the regions and for the standing professional committees have, I'm sure, found themselves saddled with equally heavy burdens of legal qualifiers. Magnified to the scale of government at the municipal, state, or federal level, infinitely more such qualifiers are required.

If nothing more than the perversity of lawyers, bureaucrats, and lawmakers were responsible for generating this buzzing swarm of legal qualifiers, it might be an easy enough matter to make it go away. But the case, I fear, is otherwise. The "except as otherwise provideds" and "notwithstandings" that envelop us are neither perverse nor accidental. They are the inevitable by-product of our desire to do things better. And they will be with us at least as long as we aspire to do things better.

If we must, then, accept the growing complexity in which our museums find themselves as the nonnegotiable price of satisfying this desire to do things better, can we at least determine those areas in which such complexities are most likely to occur? Particularly for museums, what are the kinds of things that are becoming more complex and why? Examples may be drawn from two areas that, on first impression, appear to have little connection: conflicts of interest and access by the physically handicapped.

That a trustee of a nonprofit organization should not have an undisclosed conflict of interest seems axiomatic as both a moral and a legal proposition. In fact, there is a large and healthy body of Anglo-American law, going back over several centuries, that defines the rights and obligations of various types of trustees and provides a variety of remedies for those instances in which a trustee may be deemed to have breached his trust.

Notwithstanding this existing law, there is something in the air—something like the rumble that warns of an impending avalanche—that would seem to suggest either that the rules regulating trustees' conduct are about to be significantly tightened or, in what may amount to almost the same thing, that the class of those who may question the conduct of trustees, and the manner in which they may raise such questions, is about to be immensely broadened.

From the recent report of the Commission on Private Philanthropy and Public Needs (the Filer Commission), we learn, for example, that the commission actually considered recommending an absolute legislative prohibition against business dealings of every type between a nonprofit organization and any law firm, bank, accounting firm, or other supplier with which any of its trustees might have any connection. If a local charity dealt with the only bank in town, then no one from that bank could serve the charity in a trustee capacity, regardless of how sorely it might need such a knowledgeable trustee.

The commission's ultimate recommendation was both narrower and broader. It recommended

> that all tax-exempt organizations be required by law to maintain "arms-length" business relationships with profit-making organizations or activities in which any member of the organization's staff, any board member or any major contributor has a substantial financial interest, either directly or through his or her family.

Beyond this, the commission recommended that state or federal authorities be empowered to recover any "improper benefits" that profitmaking organizations or activities might realize from their dealings with nonprofit organizations.

If we turn to what many lawyers believe to be one of the most significant decisions in recent years to affect charitable trustees—the so-called Sibley Hospital case, decided in 1974 and potentially as applicable to museums as to medical institutions—we find another element. In the Sibley case, the Federal District Court for the District of Columbia both reprimanded and assumed continuing jurisdiction over the board of trustees of the defendant hospital for, among other things, permitting relatively large sums of cash to remain uninvested, at no interest, in a bank of which one of the trustees was an officer.

The most striking element here was not the court's decision, which, in itself, does not seem particularly startling, but the manner in which the case arose. The plaintiff was the father of an adolescent who had been treated at the hospital's emergency room and charged a nominal fee. The complaint alleged that this fee, and the fees charged to all others in the class that the plaintiff represented, could have been even lower had the hospital's trustees supervised its investments with greater diligence and more disinterested care. It requires only a minor talent for fantasy to conjure up visions of the comparable class action that an equally ingenious plaintiff might some day launch against a museum. [The question of standing to sue is treated at length in "Breaches of Trust, Remedies, and Standards in the American Private Art Museum," pp. 160–88.]

There are other signs that change, and greater complexity, are on this particular horizon. The 1969 Tax Reform Act imposed heavy penalties on acts of self-dealing in the case of certain nonprofit organizations that are classified as private foundations. These apply to both trustees and employees. "Sunshine laws," applicable to some museums, are beginning to open the proceedings of trustees to closer scrutiny. And within the museum community itself there is a great scurrying of activity. Alan Ullberg of the Smithsonian Institution is working under a National Endowment for the Arts grant to study conflict of interest problems at both the trustee and staff level. The AAM also is addressing these problems through its Ethics Committee under the chairmanship of Giles Mead of the Los Angeles County Museum of Natural History.

[See "Breaches of Trust . . .," pp. 160–88.]

What about the physically handicapped? Again, it is probably axiomatic as a moral, if not yet a legal, proposition that the handicapped should, to the extent possible, have equal access to public facilities. Here the rumble is already fading to an echo and the avalanche is fully upon us. At the federal, state, and municipal level, one after another legislative scheme has been devised to sweep public buildings of any barriers that would limit their use by the handicapped.

At the state level, South Carolina was the first to take action with a bill passed in 1963. The remaining 49 states and the District of Columbia have taken action since. The first major federal legislation was the Architectural Barriers Act of 1968 (Public Law 90-480). Under this act, various of the executive agencies were given broad powers to prescribe standards for the design, construction, or alteration of buildings or facilities constructed, leased, or financed by or on behalf of the United States government.

The most recent trend is legislation at the municipal level. While the limited powers of the federal government are such that the Architectural Barriers Act covers only real property with which the federal government has some connection, the police powers of the cities are far broader. Thus, by a 1969 amendment to its building code, Minneapolis was able to mandate the removal of architectural barriers from *all* new nonresidential buildings within the city. A 1973 ordinance in South Bend, Indiana, went further. It prohibited the issuance of building permits for the construction or substantial remodeling of such public facilities as theaters, churches, and museums unless these were made fully accessible both to the physically handicapped and to the elderly.

In some cases, the pattern of this new legislation is such that specific standards are set by the statutes themselves. One California law, for example, provides that the numbers on elevator buttons in public facilities must be made accessible to the blind by requiring that such numbers be embossed in both Braille symbols and raised Arabic numerals immediately to the right of the buttons themselves. Other statutes incorporate, by reference, standards set or to be set by the American National Standards Institute. These are extremely detailed and cover building features as diverse as the maximum permitted height of those same elevator buttons, the width of lavatory doors, the design of drinking fountains, and the type of telephone receivers that must be provided for the hard-of-hearing.

I strongly doubt that we have seen the last of such legislation, and I do not doubt that museums will increasingly be brought within the scope of its coverage. To date, legislation has affected chiefly new construction and substantial alteration or remodeling, but the standards imposed could certainly be extended to existing facilities. There may even come a time when the eligibility of museums to receive grants may depend upon their ability to meet such standards. And there may come a further time when new grant programs might come into being to *assist* museums in meeting such standards. The only thing certain is that, however these laws develop, still another layer of complexity will be added to our daily museum operations and that it will be done for the best of reasons.

How can we connect these two examples— conflicts of interest and access by the handicapped—and what do they tell us? Common to both, and common to so many of the other regulatory schemes to which museums have become subject in the past, is the perceived inability of the society at large to meet—voluntarily and so broadly that failure might be seen as an exception rather than the rule—the standards of goodwill that we have set for ourselves. In one area after another, this failure to meet our rising expectations—for equal opportunity in training, hiring, and employment, for occupational safety, for the payment of promised pensions, for maintaining the integrity of the environment—has led us to abandon voluntary solutions and to reach for stronger legal remedies.

I don't think that there have been many serious abuses of their trust by those who oversee museums. Certainly, the most flagrant abuses of power in our society have been elsewhere. Likewise, I do not think that museums have been more callous or insensitive than the best of other institutions in responding to the problems of the physically handicapped. No matter. No more than we could have expected to be exempt from the Occupational Safety and Health Act of 1970 or the Employee Retirement Income Security Act of 1974 on the grounds that industrial accidents and pension abuse are not generally characteristic of museums, can we expect to escape the coming complexities of new rules as to conflicts of interest and the physically handicapped.

To understand, and to plan for, what will become complicated for museums tomorrow, we must begin by looking at what seems not to be working today in that larger society in which we are embedded. As our present complexities are rooted in yesterday's unmet expections, so tomorrow's complexities will be rooted in today's; the clues to where we may expect these are, if we can unravel them, on the front page of this morning's newspaper. The better we understand the world we live in today, the better we will be able to run our museums tomorrow.

But that, having been so simply said, is not so simply done. From the root of a problem, there may spring strange and even exotic growths; some trees don't grow the way the twig is bent.

For example, within the next few years, nearly every American museum may become subject to a new set of accounting rules. These rules will have virtually the force of law and, depending upon their final formulation, may—in several sensitive areas— prove to be very difficult for museums to live with. Even now, ten wise men—the representatives, as it happens, of ten of the largest accounting firms in the country—are engaged in preparing a first, so-called exposure draft of these rules [issued February 1, 1977].

How and why this is happening is instructive. The "why" does not, as you might suspect, lie in any general failure by museums to keep their books properly or to make adequate public disclosure of their financial transactions. Notwithstanding that they may be enormously affected by these rules, the past behavior of museums is irrelevant to the birth of the new regulations.

For some time now, the media has been giving prominence to stories about certain charitable organizations—almost invariably engaged in massive direct-mail solicitations—that spend the major share of the contributions they receive on administration and fund raising and correspondingly little on the programs that constitute their ostensible reason for being. While a majority of the states now have charitable solicitation laws, including some requiring that a certain minimum percentage of the funds an organization raises be used for its stated charitable purpose, there is no comparable federal legislation. That situation may soon change. Over the past several years, Congress has begun to look at this, and we may be no more than a year or two from national legislation that would put a similar ceiling on what any nonprofit organization soliciting funds through the United States mails could spend for other than program purposes.

That is the root; the tree, however, has an odd shape. The distinction between a "program expense" and an "administrative expense" may be a close and iffy one on which bookkeepers of goodwill could disagree. For the law to have any bite, it must be accompanied by some accounting standards. The accounting profession, fearful that such standards might be poorly or hastily conceived, determined some while ago to anticipate federal legislation in this area, and, moving on its own, it established a committee to develop an accounting guideline that would cover every nonprofit organization not already covered by one of four earlier guidelines that the American Institute of Certified Public Accountants (AICPA) had approved in 1972, 1973, and 1974.

Among the kinds of organizations to which this new guideline will apply are organized religion, parent-teacher associations, organized labor, neighborhood associations, the Girl Scouts of America, the Benevolent and Protective Order of Elks, and—oh, yes—museums. In all, if the statistics compiled by the Filer Commission are to be believed, the fifth guideline will cover more than five million organizations. As one of the accountants working on the exposure draft told me, "We are expecting interested comments from everyone, from the Teamsters to the Vatican— couched in different language, of course."

If and when this fifth guideline is issued—possibly by 1979 or 1980—no certified public accountant will be permitted to give an unqualified opinion that a museum's financial statement reflects its operations and the changes in its financial position "in conformity with generally accepted accounting principles" unless the standards of the guidelines are met. To the extent that a museum must, for any reason, present such an unqualifiedly approved financial statement, the use of the fifth guideline will for all practical purposes be mandatory. And, of course, if national charitable solicitation legislation is ultimately enacted, this guideline, or something like it, will be applicable under that as well.

Here, then, is another Red Sea that the Lord is not going to part for us. The drift of things is toward national, broadly applicable accounting standards, and no amount of pious protestation is going to exempt museums from their coverage. If the accountants don't get us, the Feds will. Our only hope is to do our best to see to it that these particular new complexities will, when they come, be as benign as possible. The AAM will follow this situation closely and, with other interested groups, attempt to moderate or eliminate whatever in the fifth guideline seems most adverse to the interests of museums. It will be a battle, but, happily, the experience recently gained in formulating our own museum accounting guidelines—those published in 1976 by the Association of Science-Technology Centers—should be of significant advantage.

However this battle comes out, though, our lives will once again have been made a little more complicated. From just this one root—the abuse, or the perceived abuse, of their public trust by a handful of charitable organizations—there will have grown a virtual banyan tree of complexities: new accounting rules, possible legislation that will restrict the proportion of our operating funds that we may spend for overhead and fund raising, and beyond that (and this is also one of the Filer Commission's recommendations) the probability that we will become subject to new and broadened financial disclosure requirements.

And, once more, as burdensome and annoying as those complexities may seem, I find it difficult to consider them unjust. It is how this world is going, and we, the museum community, are of this world, and not a thing apart.

In Number 51 of the *Federalist Papers,* written nearly two centuries ago, James Madison wrote: "If men were angels, no government would be necessary." But men are not angels, and as there get to be more and more of them—and more and more women, children, dogs, automobiles, and museums as well— there will be more and more government. As there is, the legal framework in which museums must operate will continue to tighten and change. If it is not our job as museum people to resent or regret or even necessarily to resist these changes, it *is* our job— once we have understood them—to anticipate them and, as best we can, to seek a major role in shaping them to the best interests of our institutions.

Here we must be very careful of the aloofness that the outside world too often ascribes to museums. Not only must we continue to work closely together—and harder than ever before—through our various museum associations at the state, regional, and national levels, but we must build bridges to other groups in the community that share our interests. Our particular world—the nonprofit sector—is a vast one in which there are opportunities that museums may take for assuming leadership and for working with others. Several thousand museums are simply too small a factor in the cultural world, no less a nonprofit world of more than five million organizations, to think that they can always go it alone.

We must, as Senator Claiborne Pell pointed out in a similar context at the 1976 AAM annual meeting in Washington, lose our traditional timidity about speaking out to our legislators and doing such lobbying as we legally may. We must become active participants in the legislative and rule-making processes, aggressive when need be and proud of the interests that museums represent. By doing these things, we will not stem the flow of change. But we may, with enough work, at least help to channel it in directions that we might find more congenial.

If we succeed, both in anticipating and preparing for such change before it comes and in molding it to a more comfortable fit when it does, it is very likely that no one, or at least no one but us, will ever know. One of the curiosities of the museum business is that our work, at its best, is so transparent as to be virtually invisible to the general public. In the well-run museum, the objects must seem to that public to have installed themselves, the galleries to devour their own dust every night, and the doors to swing open each morning on their own.

So it is with these legal complexities. Managing those that surround you now, and anticipating and preparing for those yet to come, will earn you no good reviews. Newspaper space is reserved for the failures, and to fail in this can be costly in the time, energy, and money that may be involved in straightening things out, in its impact on public confidence, and in terms of potential support.

You need not fail. You need not—and this is my only good news—even have to go to law school not to fail. What you do need, to begin with, *are* some practical things. You need, to begin with, someone on your staff—it may be the director, it may be a deputy or an assistant—who is charged with specific responsibility for monitoring those areas of your operations that may have legal consequences: employment and promotion practices, wage and hour law, acquisition policy, copyright, the conduct of guards, health and safety practices, and a host of etceteras.

Since, except in the very largest museums, this person—someone I think of as a sort of compliance officer—will most likely not be a lawyer, you will also need ongoing outside counsel upon whom you can call for regular help. In a number of museums, a trustee has served this function in the past but, if there is to be a further tightening of conflict of interest rules, some care must be exercised here, especially if any fees are to be paid.

Legal fees, in any case, will represent a considerable burden on your already overstrained budgets, but there are things that you can do to keep these to a minimum. Most important, since lawyers generally charge by their time and very few lawyers are specialized in this field, you can save the time of a nonspecialized lawyer by your own ability to identify those areas where museum law problems are apt to be found. Here, the compliance officer can be of enormous help. And, to the extent possible, you can also minimize legal fees by providing for some continuity of counsel so that work that has been done once does not have to be done again and paid for again.

At the cooperative level, it is of the utmost importance that at least one session dealing with the ongoing legal problems of museums be included in the program of every professional meeting. And to the extent that you can send someone to the annual Museum Law Conference given by the American Law Institute–American Bar Association and sponsored by the Smithsonian Institution and the AAM, so much the better.

These are practical steps, and they can be important. Beyond these, however, and more important still, are the understanding and the attitude of those ultimately responsible for the running of our museums: the trustees and the directors. If museums are to avoid costly entanglements with the law, it will be because those who lead them have come to face these realities:

- The thickening of life around us is neither a transient phenomenon nor the result of some villainy; it is the by-product of a process not likely to be reversed in our lifetimes.
- Museum people are not a chosen people who, by some miraculous intervention, will be exempt from the growing complexities of this world; museums are of this world and not a thing apart.

- Museums will only ignore the problems of future change at their peril. If they hope to play a role in determining the shape of such change, they will have to do it both by strengthening their own community and by making common cause with others who share their interests.

The laws that affect museums are cumulative, not successive. They do not follow one another like the slides in a carousel; they pile up like the silt in a river. Our job is to navigate. We must, of course, be practical navigators. But beyond that, we must understand why these things come to be and the shapes that they are apt to take. If we are prepared to do this, there is no reason at all why we should not be successful navigators, too, and no reason at all that we cannot guide our museums to that flourishing future that we all want so much and for which we have all worked so hard.

Afterword

Readers failing to check the dates may be impressed by the apparent prescience with which I suggested in 1976 that a time could come when the eligibility of a museum to receive future grants might depend on its adherence to certain standards of handicapped access. What neither I nor apparently any of my equally uninformed audience then realized was that that time had *already* come and that a law to that effect was *already* on the books. The law, of course, was the Rehabilitation Act of 1973, and the provision cutting off federal assistance to any recipient who failed to make adequate provision for the handicapped was the soon-to-be notorious Section 504. It provided:

> No otherwise qualified handicapped individual . . . shall, solely by reason of his handicap, be excluded from participation in, be denied the benefits of, or be subjected to discrimination under any program or activity receiving Federal financial assistance.

Except within the handicapped community, little attention had been paid to the Rehabilitation Act at the time of its passage. There was no mechanism for its enforcement, and nobody in

Washington had yet tried to tackle the complex problems that would entail. The situation changed in the spring of 1976 when President Ford issued Executive Order 11914. By this, he directed the secretary of health, education and welfare to coordinate the implementation of Section 504 by all federal departments and agencies. Following an extensive solicitation of public comment—as well as a series of dramatic and highly publicized demonstrations by organized handicapped groups—an initial set of regulations implementing Section 504 was signed by Secretary Joseph Califano on April 29, 1977. In time, other federal agencies (including those most relevant to museums) followed with regulations of their own.

For many museums, the first hard news of Section 504 came during the March 1977 sessions of the annual Museum Law Conference. That year's conference was held at the Metropolitan Museum of Art in New York, and one of the invited speakers was Anne Beckman—an attorney with the Office of Civil Rights in the Department of Health, Education and Welfare. Beckman's discussion of the department's then pending regulations was a shock. The department's approach, as she spelled it out, was to be uncompromising—even draconian. Whatever failed to measure up to the new accessibility standards would simply have to be slashed away. If the original doorways of an historic house were too narrow to admit wheelchairs, then fine: either replace them with wider doors, or punch a new entrance into the side of the building. Otherwise, forget any hope of future federal assistance. If an NEA-funded exhibition was scheduled to be shown in a spacious second-floor gallery accessible only by stairs, that was no problem: it could simply be jammed in somewhere downstairs, regardless of whether the space was suitable or even adequate. Neither aesthetics nor the concerns of preservation—not all of them, anyway—had the force of law. The rights of the handicapped did. Enforcement would be strict.

In actual practice, the impact of Section 504 on museums has been neither so definite nor so harsh. While the courts continue to wrestle with its language, its enforcement within museums has been largely by voluntary compliance, accommodation, and only occasional persuasion. Confrontations have been rare, and generally handled with tact. Typical is the case of a discrimination charge against the Museum of Modern Art that was filed with the

NEA. The complainant was a blind artist who alleged he had been discriminated against when the museum refused him permission to touch any of the sculpture in its 1980 Picasso exhibition. While sustaining the museum's position—there was no discrimination since *nobody* was allowed to touch the sculpture; there was an equal opportunity to participate in and benefit from this federally assisted exhibition since an audio tour *was* offered as an "equivalent" to what a sighted visitor might have enjoyed—the general counsel of the NEA nonetheless gently admonished MOMA for allowing the matter to reach the complaint stage and suggested that "consistent, easily available information and greater sensitivity on the part of the Museum staff" might have avoided such an incident. The hardships to museums that Section 504 once seemed to threaten now seem considerably diminished.

Whether museums, together with much of the remaining nonprofit sector, are to be embraced in a uniform set of accounting standards is still an open question. An "exposure"or discussion draft of such standards was circulated for comment by the Accounting Standards Division of the American Institute of Certified Public Accountants in early 1977 and a final statement of position (SOP 78-10) issued on December 31, 1978. Nonetheless, the last step necessary to clamp these standards into place has not yet been taken. That would be the establishment by the Financial Accounting Standards Board of an effective date for their implementation, until which time no sanctions could be imposed against an accountant who failed to follow SOP 78-10. While this document may still carry clout in the interim—particularly with the larger accounting firms that were most closely involved in its formulation—museums thus far are under only its shadow, not yet its full weight.

Curiously, while SOP 78-10 remains a looming possibility, the context in which it was born—the likelihood that there would be federal legislation to limit the nonprogram expenditures of charitable organizations that solicit through the mails and the fear that such legislation would be accompanied by accounting rules less acceptable than those that the accountants themselves might devise—seems largely to have dissolved. For the past several years, there has been little push in Washington for such a law. (At the same time, questions have been raised at the state level about the constitutionality of legislation limiting the right to solicit.) If the Congress tends to be most responsive to what is most recently in the news, then the dearth of recent scandals involving charitable organizations—the situation was otherwise in the mid-seventies—might permit museums to enjoy a few more years of grace without *this* additional dose of federal regulation.

Section 504, uniform accounting standards, and federal limitations on nonprogram expenditures—all of these are elements in what I described in 1976 as the "thickening texture of American life." My attitude then was largely clinical. I was not particularly troubled by this "thickening." It was not, I wrote at the time, "anything that is necessarily good or bad."

Since then, I have come to feel otherwise. This "thickening" now seems to me *not* to be a good thing. It strikes me as unhealthy, and perhaps unhealthy too is the degree to which we have permitted a belief in the perfectability of society to play so dominant a role in shaping our lives and institutions. By seeking to erase every last irregularity and mollify every last hurt, there may be other goals perhaps equally precious—not least, the achievement of some common good—that we are inadvertently neglecting along the way. The cost of trying to institutionalize goodness may be greater than we realize.

Nor am I any longer so sure as I once was that the lawyers—myself included—are wholly innocent. It is not our intentions that I question, but our proliferation. Lawyers may be likened to nuclear warheads. From one point of view, the more of them we have, then the greater would seem the safeguard to our liberties. From the opposing view, the endless multiplication of such potentially destructive weapons can have no consequence in the long run but to raise the general level of tension and confrontation.

Those who share this second view can look to the future with some foreboding. In September 1982, addressing the degree to which we have become a contentious rather than a cooperative people, Charles Peters—the editor of *Washington Monthly*—pointed out that during the 1981–82 academic year there were 127,530 students enrolled in American law schools. He went on to quote *Harper's* editor Michael Kinsley:

> Anthropologists of the next century will look back in amazement at an arrangement whereby the most ambitious and brightest members of each generation were siphoned off the productive work force,

trained to think like a lawyer, and put to work chasing one another around in circles.

Those who question that there can ever be too much of a good thing are referred to the legend of King Midas. For a favor to Bacchus, he was awarded with the power to transform whatever came within his reach to what he valued most—gold. As Thomas Bulfinch tells it:

> His joy knew no bounds, and as soon as he got home, he ordered the servants to set a splendid repast on the table. Then he found to his dismay that whether he touched bread, it hardened in his hand; or put a morsel to his lips, it defied his teeth. He took a glass of wine, but it flowed down his throat like melted gold.

Justice, equity, fairness, regularity, predictability—all of these are essential and all are of the greatest value. And yet, like King Midas, we may face a "glittering destruction"—or perhaps in our case worse, a gray suffocation— if we let the life around us thicken to the point where these are all we have.

Vincible Ignorance:
Museums and the Law
(1979)

L et me begin with three propositions: First, that the tangle of legal considerations in which the day-to-day operation of American museums
has become increasingly enmeshed is not a transient phenomenon. While we have some reason to hope that the federal regulatory process—one of the most constricting of the various strands
that weave through this tangle—may soon be subject to some
relaxation, there is little prospect that, for the immediate future,
we will see any significant reduction in the number of ongoing
museum activities that continue to involve one legal concern or
another.

Second, that the day-to-day responsibility for dealing with these
legal concerns—for seeing to it not only that a museum is in
compliance with applicable laws and regulations, but also that it
is able successfully to defend such claims as may be asserted
against it by government officials, by aggrieved employees, by
visitors, and by otherwise interested outside parties—falls squarely
on the director.

And third, that we have reached a point where it would be the
height of folly—or, beyond folly, where it would constitute culpable negligence and an abuse of their trust—for those entrusted
with the well-being of our museums to attempt to deal with these
legal considerations without the benefit of competent professional counsel.

*Copyright © 1979 by the American Association of Museums. A longer version of
this paper was originally delivered as the keynote address at the American Law
Institute–American Bar Association Course of Study on Legal Problems of Museum
Administration held in Fort Worth, Texas, in March 1979 and appeared as an article
in Museum News, vol. 58, no. 1 (September/October 1979).*

Over the past fifteen years we have watched, almost spell-bound, the seemingly inexorable advance of a mass of regulation, and federal regulation in particular, that today touches virtually every aspect of museum operations. The questions we may ask a prospective employee, the objects we may choose to collect, the tools we provide to our workers, the temperature at which we maintain our galleries, and the width of the aisles between exhibition cases—all of these, and far more, may today be subject to one or another law or regulation.

That it is the director of a museum who must bear the day-to-day responsibility for dealing with such regulations and other legal concerns is a harsh proposition and one that some might question. Certainly, the *ultimate* responsibility for all of the actions of a museum must be borne by its board of trustees or other governing body. And certainly, too, there are some things, particularly legal questions arising from the conduct of the board or its members, that clearly are beyond the director's control.

Nevertheless, it seems to me that there is no practical or desirable way to involve the board of trustees in that multitude of day-to-day decisions that constitutes the ongoing operation of a museum. In some areas—personnel or collections management, for example—the board, working with the director, may adopt formal, written policies that can resolve a substantial number of day-to-day situations. Nonetheless, such policies will still need to be interpreted, events will occur that no one has anticipated, and the law, ever susceptible to change, may always change faster than the policies can be changed.

Below the director, there is no one with so comprehensive a knowledge of all the museum's activities. Above the director, there is no one whose attention is focused exclusively on the museum's daily operation. Given everything else with which a director must deal, the responsibility for safeguarding the museum's legal posture does seem a cruel additional burden. And yet, unless the director is to abdicate the management of the museum, there is no other place it can rest except in—or at least very near—his office.

More self-evident, I think, is my third proposition: that a museum would be derelict in the extreme if it sought to deal with the tangle of legal considerations within which it must operate without the benefit of competent professional counsel. We are dealing here with matters which, if mishandled, can be very costly to a museum in terms of litigation, in terms of potential damages, in terms of its reputation and its consequent support in the community, and in terms of the energies that must inevitably be diverted from what should be the museum's central concerns.

Our laws are too complex, and the consequences of misunderstanding them too grave, to make it thinkable that the legal aspects of museum management should be based on anything less than the best available professional advice. None of you would risk your museum's most valued object in the hands of an untrained conservator. Why, then, should you not have a similar high regard for the reputations of your institutions or, for that matter, for the conservation of their hard-won and frequently too slender resources?

If you accept these three propositions, then, the situation in which we find ourselves is this: Short of the grotesque possibility of instantly replacing every American museum director with a versatile (and probably independently wealthy) attorney, some provision must be made to provide our present directors with regularly available access to competent professional counsel.

Such access must, moreover, be provided as a matter of course. The need for counsel must be recognized as a normal incident to the management of museums and not (as it may perhaps in the past have been) as the remedy for some directorial malfunction. If expense is to be involved, it should be anticipated as a normal cost of museum operation and provided for in the annual budget. If the board must be consulted as to the means by which legal services are to be provided, such consultation should be had in advance. Above all, the director's access to professional counsel should be timely. For all of those good reasons we crystallize in maxims about closing barn doors and stitches in time, it is *before*, not *after*, a problem may surface that professional counsel can be of greatest value to a museum director and of the least ultimate expense to the museum.

Where, then, is such counsel better located: inside or outside the museum? Given infinite resources and an infinite supply of experienced, capable attorneys, every museum might simply add to its staff such number of in-house counsel as might be needed to cover the entire spectrum of the museum's activities and its consequent legal concerns. In the corporate sector, just such a pattern has developed. General Motors, for example, has nearly 150 staff attorneys and considerable outside counsel as well. IBM employs nearly the same number. And General Electric, having chosen to do much of its own patent work in-house, employs more staff attorneys than GM and IBM combined—at last count, some 320.

Museums have neither infinite nor even comparable resources. To the best of my knowledge, there are scarcely a half-dozen museums in the United States—and they are among our largest— that have the resources to maintain an in-house legal staff. Even if such resources were available, it is questionable whether the establishment of an in-house legal staff would be the most desirable course for most museums to follow.

In many museums, particularly those where good preventive law has been practiced, there probably would not be enough day-to-day work for such inside counsel to do. Moreover, when particular problems did arise, they might well turn out to be beyond such counsel's specialization. Even at the Smithsonian, with a legal staff of eight, the largest of any museum or museum complex in the country, we frequently employ special outside counsel for matters that our attorneys think can thereby be better handled. Beyond both these considerations, good legal services are a scarce and therefore expensive commodity.

According to the *New York Law Journal* of December 4, 1978, students graduating from law school in June of 1979 and joining major big-city law firms could look forward to the following starting salaries: in New York City, $30,000; Washington, $28,000; Los Angeles, $24,000; San Francisco and Boston, $22,000; and Houston and Dallas, $20,000.

Those are starting salaries. Even if you *could* afford such an apple-cheeked law school graduate and not convulse your remaining professional staff in the process, it is doubtful that such a beginning lawyer could really provide you with the services you need.

For almost all museums, then, legal services must in all likelihood continue to be provided by outside counsel. There are many ways in which this may be done. Outside counsel may be paid or voluntary. It may be provided by members of the board or by others. General counsel may be retained for all museum purposes or special counsel may be employed for special purposes. Counsel may be provided by an affiliate organization or even, on occasion, by one or another of a museum's insurance carriers. And finally, of course, a museum may use any combination of these.

We must then turn to what seems to be the most difficult problem among these otherwise self-evident propositions.

"It is not enough," wrote Descartes in his *Discourse on Method*, "to have a good mind. The main thing is to use it well." It is not enough for a museum director to be provided with competent legal counsel. The main thing is to use it well. But knowing how to use legal counsel effectively may still not be enough. The initial requirement is to know *when* to use it. If a museum director does not know when to turn to professional counsel, the rest is irrelevant. Unless counsel is consulted, there is nothing that counsel, no matter how competent, can do.

Here, then, is the core of our problem. How is a museum director, not an attorney but charged nevertheless with day-to-day responsibility for guiding the museum through a tangle of legal complexities, to recognize those situations that require reference to outside professional counsel?

I wish there were some all-purpose answer, some clever formula that would permit you to invoke the aid of counsel on every appropriate occasion, but never otherwise. Initially, I can only suggest that it is probably better to be too cautious than too cavalier. Your attorney, your board, and the world outside will more readily forgive the telephone call that sounds a false alarm than they will your failure to have sounded an alarm when something was really smoking.

Beyond that, it seems to me a matter of blending an instinct and knowledge not unlike those that parents develop over the years of their parenting, knowing on one occasion that two aspirins are just right and on another that it's time to call the doctor. Of these two components, it may be that the first—instinct—can only be developed through experience and through an openness to sharing experiences with others.

But, to reverse Aldous Huxley's observation that "most ignorance is vincible," most knowledge—including the knowledge that museum directors need to make effective use of counsel—*is* acquirable. Helpful are seminars such as the annual ALI-ABA course of study on legal problems of museum administration, as well as the legal sessions that are increasingly included in the meeting programs of the AAM and other national, regional, and state museum organizations. Helpful too is the increased attention given to legal developments in our professional museum periodicals. Fundamental to acquiring such knowledge, though, is a clear and basic understanding of just how it is that the law does affect museums. [For an overview of the legal concerns that may affect museums, see "A Checklist of Legal Considerations for Museums," pp. 143–50.]

It has recently seemed to me that we may somehow have clouded this understanding by appearing to suggest that there is something—some monstrous, limitless, omniverous, black-cloud of a thing—called "museum law." Two recent incidents triggered this concern.

The first involved a call from a friend who directs an association of nonprofit art galleries in one of the northeastern states. The association operates a trucking service for its members and, because the demand for this service tends to vary considerably from day-to-day, the director had asked one of her drivers to agree, regardless of how many hours he might work on any given day, that he would not be entitled to overtime pay except for hours worked over forty during any given week. The driver had subsequently been discharged by the association and was now asserting a claim for unpaid overtime. What concerned me was that my friend, the director, believed that she had a "museum law" problem. She was calling to ask if I could put her in touch with some museum that had found itself in a comparable situation.

The second incident was similar. The call this time was from the director of a southwestern museum. The museum had recently fired its assistant director who, it seemed, had an employment contract providing for six-months notice. No notice had been given, and the erstwhile assistant director was now suing the museum for six-months salary in lieu of notice. Again, the question was the same: Did I know of some museum where something similar had happened? Again, the director believed the problem he had was a "museum law" problem.

In fact, with few exceptions, there is no body of law that is particular to museums. There are few laws—not even the cornerstone of our tax exemption, the blessed 501(c)(3)—that even mention museums, whether to include them or exclude them. Museums are complex entities, the various aspects or activities of which are subject to various bodies of law that, for the most part, are not interrelated.

If that sounds abstruse, an analogy may help to clarify it. Consider a person who may be at once a husband, a tenant, a father, an employee, a son, a registered alien, an author, a debtor, and a licensed driver. The fact that he is married will not affect his legal situation if he should happen to be caught while speeding. The fact that he has children will not affect his obligation to pay his rent. And the fact that he has borrowed money will certainly not affect the requirement that he maintain his alien registration. To each characteristic of his being, a particular body of law is applicable—a body of law to which he is subject in common with everyone else who shares that particular characteristic. As a driver he is subject to the same laws as other drivers, regardless of whether they share his married state, owe someone money, or have a living parent. As a tenant he is subject to the same laws as other tenants, regardless of whether they have children or hold any copyrights. And so on, down the line.

So it is with museums. For each of a museum's characteristic aspects or activities, there is a particular body of law applicable, one to which the museum is, for the most part, subject in common with a host of other organizations or individuals who share that same characteristic. What are some of these characteristics?

Virtually every museum, for example, is an employer. As such it will, depending on the number of people it regularly employs, fall under a body of state and federal laws common to all employers that may be similarly classified. Many of the same museums that have employees also import objects or specimens of foreign origin. In doing so, the body of law to which they subject themselves is altogether different than that which regulates their relationship with their employees. Moreover, depending upon just what it is they import—pre-Columbian architectural fragments or Icelandic scrimshaw—the group with which they will be classified as subject in common to this law may differ entirely from that with which they were classified as employers. It might, for instance, include private collectors who have no employees.

To extend these illustrations: Many museums accept grants or contracts from the federal government. In doing so, they subject themselves to still a different series of regulations that, again, will be common to every organization—regardless of whether it is a university, hospital, library, or other museum—accepting similar support. Many museums are also private nonprofit organizations governed by boards of trustees. Here, other bodies of law—in some cases analogous to those applicable to business corporations, in others rooted in the traditional rules of private trust administration—may be applicable.

Beyond this, a museum may also be a merchant; it may maintain public premises; it may be an instrumentality of the federal government or of a state, county, or municipal government; it may be a publisher. The list could be extended. And, for each such characteristic, the museum intersects with another body of law. If a museum operates a restaurant, the fact that paintings by Pablo Picasso hang in its galleries will not exempt it from coverage by the same local health regulations that govern Piero's Pizzeria across the street.

Beyond disabusing ourselves of the notion that there is something called "museum law," why is it so important to understand this process of characterization? For three reasons: First, by learning to characterize the museum's various aspects and activities, the boundless body of law by which museums seem to be surrounded can be reduced to a series of discrete and far more manageable concerns. By developing a sharpened sense of which legal concerns need to be considered in connection with which of the museum's particular aspects or activities, the ability of the director to make that one critical legal judgment that he is regularly called upon to make—to know *when* the services of professional counsel should be sought—can be immeasurably strengthened.

Second, by learning to apply this process of characterization to other types of organizations, a museum director may come to understand better that many situations and events that seem at first glance irrelevant to museums may have, in fact, enormous relevance to his own institution. The Sibley Hospital case, for example *(Stern v. Lucy Webb Hayes National Training School, etc.,* 1974), might, without proper characterization, have appeared to be nothing but an instance of as misleading a concept as "museum law"—"hospital law." Properly characterized, it was a stern warning to the trustees of all private nonprofit organizations, including museums that might be so classified, about the management of their finances and about what might be deemed an impermissible conflict of interest. Similarly, if your local college or library encounters a problem under the Civil Rights Act of 1964 or the Rehabilitation Act of 1973, you may, if you characterize it properly, and do not simply dismiss it out of hand as some problem of "library law" or "college law," better be able to anticipate the extent to which such a problem may ultimately be your problem too. In this way, a museum director may substantially broaden the range of experiences that can be perceived as relevant to his own institution.

Third, and this is particularly important for museums that do not retain general counsel or use affiliated counsel, this process of characterization can—when a problem impends—prove extremely useful in suggesting the sources from which the necessary help may be sought. If a wage and hour problem in a museum is viewed as uniquely a museum problem, the director may have to search far outside the community to find help in dealing with it. On the other hand, if the problem can be characterized for what it is—an employment problem occurring in a museum setting— ample guidance may be available from local resources. If you do have general counsel, it is just such a process that your counsel must follow to determine how a problem should best be dealt with. If you don't, this diagnostic function is one that you may be forced to undertake yourself.

To suggest that museum directors should reach such a basic understanding of how it is that the law affects museums is not to suggest that they ought to become amateur lawyers. That might be worse than having no counsel at all. The point, rather—to return finally to our three opening propositions—is this: Given that museums must, now and for the foreseeable future, operate in a broad context of legal considerations, given that the director must bear the day-to-day responsibility for dealing with these legal considerations, and given that—if that responsibility is to be discharged properly—the director must have the benefit of adequate legal services, the directors of museums have a double obligation. First, in conjunction with their boards they must see to it that provision is made to give them regular access to the services of professional counsel. Second, once such counsel is available to them they must be sensitive enough to learn how and when such counsel can best be used.

Too often, in the past, too many museums have had more adequate procedures for ordering legal pads—a countersigned purchase order, perhaps, or some form of requisition—than they have had for providing their directors with needed legal services. Too often, in the past, too many museums have used legal services as their pound of cure when, at a fraction of the expense, such services might have been employed to provide a good many ounces of prevention. And too often, in the past, too many museums have seen their periodic entanglements with the law as puzzling exceptions to some long-standing privilege of living outside the contentious mainstream of American life.

As all of you must know by now, attitudes such as these are luxuries that none of us who care about the healthy survival of museums can any longer afford.

A Checklist of Legal Considerations for Museums (1981)

The following is a checklist that I began compiling in 1973 and have since up-dated as occasion required. Not every item will be relevant to every museum, and, in several instances (accreditation being one), items of a nonlegal nature have been included. In no sense (even allowing for inadvertent omissions) should it be considered as final. If the past is any guide, the occasions for updating it will probably come with increasing frequency.

It is not supposed that any museum administrator (or even his general counsel) will at any time be in thorough command of all the items included. My purpose, rather, has been to furnish an aid-memoir for those responsible for the operation of museums that they might use periodically to review their total management and ask themselves about each item, "Is this relevant to our museum and, if so, who is addressing it and when was it last addressed?" Phrased otherwise, it might be regarded as the framework for a periodic "museum legal checkup."

Checklist

A. *Organization.*
   1. Conformity with applicable state law.
   2. Conformity with charter and/or other governing public or private instruments.
   3. Establishment and maintenance of federal tax-exempt

Copyright © 1981 by the National Association of College and University Attorneys. The checklist was published previously in Journal of College and University Law, vol. 7, nos. 3–4 (1980/81).

status; exclusivity of purpose, nondiversion of funds, influencing legislation, participation in politics.

4. Determination and maintenance of federal tax classification; impact of unusually large gifts on public charity status.

5. License or registration under state charitable solicitation laws.

6. Maintenance of state and local tax-exempt status; income, real estate, admission, parking, water, and sewer taxes, etc.

7. Filing of required information returns and other periodic reports: federal, state, county, municipal.

8. AAM accreditation and reaccreditation.

B. *General Endowment and Restricted Funds.*

1. Legality and propriety of investments.

2. Conformity with donor-imposed and trustee-imposed restrictions.

3. Determination of income and principal of restricted funds.

4. Propriety of expenditures from restricted funds.

5. Implementation of total return concept; Uniform Management of Institutional Funds Act.

6. Transactions with donors, including pledges, receipts, and tax determinations.

7. Preferred forms for bequests and intervivos gifts.

8. Deferred gifts; charitable remainder annuity trusts, unitrusts, pooled trusts.

9. Sale of restricted securities.

10. *Cy pres* proceedings.

C. *Trustees.*

1. Periodic review of by-laws.

2. Conformity of proceedings with by-laws; notices, minutes, resolutions, proxies.

3. Conflicts of interest: professional services, corporate opportunity, insider advantage, self-dealing.

4. Personal liability.

   a. Indemnification.

   b. Insurance.

   c. Payment of premiums; taxability.

5. Delegation of authority: executive and other committees, officers, staff.

6. Written consent for use of names of honorary trustees and officers.
7. "Sunshine," Freedom of Information, and similar disclosure laws.
8. Audit committee.

D. *Staff.*

1. Wage and hour laws, minimum wage laws, Bureau of Labor Standards wage rates (NEA grants), child labor laws.
2. Wage and price and similar guidelines.
3. Fair employment practices and affirmative action programs: race, color, religion, national origin, sex, age, handicap, sexual preference.
4. Methods of recruitment, permitted selection interview techniques.
5. Employee unions.
   a. Unfair labor practices.
   b. Recognition, NLRB or state jurisdiction.
   c. Exclusion of "managerial" titles.
   d. Negotiation.
   e. Grievances and arbitration.
6. Employee Retirement Income Security Act of 1974 (ERISA).
7. Other insured fringe benefits: hospitalization, group health, major medical, dental, disability and life insurance, special 403(b) annuities.
8. Absence-with-pay fringe benefits: vacation, holidays, sick leave, death in family, jury duty, personal leave, maternity leave, voting time.
9. Leave-of-absence (without pay) fringe benefits: impact on pension calculations, seniority, tenure.
10. Unemployment insurance, claims.
11. Workman's compensation insurance, claims.
12. Occupational Safety and Health Act of 1970 (OSHA).
13. Royalties on museum-generated publications, agreements with employees, ownership of employee work-product.
14. Conflicts of interest: corporate opportunity, insider advantage, self-dealing, personal collecting.
15. Outside employment.
16. Civil Service regulations, dual compensation.

17. Use of CETA employees.
18. Employment contracts.
19. Fidelity insurance.
20. Independent contractors, Form 1099.
21. Withholding taxes: deposits, W-2's.
22. Administratively established grievance procedures.
23. Termination procedures, disciplinary procedures.
24. Control of personnel files.
25. Rights on termination, insurance conversions.
26. Waiver of Social Security exemption.

E. *Volunteers.*
1. Liability for injuries to volunteers.
2. Liability for acts of volunteers.
3. Deduction of volunteers' unreimbursed expenses.

F. *Collection.*
1. Acquisition by purchase.
   a. Authority.
   b. Works originating outside the United States: laws of country of origin, legality of export, legality of import, customs.
   c. Objects constituting or incorporating (in whole or in part) endangered species.
   d. Warranties: authorship, title, condition, provenance.
   e. Safety standards.
   f. Acquisition and retention of reproduction rights.
   g. Obscenity, invasion of privacy, defamation.
   h. Reserved Right Transfer and Sale Agreement and similar contracts.
   i. Arrangements for shared ownership.
2. Acquisition by gift.
   a. Authority to accept.
   b. Year-end procedures.
   c. Custody, insurance, and conservation of fractional gifts.
   d. Restrictions.
   e. Donor's tax considerations: valuation, exempt purpose, attribution, valuation by museum.
   f. Bequests: renunciation, precatory language.
   g. Bargain sales.

   h. Provenance.

   i. Status of reproduction rights.

  3. Acquisition by exchange.

   a. Propriety of accompanying disposition.

   b. Valuation.

   c. Continuing identification of donor.

   d. Resale royalties (California).

  4. Field collections.

   a. Endangered species and similar legislation.

   b. Antiquities Act of 1906 and similar legislation.

   c. Archeological Resources Protection Act of 1979.

   d. Public Health Service Act.

  5. Acquisition by adverse possession.

  6. Disposition.

   a. Authority.

   b. Restrictions.

   c. Method of disposition: public or private auction, private sale, exchange, transfer, destruction.

   d. Public notice requirements.

   e. Application of proceeds, retention of credit to original source.

   f. Resale royalties (California).

  7. Insurance: risks, ransom, values, currency fluctuations, deductibles, transit and other limits.

  8. *Cy pres* proceedings.

  9. Outgoing individual loans: authority, insurance, loan agreements, uniform availability.

 10. Contracts for outgoing loans of entire exhibition.

 11. Conservation, *droit moral* (California).

 12. Access to reserve collections.

 13. American Indian Religious Freedom Act of 1978.

G. *Exhibition Program.*

  1. Incoming individual loans.

   a. Insurance: insurance by lender and waivers of subrogation.

   b. Obligation to exhibit.

   c. Sales from exhibition.

   d. Death of lender: rights of heirs, tax waivers.

   e. Reproduction: catalogs, slides, publicity.

   f. Attachment: immunity statutes.

       g. Alteration, restoration, reframing.

       h. Customs, temporary entry.

       i. Failure to accept return.

       j. Loans for indefinite term.

  2. Contracts for incoming loans of entire exhibition.

  3. Safety standards.

  4. Obscenity, invasion of privacy, defamation, desecration, prohibited images.

  5. Federal indemnification.

  6. Protection of lender's copyright, photography by public.

H. *Visitors.*

  1. Admission fees, receipts for voluntary donations.

  2. Handicapped access: physical and programmatic, Sections 502 and 504 of the Rehabilitation Act of 1973.

  3. Illness or injury in museum.

  4. Accidents: insurance, reporting.

  5. Assault, battery, and false arrest.

  6. Check-room liabilities.

  7. Openings: sale of liquor on premises; liquor law liabilities, minors.

  8. Rules and regulations: smoking, strollers, photography, political demonstrations.

  9. Anti-defacement statutes.

  10. Visitor surveys: National Research Act of 1974, protection of human subjects.

I. *Membership.*

  1. Extent of deductibility of dues.

  2. Member's activities.

       a. Charter flights: liabilities, unrelated business income (Revenue Ruling 78-43).

       b. House tours.

       c. Authority to bind museum.

  3. Regularity of proceedings.

  4. Written consent for use of names.

  5. Parallel organizations.

J. *Auxiliary Activities.*

  1. Unrelated business income: Revenue Ruling 73-104, 73-105 and 74-99; exclusivity test.

  2. Sales taxes.

3. Publishing contracts: copyrights, royalties, late delivery, subsidiary rights.
4. Reproductions, slides, post cards.
5. Film and television licenses.
6. Restaurants: local regulation, liabilities.
7. Parking lots.
8. Recorded tours.
9. Art lending or sales gallery.
10. Franchise operations.
11. Rental of premises, uniform standards.
12. Sales of membership lists.
13. Unrelated debt-financed income.

K. *Building.*
1. Violations.
2. Sanitary codes.
3. Alteration or new construction: permits, zoning, handicapped considerations, historic structures.
4. Leased premises.
5. Sidewalk responsibilities.
6. Maintenance contracts.
7. Professional licenses.
8. Insurance.
9. Fuel priority.
10. Outside signs, Federal Flag Code.
11. Thermostat Control Act of 1979, exemption certificates.

L. *Financing.*
1. Use of debt instruments: tax-exempt bonds, arbitrage bonds, and Section 109(d).
2. Sales of air rights.
3. Special taxes and tax districts.

M. *Miscellaneous.*
1. Expert opinions.
2. Public grant applications, administration, and accountability.
   a. Eligibility.
   b. Matching funds, challenge grants, Treasury Funds methods.
   c. Indirect cost rates.
   d. Reporting.

3. Museum vehicles.
4. Credit card arrangements.
5. Postal regulations.
6. Public solicitation, statutory limit on expenses.
7. Lobbying, Section 501(h) election.
8. Validation of expenses incurred on behalf of museum by donors.
9. Archival material: publication, permission to use, oral history.
10. Use of licensed carriers.
11. Conformity of accounting procedures with AICPA or other standards.
12. Procurement procedures.

Custody Without Title
(1977)

Once upon a time—when life was much simpler—it was relatively easy to describe a museum's relationship to the objects in its possession. The museum either *owned* these objects–in which case we referred to them as the "collection"—or it had *borrowed* them.

If the objects belonged to the museum, then, unless some crackpot newspaper came along to raise a fuss, the museum could do whatever it wished with them—it could exercise all of those sovereign rights of dominion that ownership generally confers. On the other hand, if the objects were borrowed, then a loan agreement or some similar arrangement would presumbly specify what the museum might or might not do.

What we have been seeing recently, though—and what we will be talking about today—is the introduction into museums of new and unprecedented relationships to the objects in their care. In some instances, these involve a split between the actual legal title to an object and the right to its custody; in others, museums may continue to retain technical title but must relinquish one or more of what might be considered the normal incidents of ownership.

What we are finding, in other words, are instances of objects that a museum may "less than own" and "more than borrow." Or, in still other words: owning and borrowing have been the traditional black and white polarities for museums; there is now emerging an area of gray, full of pitfalls, but full of opportunities as well.

This paper was originally prepared for the American Law Institute–American Bar Association Course of Study on Legal Aspects of Museum Operation, given in New York City, March 23–25, 1977.

Some things fall into this gray area because they must—by reason of law or public policy. But others, as we shall see, have been put there as a matter of conscious choice. By deliberately locating their relationship to objects in this gray area between outright ownership and a transient loan, museums have been able to obtain access to objects that might have otherwise been unavailable to them—because of cost or, again, because of law or public policy.

To begin with a simple example of the first kind—a case in which a museum has no choice but to accept something less than outright ownership—we have the still unfolding story of the Van Buren County Historical Museum in Keosauqua, Iowa.

Those of you who have followed this story in *Aviso* will recall that in November 1976 agents of the Federal Bureau of Alcohol, Tobacco and Firearms swooped down on the museum to confiscate four World War I machine guns—the gift of a local American Legion Post—on the grounds that these weapons had never been properly registered under the National Firearms Act. (It was, by the way, a good faith effort by the museum's curator to register these guns that alerted the Feds to their existence in the first place.)

While the bureau continues to insist that there is now no way in which the museum may retain the ownership of these objects, a compromise appears in prospect. Under the regulations to the National Firearms Act, the several states and their political subdivisions may acquire and retain such weapons. Accordingly, if Van Buren County–in which the museum is located but of which it is *not* an instrumentality—will accept the ownership of these machine guns and put them back in the museum on long-term loan, justice and equity will both have been done. The museum will retain custody without title, and the Feds will leave it alone. [Eventually, with the same effect, the Iowa State Historical Department accepted title and returned the guns to the museum on "permanent loan."]

More interesting, though—to me, at least—are examples of the second kind where new, gray areas of less-than-ownership are deliberately sought as being to a museum's benefit. A recent and extraordinary example of this is the formation, in the state of Washington, of a five-museum consortium for the express purpose of acquiring a collection of American drawings and other works on paper that might have been beyond the means of any one of the participating museums to acquire on its own.

Organized in early 1975, the Washington Art Consortium now includes as members Western Washington State College in Bellingham, the Washington State University Museum of Art in Pullman, the Cheney Cowles Museum of the Eastern Washington State Historical Society in Spokane, the State Capital Museum in Olympia, and the Tacoma Art Museum. For legal reasons peculiar to the state of Washington, the Tacoma Art Museum was unable to act as one of the original organizers but was "plugged in" to the consortium immediately after its formation.

In June 1975 the National Endowment for the Arts—which looks with favor on cooperative programs—awarded the consortium a purchase grant of $100,000. This amount was matched by an equal grant from a local foundation, the Virginia Wright Fund, and the consortium was in business. In September, a governing committee was established—including representatives of the State Arts Commission and the Seattle Art Museum as well as of the participating museums—and by-laws were adopted.

The life of the consortium is to be ninety-nine years, and, during that period, all decisions about purchases and sales are to be made by the governing committee. In general, the collection is to be maintained as a single unit and exhibited—on a rotating basis—among the participating museums. While the collection, or individual works from it, may occasionally be shown outside Washington State, each of the participants is guaranteed the right to show the entire collection for at least four months during any two-calendar-year period. At the end of ninety-nine years, the collection—together with any other remaining assets—is to be divided among the participants.

In entering the Washington Art Consortium, the participating museums not only agreed to share its operating expenses but undertook, as well, to meet a very specific set of conditions under which the consortium's collection could be shown. These included, among other things, limits on the level of illumination that could be employed, specifications of allowable temperature and humidity, and procedures for art handling. In fact, the standards specified were good museological ones—and by agreeing to these, as well as to the continued support of the consortium, the participants gained the ongoing regular use of, if not the immediate title to, a significant collection. And some time around 2074, they will each get outright title to one-fifth of it as well.

In the case of Washington State, the consortium arrangement permitted the formation of a new collection. In another case, a different—and novel—arrangement was employed to salvage an existing collection that was about to be dispersed.

The case involved 112 drawings by George Caleb Bingham, Missouri's best-known nineteenth-century artist and certainly one of the most popular American artists of any time. Executed between 1844 and 1849 as a reference portfolio for Bingham's paintings, the sketches were given to the St. Louis Mercantile Library Association in 1868. Faced with an annual operating deficit and advised by a New York art dealer that, if sold separately, these sketches might fetch a price in excess of $3 million, the library association apparently began, in 1974, to explore the possibility of selling the collection piecemeal. As word of its plan spread, opponents began a movement to assure that the collection would not be broken up and that it would not leave the state of Missouri.

Under the leadership of Governor Christopher Bond, a nonprofit corporation—Bingham Sketches, Inc.—was formed with the dual purposes of negotiating an agreement to purchase the sketches from the Mercantile Library and of raising the funds by which to do this. Bingham Sketches came into being on January 15, 1975. Eight months later, on August 18, 1975, the Mercantile Library agreed to sell all 112 of the sketches for $1.8 million. If this entire amount could not be raised by June 30, 1976, the nonprofit corporation would still be entitled to purchase part of the collection— but at a considerably higher price per item than if they bought all.

A remarkable fund-raising campaign followed. It has been estimated that more than 100,000 people—including 50,000 school children—contributed either money or time to this effort. The largest contributor was the state itself, which gave $500,000. The goal of $1.8 million was reached within a week of the deadline this past June.

Bingham Sketches was, however, simply a temporary device. By the terms of its articles of incorporation, it was required to turn those 112 drawings over to the state of Missouri "within a reasonable time after their acquisition." Then it was to self-destruct.

And what of the drawings themselves? According to the most

recent (but not final) plans that I have seen, they will be deposited with the state's two major art museums—the St. Louis Art Museum and the Nelson Gallery–Atkins Museum in Kansas City. The museums will in no way be free to do what they want with these drawings. There are to be elaborate restrictions on how the drawings are framed, on how they are glazed, and even on their labels. There will be continuing controls of temperature, humidity, and exposure to light; and loans outside the state will be subject to certain limitations.

No matter. Through this arrangement, the Missouri museums will be able to make permanently available to their publics—through their custody of these works, not by holding title to them—an important and remarkable group of drawings that would otherwise have been forever scattered. Complicated, yes—but worthwhile, too.

It was only seven years ago that the Accreditation Commission of the American Association of Museums, in formulating its first definition of a museum, put heavy emphasis on the notion that collections must be "owned." In the years since, it has found it necessary, in case after case—for science centers, planetaria, and art centers—to recede from this position and to recognize that the ownership of objects may not be a necessary criterion for the inclusion of an organization within the museum community. In that gray area between what is fully "owned" and what is "borrowed," new possibilities are emerging. If these serve our publics, then we in museums should be willing to explore them—and not turn our backs simply because it isn't the way things used to be done or because it seems too complicated.

––––––––––––––––

Afterword

The collection of American drawings formed by the Washington Art Consortium is superb—I saw a portion of it on loan to the Seattle Art Museum in 1977—and, when last heard from, the consortium itself was moving smoothly along toward its destined dissolution in 2074. Encouraged by their first cooperative venture, the participants—with several additional members—have meanwhile formed a second consortium to assemble a collection of contemporary American photographs. This, too, was funded by a combination of the NEA and a local donor.

Bingham Sketches also remains a going concern. Rather than self-destruct immediately, it has been kept alive to supervise a lending program through which the sketches it acquired in 1976 have been circulated both locally and to other parts of the country. When not in circulation, the sketches—as planned—remain on deposit at the art museums in St. Louis and Kansas City. Title, though, is still ultimately intended to go to the state of Missouri.

For museums interested in exploring two-party joint ownership arrangements—custody with only half a title—a growing number of models is available, most of recent date:

• In 1973, the Metropolitan Museum of Art and the Louvre jointly purchased at auction in Paris for $56,000 a medieval carved ivory comb depicting the Tree of Jesse. A coin was tossed to see which museum would show it first. The Metropolitan won, and it was shown first at the Cloisters for five years before being sent off to Paris for the next five. This rotation is slated to continue indefinitely.

• In 1976, the New Jersey State Museum in Trenton and the Newark Museum accepted the joint ownership of a Childe Hassam painting, *Les Bouquinistes du Quai Voltaire, Avril*, as a gift from a couple in Far Hills, New Jersey.

• In 1980, the Smithsonian Institution's National Portrait Gallery and the Boston Museum of Fine Arts jointly purchased Gilbert Stuart's portraits of George and Martha Washington from the Boston Atheneum for $4,875,000. The paintings had been on loan to the Museum of Fine Arts since 1876, and the joint purchase settled a bitter dispute that was set off nearly a year earlier when the Atheneum—strapped for money—undertook to sell the paintings outright to the Portrait Gallery for $5 million. Under the settlement, the two museums are to rotate custody on a three-year basis.

• In 1981, acting through Wildenstein, the J. Paul Getty Museum and the Norton Simon Foundation—both based outside of Los Angeles—jointly purchased at auction in London a Nicholas Poussin painting, the *Holy Family*, for approximately $4 million.

• In 1982, the Minneapolis Institute of Arts and the Des Moines

Art Center jointly purchased (for an undisclosed price) Grant Wood's painting *The Birthplace of Herbert Hoover*. Referring to the joint purchase, Samuel Sachs II, director of the Minneapolis Institute, described it as "a new method of acquiring significant works at a time when soaring prices and limited art funding have made such purchases by individual museums less feasible."

• Also in 1982, the National Portrait Gallery and the Thomas Jefferson Memorial Foundation—which operates the Jefferson home at Monticello—jointly purchased Gilbert Stuart's so-called Edgehill portrait of Jefferson from a New York City private collection for $1 million. The painting is to rotate on a three-year basis. Commenting on this and other joint purchases, Charles Blitzer, the Smithsonian's Assistant Secretary for History and Art, called them a "welcome form of cooperation" and a way "to overcome the staggering cost of major works of art."

A variation on the theme of joint ownership is the "standing loan agreement." By regularly rotating custody of the separated parts of a work of art that is no longer intact, each of the participating museums can, while still retaining title to its own fragment, have the opportunity to exhibit the work as a reunified whole. Typical of such arrangements was that announced in 1974 between the Metropolitian Museum of Art and the Louvre. Under this, the head (from New York), and the body (from Paris) of an alabaster neo-Sumerian statue—believed to have been separated in ancient times—were to be reunited and shown at the two museums for alternating periods of three years. A similar agreement that the Metropolitan had earlier pursued with the Oslo Museum of Applied Art—one under which the Metropolitan's great Bury St. Edmund's cross would have been reunited with the ivory figure of Christ then believed to be the cross's missing corpus—was allowed to languish after doubts developed that the fragments involved were actually parts of the same original object.

Inherent in both joint ownership and "standing loan agreements" is the likelihood that the objects themselves will have to be transported more frequently than they might otherwise. While this is to be regretted—"All valuable art objects are better off if they are never moved," the National Portrait Gallery's registrar said at the time of its 1982 acquisition of the Stuart portrait of Jefferson—there is arguably a trade-off, particularly in the case of objects acquired from private sources. Held by museums, they will generally be more accessible and—notwithstanding occasional travel—undoubtedly better protected than if left to the hazards of the outside world. Nonetheless, in selecting objects suitable for joint ownership, their ability to withstand repeated transport should be an important consideration.

To date, most joint acquisitions appear to have originated out of either the settlement of a dispute (as in the case of the Stuart portraits of George and Martha Washington) or the need to meet a purchase price that neither party could manage by itself (as in the case of Grant Wood's *Birthplace of Herbert Hoover*). There is a third possibility, however, of which museums should be cautious. It would be the case where two or more museums combined to limit the price that an object might otherwise have fetched if the museums had instead been competing for—and not cooperating in—its purchase. Such a combination could well be interpreted as a restraint of trade and could make the participating museums subject to a claim for damages.

This is not so fanciful as it may seem. During a 1979 auction at Christie's London salesroom, three dealers—Thos. Agnew and Company, E. V. Thaw and Company, and the Artemis investment group—combined to purchase for $360,000 a marble portrait bust by the seventeenth-century Italian artist Alessandro Algardi. They were subsequently indicted on criminal charges under Great Britain's Auction Act of 1927, which forbids the formation of undisclosed partnerships for the purpose of holding down bids. (The act was originally aimed at "ring" operations—in no event the case here—in which the purchased object would have subsequently been re-auctioned among the members of the "ring.") The dealers were tried in 1981 and acquitted when the magistrate accepted their contention that none of them would have bought the bust individually and that the only effect of combining their effort had been to *increase*—not decrease—the price that the consignor received for the work. While the United States has no law exactly comparable to Great Britain's Auction Act (and a distinction might be drawn between dealers and museums, anyway), it would nonetheless behoove museums—particularly in the case of purchases at auction—to ensure that any joint purchase they make can be demonstrated to arise from a good faith pooling of funds and not from an effort to suppress competition.

There remains room for still more ingenuity than the museum community has yet exercised in bringing important objects within its protective compass and—once there—devising means to share them with a larger public in ways that are reasonably consistent with their proper care. Such ingenuity should, though, be exercised with forethought, care, and—most appropriately—all the artfulness that museums can muster.

Breaches of Trust, Remedies, and Standards in the American Private Art Museum (1982)

From its founding in 1930 until 1965, the George F. Harding Museum occupied a publicly accessible building on the South Side of Chicago. Its contents included an arms and armor collection believed to be one of the finest in the world, a distinguished collection of musical instruments, Western Americana, and important European paintings from the seventeenth through nineteenth centuries. Recent estimates of the current value of these and its other collections range from $25 million to $100 million.

In 1965 the museum closed its doors to visitors and removed the bulk of its collections to storage. The larger part was left in crates, with only a small portion unpacked and made available to the public on a limited basis, by appointment only.

In October 1976 the state of Illinois—at the request of the state attorney general—commenced a civil suit against five of the museum's trustees[1] as well as the museum itself.[2] The complaint alleged, among other things, that:

a) The continuing failure to make the museum's collections generally accessible to the public violated the museum's intended purposes;

b) The manner in which the collections were being stored threatened them with irreparable harm;

c) Through intentional and reckless mismanagement, the

Copyright © 1982 by Stephen E. Weil. All rights reserved. This paper was originally delivered at a seminar on "The Penal Protection of Works of Art" organized by Judge Shoshana Berman of Rehovot, Israel, and sponsored by the International Institute of Higher Studies in Criminal Sciences in Syracuse, Italy, in April 1982. It has been published in condensed form in ARTnews (December 1982).

museum had been operated from 1972 through 1974 at deficits ranging from $200,000 to $300,000 annually;

d) Notwithstanding such deficits, four of the trustees, as officers of the board, had voted themselves salaries totaling $95,000 for each of those years;

e) The deficits thus incurred were being met or were intended to be met by selling objects from the museum's collections; and

f) The chairman of the board, who, together with some associates, owned the controlling interest in a local Chicago bank, had involved the museum in a series of loan transactions with the bank that constituted prohibited acts of self-dealing.

By way of remedies, the attorney general demanded that the court restrain the museum from making any further sales out of its collections, that it appoint a receiver to make an inventory and appraisal of the remaining collections, and that it remove the individual defendants as trustees and replace them with persons better able to carry out the museum's original purposes. In addition, he asked the court to require an accounting for all of the museum's assets (including the interest paid on the loans taken from the local Chicago bank), to impose a constructive trust over any moneys or other assets wrongfully obtained by the individual defendants, and to hold such defendants personally liable to the museum for whatever losses it might have sustained.

Noteworthy in the Harding complaint is the fact that the particular remedies sought all focused on the restoration of the museum to the purposes for which it was founded. While the trustees were alleged to have committed a number of wrongful acts, the attorney general did not ask that they be punished. Neither did he ask that the museum itself be fined or in any way deprived of some special status—such as tax exemption—that it might previously have enjoyed. At the most, the complaint demanded that the individual defendants be removed from their positions of trust, required to return to the museum such moneys as they had wrongfully obtained, and/or be made to reimburse it for such losses as might have been incurred through their mismanagement.

To understand the reasons for this, as well as the role played by the state attorney general in this and similar situations, one must begin by considering both the organizational structure of American art museums and the nature of the private nonprofit sector to which the majority of such museums belong. Brief consideration must also be given to the historic legal background, particularly as it pertains to the doctrine of equity as developed in the English Courts of Chancery from the fifteenth century onward and the employment by these courts of equitable remedies for the enforcement of charitable trusts.

I

Nobody knows, with any certainty, how many museums there are in the United States. A reasonable estimate, based on a 1979 survey made by the National Center for Education Statistics under contract to the United States Department of Education, would put the figure at approximately forty-five hundred.[3] Close to 60 perent of these were founded after World War II. Less than 10 percent date from the last century.

While only 14 percent of American museums—something just over six hundred—can be classified as primarily art museums, another 8 percent (chiefly history and so-called general museums) responded to the survey that works of fine art constituted an important part of their collections. In total, then, it may be estimated that there are some one thousand museums throughout the United States that are, to one degree or another, responsible for collecting, preserving, and exhibiting works of fine art.

Of the six hundred institutions that are primarily art museums, roughly one-fourth are controlled—directly or indirectly—either by the federal government or by a state, county, or municipal government. While a considerable number of these museums may have boards of trustees with greater or lesser advisory powers, and while some may use contributed (or endowment-derived) income to supplement the appropriated tax-generated funds through which they are primarily financed, they remain essentially "public" in their governance and in the rules that apply to the conduct of their staff. Hereafter, these will be referred to as "public museums."

The remaining three-quarters of the institutions that are primarily art museums are—directly or indirectly—privately governed and supported largely through voluntary contributions. In general, the overall responsibility for their day-to-day management is vested in a self-perpetuating body of private citizens whose members may variously be denominated as "trustees," "directors," "governors," or "regents." For convenience, they will hereafter be referred to as "trustees," and the museums themselves—notwithstanding their public purpose—will be referred to as "private museums."

Private museums constitute but a small part—by any measure, certainly less than 1 percent—of a broad aggregate of private nonprofit organizations that, after business and government, is often referred to as the "third sector" of American life. Included as well are the country's great private universities and hospitals and a broad array of religious, cultural, and social welfare organizations that range from the American Cancer Society and Metropolitan Opera to the smallest of neighborhood block associations. Characteristic of them all, one commentator has noted, is "that they are private, do not operate for profit, and are devoted to serving the general welfare—not simply the welfare of their members or supporters."[4] In law—for lack of a better term—these organizations, including museums, are generally referred to as "charitable."

The "third sector" has been called a distinctive feature of American life. As de Tocqueville observed a century and a half ago. "In no country in the world has the principle of association been more successfully used, or more unsparingly applied to a multitude of different objects, than in America."[5] In general, these objects—such charitable purposes as education, health care, and social and cultural nurturing—are those that, in most other countries, are the province of either government or religion.

In the pursuit of its charitable objectives, the "third sector" has—like government, its counterpart—grown to enormous size. It is today believed to include well in excess of a million organizations. The total funds that flowed through it in 1980 were recently estimated at $128 billion. The value of volunteer services donated for that year was estimated at an additional $64.5 billion.[6] As of the mid-1970s, it was estimated that the private organizations of the "third sector" owned one-ninth of all of the property in the United States.[7]

The effective management of such enormous assets necessarily requires that the private trustees of the "third sector" exercise a broad discretion. At the same time, as the allegations in the Harding case suggest, the very breadth of this discretion carries with it a substantial possibility of abuse. In a public museum, the situation would have been simpler. The board, had there been one, in all likelihood would have played only an advisory role and not exercised plenary authority over the museum's property. Beyond that, those actually working for the museum would have been bound, in the same manner as public servants in any branch of government, by an elaborate network of anticorruption, anti-bribery, and anti-conflict-of-interest statutes. So flagrant a diversion of the museum's assets could well have involved criminal penalties.

Equally, had the allegations in Harding involved some less subtle form of wrongdoing—if, for example, the trustees had falsified the museum's books of account or secretly appropriated objects from the collection—they might have been charged with the crime of embezzlement. Museum employees enjoy no special privilege. A public servant who abuses his position in a public museum can be treated as any other public servant. A trustee or employee who steals from a private museum can be treated as any other thief. Within the past two years, employees of the Art Institute of Chicago, the Museum of Fine Arts in Boston, and the Smithsonian Institution in Washington have received substantial jail sentences for stealing objects from the collections of their respective museums.

In Harding, however—and in other museum-related cases to be dealt with later—we are confronted with a different kind of wrongdoing. Aside from the self-dealing charge against the chairman of the board, the trustees in Harding were not alleged to have violated any specific laws. They were charged, rather, with a failure to exercise properly the broad discretionary powers vested in them as fiduciaries and, moreover, with using their fiduciary positions for selfish advantage. For a charitable trustee to violate the obligation he undertakes in holding property intended for a public purpose is, in short, a breach of trust.

Here the historic background becomes important. The American private museum—in common with other organizations of the "third sector"—is a direct descendant of the English charitable use or trust. This is not changed substantially by the fact that the majority of such organizations are today organized as not-for-profit corporations instead of actual trusts. Although traces of the charitable use—the conveyance of property to one person for the use of an indefinite class of others—have been found from as early as the thirteenth century, the major developments in the applicable law date from the early fifteenth century, when the jurisdiction over uses passed to the newly established Court of Chancery. As described by Marion R. Fremont-Smith:

> This Court based its decisions on ethical principles, not legal prec- edents. Its procedure was more flexible than that of the common law courts; and its freedom from fixed forms of action and its power to enforce a defendant's duties, not merely to uphold a plaintiff's rights, made it particularly suited to assuming jurisdiction over uses.[8]

The jurisprudence practiced in the Court of Chancery was eq- uity, a system characterized by "fairness, justness and right deal- ing."[9] Also characteristic of equity were the variety and flexibility of the remedies it provided. It allowed the court to enjoin a de- fendant from following a specific course of action or to command him to do something else. It permitted the court to nullify existing agreements. It empowered the court to require accountings. In essence, it could provide virtually any remedy that "fairness, just- ness and right dealing" required.

When the English colonists came to America, they brought the principles of equity jurisprudence with them. Four centuries later, the remedies provided by equity remain available in most Amer- ican jurisdictions to cure the breach of a charitable trust. They are precisely the remedies that the Illinois state attorney general sought from the court in the case of the Harding Museum.

No less historic was the role that the attorney general played in initiating the Harding case. Since a charitable trust was, by definition, intended to benefit an indefinite class of beneficiaries, the enforcement of such a trust presented a problem in that there might be no particular individual with a sufficient or certain enough interest to bring an action in case the trust was breached. Fremont- Smith has described how, beginning in the fifteenth century, this problem was solved:

> The need for a situs for the enforcement power was answered . . . by considering that it was lodged in the King, the *parens patriae*, and carried out by his chief legal officer, the Attorney General. In the language of trusts, this power is described as the power of enforce-

ment, and implies the duty to oversee the activities of the fiduciary who is charged with management of the funds, as well as the right to bring to the attention of the court any abuses which may need correction. Thus, a duty to enforce implies a duty to supervise (or oversee) in its broadest sense. It does not, however, include a right to regulate, or a right to direct either the day-to-day affairs of the charity or the action of the court.[10]

With this background in place, it can be seen that the approach undertaken to correct the abuses alleged in the Harding case falls squarely within the traditional pattern for curing the breach of a charitable trust and, as such, would be applicable to most American private museums. What must then be asked is whether this approach is effective and, if not, what alternatives might be available.

II

It must, from the outset, be acknowledged that the ability of the state attorney general to supervise the operation of charitable trusts has been considerably greater in theory than in practice. While virtually every American state recognized that the attorney general had a common law power of enforcement, a power strengthened in most jurisdictions by a series of legislative enactments, serious difficulties impeded any effective program of enforcement.

For one, the supervision of charities was but one of a broad range of duties—and by no means considered the most important—with which the attorney general was charged. For another, there was no mechanism by which the attorney general could obtain any regular knowledge of what charitable organizations were present within his jurisdiction or learn of the activities in which these organizations were engaged. The trustees of charitable organizations tended to be drawn from the ranks of the socially powerful and were resistant to supervision. Almost no public moneys flowed into such organizations, and there was little popular pressure to allocate to the attorney general the funds or personnel that any effective oversight program would have required. Enforcement was so lax that, as recently as 1966, a commentator could note, "The net effect of those factors is that under the common law in [the United States] trustees and administrators of charitable trusts have been virtually exempt from supervision."[11]

This situation, nonetheless, had begun to change—albeit ever so slowly—as early as 1943, when New Hampshire became the first state to adopt a statute that required the registration of every charitable organization within the state and the submission thereafter of an annual report by every such organization. By the late seventies, at least fourteen additional states had adopted similar legislation. These included New York, Massachusetts, and California, the three most heavily museum-populated states, which have among them more than nine hundred of the country's forty-five hundred museums. In the early fifties, the National Association of Attorneys General collaborated with the Commission on Uniform State Laws to draft a Uniform Act for Supervision of Trustees for Charitable Purposes that has since been adopted in several states and served as a model in others. Within the past two decades, a number of attorneys general have established divisions of charitable enforcement, often staffed by accountants and investigators as well as attorneys. Throughout the seventies, both the attorneys general and the courts have shown a steadily increasing willingness to examine—and, where necessary, correct—the conduct of charitable fiduciaries in "third sector" organizations of every kind.

While the gap between the attorney general's theoretical and practical powers of enforcement would thus appear to have started narrowing over the past forty years, it has nonetheless done so only slowly and unevenly. Other problems remain.

One of these, so far as the supervision of private museums is concerned, has been the lack until very recently of any generally agreed upon standards by which the conduct of trustees and staff might be judged. In seeking to determine whether those charged with the management of museums are exercising their discretion within the bounds of reasonable judgment, then—as Austin W. Scott has pointed out—a key element may be "the existence or non-existence, the definiteness or indefiniteness of an external standard by which the reasonableness of the trustee's conduct can be judged."[12] Absent such a standard, any such judgment may be difficult to make.

Although it involved a public, rather than a private, museum, a recent incident at the Greenville County Museum of Art in South Carolina is indicative of the role that the existence or nonexistence of standards can play.[13] At issue was a total of $200,000 that the museum's director had received during 1978 and 1979 in connection with the sale by various art dealers of more than $4 million worth of art (including a large group of paintings by Andrew Wyeth) to a Greenville resident who was also the museum's principal donor. It was generally understood that these paintings were ultimately to be given to the museum. In a hearing before the county museum commission, the director claimed that this money, which he had received directly from the dealers, had been earned by him during the course of "outside employment" and—notwithstanding that the payments were apparently contingent on the sales being completed—that it was paid to him for "consulting" rather than as any kind of a "commission" or "kickback." In the absence of any written guidelines applicable to the situation, the commission took no action beyond securing the director's resignation. Five months later, in March 1981, it adopted an operational code of ethics that clearly established such conduct as violating the standard of duty owed to the museum by its employees.

Nowhere might the establishment of generally agreed upon standards be more important than in what might be called the "neglect" situations where trustees have been charged with violating their fiduciary obligations not through any failure to act with undivided loyalty to their trust but, rather, through their failure to act at all. The two most widely publicized cases of recent years—each of which ultimately involved intervention by the attorney general of its resident state—were those of the Museum of the American Indian in New York City[14] and the Maryhill Museum in Klickitat County, Washington.[15] In each, there was evidence that the trustees had simply disregarded their duties to such a reckless degree that the institutions in their care were seriously endangered.

In 1975, following a two-year investigation, the attorney general of New York commenced an action against the director and trustees of the Museum of the American Indian, alleging improper care of its collection and a failure to supervise its operation adequately. What seemed in fact to have happened was that the museum—with a collection of nearly one million objects—had slipped out of control. There were inadequate records and improper storage. Members of the board were permitted on occasion to purchase works from the collection. On other occasions, important works were apparently given to outside parties in gratitude for their contributions to the museum.

Following the attorney general's action, the director was removed, six of the trustees resigned, a computerized inventory of the collection was compiled, and an effort was launched to put the museum—virtually reconstituted—into a new facility. In January 1980—having left the museum impressed with a set of professional standards it had previously been incapable of generating by itself—the attorney general stipulated the matter as closed. That such standards were meanwhile developing elsewhere in the museum community was a significant factor in turning around what had been a deteriorating situation.

So complete a renaissance would not seem in prospect for the Maryhill Museum. The neglect there was even more shocking. After the museum first opened in 1940, the trustees left its direction for thirty-five years in the hands of a local carpenter (the relative of one of the trustees) and then hired his son, a gardener, to replace him. The collection, which included unique works by Rodin together with important American Indian artifacts, could not be accounted for. Some objects had been sold, some had been traded for worthless substitutes, some had fallen apart, and some had actually been defaced. Real estate adjacent to the museum had been mishandled, and the museum building itself allowed to fall into disrepair. It was only in 1977, after the board—confronted by considerable publicity about these facts—still failed to take corrective action, that the attorney general of Washington State filed suit against the trustees. The matter has never been resolved in a manner calculated to restore the losses to the collection.[16]

Once more, had a well understood set of standards been in place, the trustees of the Maryhill Museum—presumably people of goodwill—might sooner have realized what was expected of them. If not, then the attorney general himself might sooner have been made to understand how great a discrepancy there was between those standards and the neglect with which the Maryhill trustees were carrying out their duties.

To some critics, another problem with the current system of

supervision is the rule prevailing in the majority of American states that the attorney general has the exclusive authority to initiate an action to enforce a charitable trust.[17] While some of these states relax this rule, if only slightly, to permit an "interested party"— a dissenting trustee, for example—to bring an action on his own, the general public, nonetheless, remains largely excluded.

John Merryman has been one such critic. That the attorney general functions in the case of museums as an effective supervisor on behalf of charitable beneficiaries is, in his view, a "fiction." It is, he says:

> a fiction for a variety of reasons, only one of which is that most attorneys-general have neither the staff nor the expertise for the active exercise of such supervision. The result is that there is little effective legal regulation of museum trustees. The law is on the whole clear. It is just not enforced.[18]

This lack of enforcement, he suggests, may also be connected with the political influence and social prominence of many of those who typically serve as museum trustees. Critics such as Merryman, frustrated by this gap between theory and performance, would extend the standing to begin an action against a charitable trust to include all of the intended beneficiaries of that trust—i.e., the public at large.

The traditional opposition to so broad an extension of the standing to sue is not so much theoretical as it is practical: that it would, as Fremont-Smith says, make it "impossible to manage charitable funds, or even to find individuals to take on the task, if the fiduciaries were constantly to be subject to harassing litigation."[19] The danger of such harassment would seem particularly acute in those cases where the members of the public most likely to be drawn into confrontation with the museum might be as much motivated by ideology or self-interest as by any concern for the public good. Consider two examples involving private museums.

Between 1942 and 1944, the Museum of Modern Art in New York was under almost constant attack from the Federation of Modern Painters and Sculptors, on the grounds that its collecting and exhibition policies were biased in favor of Picasso, Matisse, and other School of Paris painters to the detriment of the local artists whom the federation represented.[20] In the early seventies, the Whitney Museum of American Art, also in New York, came under heavy fire from certain women's groups for its refusal to adopt affirmative action procedures sufficiently strict to guarantee that the work of female artists would occupy at least half the places in its annual survey exhibitions of American art. The choice, in each case, was between a legitimate policy that those responsible for the management of the museum were pursuing and an equally legitimate policy that another group, not so responsible, would have preferred that they pursue. Absent the broadened standing that critics of the attorney general's exclusive authority have proposed, these and many similar battles were fought by appeals to public opinion rather than in a courtroom. Given broadened standing, they might well have been the subject, and to no good end, of long and potentially wasteful litigation.

A recent California case is instructive. It involved an action brought by three former trustees of the Norton Simon Museum (formerly the Pasadena Museum) who had resigned from the board following a series of policy disputes and who (albeit through some alleged irregularity) were permitted to commence an action without the prior involvement of the attorney general.[21] The issue at bottom was whether the museum would continue to be one of contemporary art, as the plaintiffs demanded, or whether its character could be changed according to the wishes of the Norton Simon group, who had assumed a dominant place on the board after Simon, a wealthy California collector, had stepped forward to save the museum from insolvency. This and related issues were framed in terms of breach of trust. In the fall of 1981 the court found against the plaintiffs on every issue. Particularly striking—and relevant to the question of broadened standing—was an admonition that the court included in its Memorandum of Intended Decision:

> The court has not intended by any of its comments to indicate that the plaintiffs have acted in bad faith or for selfish purposes in attempting to impose their views upon the board of trustees. While their judgment in bringing this action may be questionable, the court is satisfied that the plaintiffs sincerely believe in good faith that what they urge is required for the best interest of the museum. On the other hand, the court is equally satisfied that the present trustees have conducted themselves with the highest motives and with the best interest of the museum in mind. . . . It is indeed unfortunate and even tragic that a museum which must be one of the finest museums of its

kind in the world of art should become the center point of a contro-versy such as has been brought by this action because former trustees simply disagree with the policies of the present board of trustees, particularly where the present board consists of . . . members of the community . . . who have unselfishly devoted many hours of their valuable time to the affairs of the museum.[22]

A central theme in shaping the remedies for abuse of charitable trust has been the preservation, to the extent possible, of the assets set aside for a charitable purpose. A conscientious attorney general, before engaging a private museum in the considerable expense of such a proceeding, should feel obligated to consider the extent to which the proceeding itself might involve a waste of the museum's assets. A third party, motivated only by self-interest, might feel no similar constraint. Therein, it may be said, lies a substantial weakness in the argument for broadened stand-ing.

Another approach to strengthening (if not wholly superseding) the present system of charitable enforcement would be through the federal income tax system. Because "third sector" organiza-tions are funded chiefly through contributions, federal tax-exempt status is vital to their continued operation. Not only does such status exempt whatever income they have from tax, but, more important, since 1917 it has permitted those who make contri-butions to such organizations to deduct—within certain limits—such charitable contributions from their own taxable income.

More stringent charitable enforcement was among the issues considered in drafting the Federal Tax Reform Act of 1969. Before that, the only option available to the Internal Revenue Service in dealing with an organization in which the trustees had violated their fiduciary obligations was to terminate the organization's ex-emption. According to Paul Treusch and Norman Sugarman:

> This was a weapon that both the Internal Revenue Service and the courts were reluctant to use because it was an "all or nothing" ap-proach, and the denial of exemption had the effect of penalizing a charity because it would result in a tax on funds intended for charitable purposes and discourage future contributions for such purposes. . . . Therefore, some advocated that there should be a strengthening of enforcement under state law so that state attorneys general would take a more active role in correcting abuses, including removal of trustees when the improper use of charitable funds was discovered.

The record of state action, however, was not such as to give Congress confidence that abuses would be corrected and, in any event, state practices varied and were likely to vary widely in the future.

The alternative route that Congress consequently took is described by Treusch and Sugarman:

> An ingenious system of reporting and enforcement devices was established in the 1969 Act, building on the existing tax structure but designed primarily to preserve charitable funds and make [trustees] more accountable to the government and the public.[23]

Among the most important of these enforcement devices was a prohibition against self-dealing. Coupled with this was an escalating range of penalty taxes that might be imposed not only on the trustee or other "disqualified person" found to be engaged in self-dealing but, if such self-dealing was not corrected, on the remaining trustees as well. This provision was aimed largely at family and company foundations. While it does not currently apply to most private museums—which were classified by the 1969 act as "public charities"and treated in a less restrictive manner—it is nonetheless suggestive of how the reach of the federal tax laws might one day be extended to deter an even wider range of charitable abuses.

A different question about the prevailing system of charitable enforcement concerns the extent to which it might permit the attorney general to reach beyond those traditionally held to a fiduciary standard (i.e., the trustees) and impose a similar standard on a museum employee. This question underlies an action commenced by the attorney general of New York in January 1978 on behalf of the Brooklyn Museum.[24] The defendants included the museum's former curator of primitive art and several New York City dealers who specialized in that same field.

The complaint alleged that, as the result of a series of arrangements among the defendants, the museum was induced to relinquish in an exchange with the dealers a considerable number of American Indian artifacts at "attributed values" that were only a fraction—in some instances as little as one-thirtieth or one-fortieth—of their actual market values. Concurrent with these exchanges had been a series of personal transactions between the curator (who maintained a personal collection that paralleled the museum collection in his care) and one or more of the same dealers. These personal transactions, which were not disclosed to the museum, involved some $25,000 worth of objects and, in the language of the complaint, "were all to [the Curator's] advantage."

As might be expected, the complaint charged that the defendants "willfully and maliciously acted in concert to fraudulently obtain works of art from the Museum." Unusual, however, was the additional charge that the curator, as a trusted employee, had breached a "fiduciary duty of loyalty to his trust" by engaging in personal transactions that had impaired his ability to act with the requisite degree of fidelity, prudence, and care in the performance of his official duties. The negligent performance of his duties and his failure to protect the interests of both the museum and its ultimate charitable beneficiaries had, so the complaint concluded, resulted in substantial damages to the museum and to the public.

Even more unusual was the judgment the attorney general sought. In addition to the traditional equitable remedies that might have been anticipated—recision of all of the outstanding transactions; the return, to the extent possible, of whatever objects the dealers had not yet sold; the payment of damages by the curator and the dealers for those objects that could not be returned; and an accounting for all of the underlying transactions—the attorney general also asked that exemplary damages of $750,000 be assessed against each of the dealers and that exemplary damages of $1.5 million be assessed against the curator.

The Brooklyn Museum case has yet to come to trial, and many observers believe it will ultimately be settled without the imposition of such extraordinary damages. Nonetheless, beyond the possibly novel question it presents about the fiduciary duty of a museum employee, it has aroused widespread interest and some concern. If such heightened demands for exemplary or punitive damages (or, for that matter, some of those penalty taxes now assessable against the trustees of certain foundations under the Tax Reform Act of 1969) should become common, there might be serious consequences for private museums.

It must be recalled, as the court did in the Norton Simon Museum case, that service on boards of trustees is largely voluntary. The maintenance of competent boards is essential to the survival of the "third sector" system of decentralized privately governed organizations, and the efficacy of an enforcement mechanism that might so thoroughly chill the willingness of qualified individuals to serve on such boards would certainly be open to question. Trustee liability insurance, as presently written, would offer little protection in any case where a trustee was found culpable. In the same manner, state not-for-profit corporation laws, as a matter of public policy, generally prohibit charitable organizations from indemnifying their trustees for either the legal expenses or damages incurred in any instance where there is a finding of actual negligence or misconduct in the performance of their duties.

Similar arguments would pertain to the broadened imposition of criminal penalties. This is not to suggest that the punitive sanctions for aggravated acts of deliberate misconduct within the museum community should be less than those that would be applicable in other settings where "breach of trust" would not be an issue. In these gray areas of fiduciary negligence, bad judgment, or nonperformance, however, it does seem preferable to rely chiefly on those more flexible equitable remedies that—while they may in fact be incidentally punitive or function as effective deterrents—focus primarily on the restoration of the museum to operational or financial health. That the attorneys general—the Brooklyn Museum case excepted—have customarily sought reparation rather than punishment may be evidence of the wise administration of their offices.

If the American system of charitable enforcement is theoretically sound but often weak in practice, the question remains concerning how it can be made more effective. Here we must return to the matter of standards. Without some consensus about what is considered appropriate conduct in the operation of a museum, neither the trustees charged with its management nor the attorney general charged with its supervision can have any firm basis on which to identify and either avoid or correct what may be abuses.

How are such standards to be developed? Neither the attorneys general nor, for that matter, the courts are well-positioned to do this, and there are special aspects to museums—particularly the central role of objects and the obligation to care for them properly—that preclude the wholesale adoption of standards from such cognate institutions as private universitites or hospitals. The imposition of standards by legislative action remains a possibility, and certainly a last resort, but there is widespread doubt that such legislative standards could properly take into account the enor-

mous diversity among American museums. Most desirable would
be for the museum community—unless and until it proved incapable of doing so—to undertake this task itself.

III

While the evolution of an expanded system of charitable supervision in the United States can be said to date from 1943, the
development of museum standards—an essential ingredient if this
system is to be applied effectively to museums—did not begin in
earnest until the mid-sixties, some two decades later. It is perhaps
more than coincidental that this same period saw the creation of
the National Endowment for the Arts, the National Endowment
for the Humanities, and a substantial number of the state arts
agencies. These were all vehicles through which, for the first time,
public tax-generated funds could be channeled to private museums in significant amounts. It was all but inevitable that such
a development would be accompanied by an increased demand
for public accountability.

In developing these standards, the Washington-based American Association of Museums (AAM) has played (and continues to
play) a major role. Founded in 1906 as a voluntary national service
organization for both museums and affiliated individuals, the AAM
has also served as an "umbrella" for a variety of smaller museum-
related groups with narrower professional interests. Its current
membership includes some fifteen hundred institutions, forty-
five hundred museum staff members, and more than six hundred
museum trustees.

In May 1968 the president of the AAM appointed a committee
to consider the establishment of an accreditation program that
might—in a manner comparable to those already in use among
American hospitals, colleges, and universitites—be used to certify
museums as currently meeting accepted minimum standards.[25]
Additional impetus was given the following November when the
Federal Council on the Arts and Humanities—asked by President
Lyndon Johnson a year earlier to investigate and report to him on
the condition of American museums—concluded that it was "urgent that the American Association of Museums and its member

institutions develop and agree upon acceptable criteria and methods of accrediting museums."[26]

The establishment of a museum accreditation program was approved by the AAM's membership in June 1970. Implementation of the program was entrusted to an independent seven-member commission that operates under its own published procedures, which include safeguards intended to assure that its proceedings are confidential. The commission's powers are broad: it may grant or refuse accreditation; it may table applications for up to one year; and in the case of museums previously accredited, it may either suspend their current accreditation or refuse to reaccredit them. It may also consider appeals, and, absent judicial intervention, its decisions are final. As of March 1, 1982, accreditation had been granted to 497 museums, and applications from an additional 108 were in various stages of processing.

In legal terms, the AAM's accreditation program is thus far nothing more than the internal undertaking of a private voluntary association. It has, nonetheless, the potential—at least if the longer-established accreditation programs of hospitals, colleges, and universities can be taken as models—to intersect at a number of points with the existing systems of both public support and public supervision.

Under certain federal programs of aid to higher education, for example, eligibility is virtually dependent upon an applicant's status as an accredited institution.[27] In a similar manner, the only hospitals that can automatically be certified by the federal government as eligible for Medicare and Medicaid funds are those that have received accreditation from the Joint Commission on the Accreditation of Hospitals, a wholly private agency.[28] As the number of American museums able to complete the accreditation process increases, a similar eligibility requirement might well be provided in the case of grants from state and federal agencies. Commenting on the AAM's then proposed accreditation program in 1969, Congressman John Brademas said, "Federal support should not be provided to museums which have not reached a level of quality accepted in the museum field.[29]

Such a development would add another sanction—in this case an economic one—to those already available for enforcing an appropriate standard of conduct in the governance of private museums. An incidental effect might be to make the accreditation process itself the subject of periodic judical review, at least of its procedural regularity. To the extent that educational accrediting agencies have been found to exercise some delegated governmental power or function in a "quasi-governmental" way, the courts have long held that their actions may be subject to such review.[30] The AAM's Accreditation Commission does not presently exercise such power, and, in only one instance to date has a museum—the Vanderbilt Museum on Long Island, New York, which had its accreditation suspended in 1980—sought judicial relief from a commission action. The local court has thus far been unwilling to intervene on the museum's behalf. Should the court ultimately do so, however, the action would not necessarily be detrimental to the commission's work and might even be perceived as strengthening it.

As we have seen earlier, accreditation may also intersect the system of attorney general supervision by providing standards against which the operation of a museum may be judged. Neither the Harding nor Maryhill museums could likely have passed even the initial review procedure used by the Accreditation Commission. They would not have met the basic definition of a "museum"—Harding because, among other things, it was not open to the public on any regular schedule; Maryhill because it did not employ a professional staff.

Finally, notwithstanding that accreditation applies basically to institutions and their governance, it can also be effective in controlling staff misconduct by encouraging closer supervision and/ or a more definite response to suspected wrongdoing. In the case of the Greenville County Museum of Art, the point was made by H. J. Swinney, a witness called during the County Museum Commission's hearing, that although the individual unethical act of the museum's director could not in itself pose a threat to the institution's accreditation, the failure of the members of the museum's governing body to take corrective action could have a substantial effect. They were, he said, "obligated . . . to do something rather than merely to accept the situation and go on.[31]

A natural complement to the establishment of the accreditation program—which dealt with the maintenance of institutional standards—was the development of ethical codes prescribing standards of conduct for individual trustees, emloyees, and volunteers. The AAM had, in fact, adopted such a code as early as 1925, but, from all accounts, it was soon forgotten.[32] In 1966 the Association of Art Museum Directors (AAMD) adopted a brief code of ethics, which still remains in force. [33] Its chief virtue—a provision requiring the reprimand, suspension, or expulsion from the association of any member violating its canons—was also its principal weakness. The code applied basically to the AAMD's own relatively small membership and made little effort to establish comparable standards of conduct for either trustees or staff members below the level of director.

The AAM moved again into this area in 1974 when a committee on ethics was established and charged with identifying "the ethical issues underlying museum operations." The committee, supported by grants from the National Museum Act and the Rockefeller Brothers Fund, spent nearly four years in preparing a report that was published in March 1978 under the title *Museum Ethics*.[34] The following May, the AAM adopted the report as the official basis on which institutional members might further develop their own codes of ethics.

As Alan D. Ullberg, who served on the committee and acted as technical editor of its report, has pointed out, *Museum Ethics* was intended to be not a set of specific prescriptions but, rather, a guideline "against which current museum policy and practice can be tested for ethical content."[35] Its coverage is broad. In the areas of most evident abuse, it deals with conflicts of interest, personal collecting, self-dealing, dual compensation, the use of insider information, and the receipt of gifts, favors, and discounts. Other sections cover obligations toward collections, personnel practices, acquisition and disposal policies, and a host of related topics. Typical are the following extracts from the sections that address conflicts of interest among trustees. For example, in lieu of flatly prohibiting an art dealer from sitting on the board of trustees of an art museum, the approach is to identify the problems that might be anticipated and suggest several ways in which these might be resolved.

> Individuals who are experienced and knowledgeable in various fields of endeavor related to museum activities can be of great assistance to museums, but conflicts of interest or the appearance of such

conflicts may arise because of these interests or activities. Guidelines for the protection of both individual and institution should be established by the governing board of every museum.

*   *   *

Whenever a matter arises for action by the board, or the museum engages in an activity where there is a possible conflict or the appearance of conflict between the interests of the museum and an outside or personal interest or a trustee or that of a person close to him, the outside interest of the trustee should be made a matter of record. In those cases where the trustee is present when a vote is taken in connection with such a question, he should abstain. In some circumstances he should avoid discussing any planned actions, formally or informally, from which he might appear to benefit. Sometimes neither disclosure nor abstention is sufficient, and the only appropriate solution is resignation.[36]

Since its publication in 1978, more than twenty thousand copies of *Museum Ethics* have been distributed. Regardless of the degree to which particular American museums themselves have used it to develop their own codes of ethics, so broad a dissemination ought to make it increasingly difficult for the trustees or staff of *any* museum charged with a violation of their public responsibilities to plead by way of defense either that there are no generally accepted standards by which their conduct can be judged or, if there are such standards, that they neither knew of them nor had any reasonable means by which to acquire such knowledge.

A third development of recent years has been the increasing adoption by American museums of formal, written policies dealing with collections management and other areas of potential abuse. In some instances, museums have generated these on their own initiative. In others, the instigation has come from outside. In New York State, the attorney general's office has shown a strong preference for negotiated settlements—on the grounds that they are more cost effective than litigation for both that office and the charitable organizations it supervises—and has frequently required, as a part of these settlements, that such internal guidelines be adopted.

Illustrative of this approach was the attorney general's disposition of a 1978 case that involved self-dealing by one of the trustees of the Brooklyn Museum. During 1975 and 1976, this trustee (who was also the vice chairman of the board and a member of its Acquisitions Committee) had voted to approve the purchase from a dealer of a number of works of African and Oceanic art. Not disclosed to the board (and not required to be disclosed under any museum policy then in effect) was that these works came directly from the trustee's own personal collection and that the dealer was acting as his agent.

Following an investigation, the attorney general, the trustee, and the museum entered into a stipulation pursuant to which the museum was given the right to reconsider these purchases and, if it so determined, recover the purchase price plus interest; the trustee agreed to refrain from any further such transactions except with advance written notice to the attorney general; and the museum agreed to adopt a "comprehensive and adequate" code of ethics intended to prevent such situations from recurring.[37] In a similar fashion, the finely detailed procedures for deaccessioning and disposing of works from its collection that the Metropolitan Museum of Art adopted in 1973 were developed in consultation with the Attorney General's Office following a series of episodes in which the museum's deaccessioning practices had drawn widespread public criticism.[38]

While space precludes mention of many other contributions made since the mid-1960s toward the development of museum standards, a special note must be made of *Museum Trusteeship*, a handbook published by the AAM in 1981 and intended to summarize in comprehensive form "the major responsibilities of museum trustees and . . [to] relate those duties to the potential for legal liability if they are neglected."[39] *Museum Trusteeship* brought together for the first time a body of information previously available only from widely scattered sources. As was the case with *Museum Ethics*, its publication and wide distribution ought to leave little room for those charged with the management of America's private museums to argue that they never understood the nature of their trust.

IV

No one would suggest that the development of museum standards will by itself make bad men good or deflect those of criminal inclination toward a more charitable purpose. The impact of their development, though, should be twofold.

First, a good deal of the wrongdoing in American private art museums appears to be due as much to ignorance as to wicked intent. Too often, service as a trustee has been viewed—in Merryman's phrase—"more as an honor than a set of obligations."[40] This has been particularly true of museums such as Maryhill and the Museum of the American Indian, which were founded at the whim of a private collector, left under the governance of his friends and associates, and never given any firm institutional base. The broad dissemination of the standards developed in recent years must inevitably dispel the ignorance of all but the most indifferent or negligent trustees. Where it fails to do so, then the availability of such standards will provide a yardstick against which such indifference or negligence can be measured and a basis on which trustee liability can be assessed.

Second, where there *is* actual wrongdoing of less than criminal magnitude, the merger of these developing standards with the existing mechanisms for charitable enforcement should provide those responsible for oversight with the long-needed means to close what in the past has been widely perceived as a gap between theory and performance.

A last ingredient, though, is necessary: a broad public concern. It would be unrealistic to expect that the responsible authorities will devote any significant portion of their resources to remedying abuses within American private museums unless they believe that there is some public demand that they do so. Here, though, a happy synergism has been at work. To secure public support— whether through the grant of tax-generated public funds or through increased contributions—the private museums have, over the past fifteen years, eloquently made the argument that, notwithstanding their private governance, they are essentially public institutions. To the extent that they have been successful in this, they have incidentally triggered a corresponding demand that those who govern them be publicly accountable for their stewardship of a public resource.

The system for dealing with wrongdoing in American private museums has evolved slowly and been the subject of justifiable criticism. Whatever its past shortcomings, though, it would seem that the elements should now be in place to make it effective: a

legal framework employing criminal sanctions for outright violations of law and a battery of flexible, equitably based remedies
for less aggravated breaches of trust; a broad consensus about
the standards that those in positions of trust will be expected to
meet; and an enlarged public demand that such private museums
truly be operated in the public interest.

To end where we begin: this past March 1—more than five
years after it was commenced—the Harding Museum case finally
came to trial. While a tenacious defense and an aborted effort at
settlement kept it out of the courtroom for many years, they also
kept it fresh in the collective consciousness of the American museum community. It has been regularly discussed, and written
about widely. It has served as a further spur toward examining
and seeking to improve the system of charitable enforcement.
Whatever the case's final outcome, the defendants will have made
a substantial, if unintended, contribution to the betterment of
American museums.

Afterword

The complexities of the Harding Museum case were dramatically simplified in May 1982 when it was announced that all of the
Harding's assets—its collections together with any moneys then
on hand or thereafter to be received from the defendants—would
be turned over permanently to the Art Institute of Chicago. When
the trial was over, the Harding Museum would, in effect, cease
to be. Under an arrangement approved by both the Illinois attorney general and the Circuit Court for Cook County, the transfer
of the collections began immediately. Throughout the summer
trucks carrying the Harding's largely hidden treasures rolled from
a downtown warehouse to the Art Institute's lakefront site. In
early September—with the opening at the institute of an exhibition
of thirty paintings and sculptures by Frederic Remington—works
of art from the Harding Museum were restored to general public
view for the first time in seventeen years.

From the attorney general's viewpoint, this was a significant victory. In initiating the original suit, he had three principal objectives: to make the collections (without further loss from either deterioration or deaccessioning) once more publicly accessible to the people of Chicago, to restore to the museum the moneys he alleged it had lost through the financial mismanagement of the defendants, and to recover from its chairman and other board members any moneys they might have wrongfully obtained through the alleged abuse of their fiduciary positions. In his view, the arrangements with the Art Institute met the first of these objectives superbly. The collections would neither be scattered, kept indefinitely in storage, nor moved to some other community.

For the Art Institute, it was an equally satisfying outcome. In a single stroke, it was enriched with an arms and armor collection that might only be equalled in the United States by those of the Metropolitan or Philadelphia museums. This it planned to keep together as a unit—the "Harding Collection." Also included in the approximately three thousand objects it was to receive were a rich variety of works of fine and decorative art that could—while still bearing a donor credit to Harding—be dispersed to strengthen a number of the institute's existing departments. Finally, there would be funds—in an amount still to be determined—to help support the study, care, and exhibition of these new acquisitions.

Meanwhile, the trial continued. In June 1982 the attorney general—citing the discovery of thitherto undisclosed evidence—asked the court for, and was given, permission to file an amended complaint. To the earlier charges against the chairman and his four co-trustees was added a new one: that in 1967 the trustees had acquiesced in a $250,000 interest-free loan from the Harding Museum's investment account to the chairman. It was the proceeds from this loan, repaid the following year, that had enabled the chairman to acquire control of the local Chicago bank with which the museum later became involved in the series of loan transactions referred to in the attorney general's original complaint.

A decision in the Harding Museum case is unlikely before early or mid-1983. Whichever way it may be decided, protracted appeals are almost a certainty. The defendants will claim that their conduct did not, in the long run, damage the museum. As the result of a profitable real estate venture—financed with moneys borrowed from the bank that their chairman controlled—the museum was ultimately restored to solvency, and more. By the time agreement was reached to turn its assets over to the Art Institute, it was carrying a balance of $3 million—all of it safely invested in Treasury Bills and neatly frozen by the court.

While the attorney general can be expected to dispute this contention—if $1 million or more had not been wasted through the defendants' financial mismanagement, he would argue, then an even larger balance would ultimately have been available—the most serious of his charges is now more than ever directed elsewhere: that through acts of self-dealing the chairman and his co-trustees abused their position in the museum for their own unjust enrichment. Charged with a duty to the public, they chose instead to pursue their personal advantage. The underlying question is this: under such circumstances, and regardless of whether such self-dealing eventually proved to be a benefit or detriment to the institution, can a charitable organization recover only the amount of any losses it may have suffered, or may it also be awarded a further amount to reflect any gains that its trustees may as a consequence have enjoyed? How the Illinois courts deal with this question may well be a test of whether the American system of charitable enforcement has truly come of age.

*   *   *

A follow-up note is needed concerning the situation of the Vanderbilt Museum on Long Island, New York.

In April 1982 the New York State Supreme Court, responding to the Vanderbilt's claim that it had been given no adequate opportunity to defend itself when its accreditation was suspended in 1980, annulled this suspension and ordered that the AAM's Accreditation Commission hold a hearing at which the museum might present witnesses and other evidence on the question of whether its accreditation should be continued. Among the questions at issue was whether the Vanderbilt was giving adequate care to its collection. In 1980, on the basis of an on-site inspection, the commission had concluded that it was not.

The museum and the Accreditation Commission meanwhile agreed that this hearing might be deferred until after the museum, in accordance with the commission's regular procedures, was reinspected by a visiting committee. The visiting committee conducted an on-site evaluation in July 1982. Based on its findings, together with current information provided by the museum, the accreditation commission—commending the progress made over the intervening two years in raising the standards by which it cared for and conserved its collection—voted in August that Vanderbilt's accredited status be continued.

It is to be noted that the New York Supreme Court did *not* give the Vanderbilt Museum the relief for which it originally petitioned, i.e., that the court itself review the Accreditation Commission's 1980 decision and direct that the museum be returned to an accredited status. What it *did* do was examine the record to determine whether the commission properly followed its own procedures and whether these, in turn, met a standard of "fair play." (The museum had proposed that "due process"—not just "fair play"—should be the measure, but the court rejected this on the grounds that the Accreditation Commission, unlike comparable bodies in the field of higher education, did not exercise any delegated governmental authority.) In the instant case, the court found that this "fair play" standard had not been met and that the Vanderbilt Museum should at a minimum have been given notice of its alleged deficiences as well as the opportunity to be heard on the merits. Significantly, the court's conclusion was based on a finding that accreditation was a valuable right, one that ought not to be suspended without appropriate procedural safeguards.

NOTES

The author is deeply indebted to Ms. Deborah DePorter, who served as his principal researcher in the preparation of this paper. Her diligence and insights have been of enormous value. The author also gratefully acknowledges assistance from Ms. Roberta Faul, public information officer of the Institute for Museum Services; Laura Werner, Esq., assistant attorney general of the state of New York; and Alan D. Ullberg, Esq., associate general counsel of the Smithsonian Institution, Washington, D.C.

1. Referred to in Illinois as "Directors."
2. People ex rel. Scott v. Silverstein, et al., No. 76 CH 6446 (Circuit Court, Cook County, Ill., County Dept., Chancery Div., October 28, 1976).
3. These and the figures that follow are taken from *Museum Program Survey,* 1979, National Center for Education Statistics (1981), and Lee Kimche, "American Museums: The Vital Statistics," *Museum News,* October 1980, pp. 52–57.
4. Waldemar A. Nielsen, *The Endangered Sector* (New York, 1979), p. 3.
5. Alexis de Tocqueville, *Democracy in America* (New York: The Colonial Press, 1900), 1:191–92.
6. *Tax Exempt News,* February 2, 1982, p. 4.

7. *Giving in America*, Report of the Commission on Private Philanthropy and Public Needs (Washington, D.C., 1975), p. 11.
8. Marion R. Fremont-Smith, *Foundations and Government* (New York, 1965), p. 20.
9. *Black's Law Dictionary*, 4th ed., s.v. "equity."
10. Fremont-Smith, *Foundations and Government*, p. 198.
11. Luis Kutner and Henry H. Koven, "Charitable Legislation in the Several States," *Northwestern University Law Review* 61 (1966): 412.
12. Austin W. Scott, *The Law of Trusts*, 2nd ed. (Boston, 1956), sec. 187.
13. For a full acccount of this episode, see Patricia Ullberg, "What Happened in Greenville: The Need for Museum Codes of Ethics," *Museum News*, November/December 1981, pp. 26–29.
14. Lefkowitz v. Museum of the American Indian (Heye Foundation) No. 41461-75 (Sup. Ct., N.Y. Co., 1975).
15. State of Washington ex rel. Gordon v. Leppaluoto, et al., Nos. 11777 and 11781 (Super. Ct., Klickitat Co., Wash., 1977).
16. The history of the Maryhill Museum and its problems is described in Patricia Failing, "The Maryhill Museum: A Case History of Cultural Abuse," *ARTnews*, March 1977, pp.83–90.
17. Kutner and Koven, "Charitable Legislation," pp. 420–24.
18. John Henry Merryman, "Are Museum Trustees and the Law out of Step?" *ARTnews*, November 1975, pp. 24–27.
19. Fremont-Smith, *Foundations and Government*, p. 200.
20. Russell Lynes, *Good Old Modern* (New York, 1973), p. 230.
21. Rowan, et al. v. Pasadena Art Museum, et al., No. C322817 (Superior Court of the State of California for the County of Los Angeles), Findings of Fact and Conclusions of Law dated November 24, 1981.
22. Idem, Memorandum of Intended Decision dated September 22, 1981.
23. Paul E. Treusch and Norman A. Sugarman, *Tax-Exempt Charitable Organizations*, Publication of the American Law Institute–American Bar Association Committee on Continuing Professional Education (Philadelphia, 1979), p. 231.
24. Lefkowitz ex rel. The Brooklyn Museum v. Kan, No. 40082/78 (Sup. Ct., N.Y. Co., 1978).
25. Marilyn Hicks Fitzgerald, *Museum Accreditation: Professional Standards*, Publication of the American Association of Museums (Washington, D.C., 1973), pp. 1–6. First published 1970 under the title *Museum Accreditation: A Report to the Profession*. Revised 1978, H. J. Swinney, ed., under the title *Professional Standards for Museum Accreditation*.
26. *America's Museums: The Belmont Report*, Publication of the American Association of Museums (Washington, D.C., 1969), p. 62.
27. Steven Thal, "First Amendment Limitations on Accrediting Agencies in Determining Eligibility for Federal Aid to Education," *Journal of Law and Education* 8 (1979): 327.
28. See Frank P. Grad, "Upgrading Health Facilities: Medical Receiverships as an Alternative to License Revocation," *University of Colorado Law Review* 42 (1971): 424–31.
29. Fitzgerald, *Museum Accreditation*, p. 3.
30. See generally "The Legal Status of the Education Accrediting Agency: Problems in Judicial Supervision and Governmental Regulation," *Cornell Law Quarterly* 52 (1966): 104.
31. Ullberg, "What Happened in Greenville," p. 28.
32. This code is reprinted in Marilyn Phelan, *Museums and the Law*, Publication

of the American Association for State and Local History (Nashville, Tenn., 1982), pp. 252–57.

33. Reprinted in *Professional Practices in Art Museums,* Publication of the Association of Art Museum Directors (Savannah, Ga., 1981), pp. 27, 28.

34. *Museum Ethics: A Report to the American Association of Museums by its Committee on Ethics,* Publication of the American Association of Museums (Washington, D.C., 1978).

35. Alan D. Ullberg, "Recent Developments in Ethical Codes and Practices among Museum Staff in the United States," *Transactions No. 16: Towards a Code of Ethics in Museums,* Publication of the Museum Professionals Group (London, 1981), pp. 57–69.

36. *Museum Ethics,* pp. 28, 29.

37. "Lefkowitz Urges Change at Brooklyn Museum," *New York Times,* June 23, 1978, p. C18, col. 1. The settlement stipulation is reprinted in American Bar Association–American Law Institute Course of Study Materials, *Legal Problems of Museum Administration* (Philadelphia, 1981), pp. 81–83.

38. Franklin Feldman and Stephen E. Weil, *Art Works: Law, Policy, Practice,* Publication of the Practicing Law Institute (New York, 1974), pp. 1115, 1123–28.

39. Alan D. Ullberg with Patricia Ullberg, *Museum Trusteeship,* Publication of the American Association of Museums (Washington, D.C., 1981), p. xi.

40. Merryman, "Are Museum Trustees and the Law out of Step?" p. 27.

ART, THE LAW,
AND THE MARKET

Beauty and the Beast
(1975, 1977)

Among the stories that are almost as old as Western civilization itself is that of the Minotaur—a monster, half-human and half-animal, who dwelt in the depths of the labyrinth and devoured all who came near him.

In some versions of this legend, the Minotaur was a child of Europa and Zeus who, disguised as a bull, stole Europa from her home in Phoenicia and carried her off to Crete. In others, it was the Queen of Crete herself who bore the Minotaur; the father, again, was a bull. All agree, however, that this monster was born from the unnatural coupling of beauty and a beast.

The story of how art and the law came to be related is, in some respects, another tale of such an unnatural coupling—another story, if you will, of beauty and the beast. Whether its outcome may prove to be as monstrous as the Minotaur is a question to be considered later.

From at least one point of view, art and the law can be seen as standing at opposite poles of the human experience. The qualities that we most prize in art—the unexpected quirks, flights, and fancies of imagination, the intoxication that comes from challenges accepted and overcome, and, above all, the artist's fierce insistence that his aspiration is the sole authority by which his work may be judged—are the very antitheses of those elements for which we value the law: its sober clarity, its reasonable pre-

Copyright © 1977 by the Law Librarians' Society. Reprinted from Law Library Journal, vol. 70 (February 1977), by permission of the Law Librarians' Society. This paper was originally presented at a meeting of the Law Librarians' Society of Washington, D.C., on September 16, 1975.

dictability, and the constant necessity that it arrive at rules of general application to resolve the urgent day-to-day problems of real people in a real world.

In 1903 Justice Oliver Wendell Holmes took occasion to comment on the gap between these contrasting sensibilities. Writing in *Bleistein v. Donaldson Lithographing Co.* (188 U.S. 239, 251), a copyright case, he cautioned:

> It would be a dangerous undertaking for persons trained only to the law to constitute themselves final judges of the worth of pictorial illustrations outside of the narrowest and most obvious limits. At the one extreme, some works of genius would be sure to miss appreciation. Their very novelty would make them repulsive until the public had learned the new language in which their author spoke. It may be more than doubted, for instance, whether the etchings of Goya or the paintings of Manet would have been sure of protection when seen for the first time. At the other end, copyright would be denied to pictures which appealed to a public less educated than the judge. Yet, if they command the interest of any public, they have a commercial value—it would be bold to say that they have not an aesthetical and educational value—and the taste of any public is not to be treated with contempt.

Today, nearly three-quarters of a century later, we find that the gap between art and the law has been, and is being, bridged at half-a-dozen places. Art and the law—beauty and the beast—have become deeply intertwined, and they threaten to become more so with each passing year.

The story—at least in its Anglo-American version—begins innocently enough and, as any good story should, with: "Once upon a time and in a certain place. . . ." In this case, the time was the 1790s, and the place was London. The European art market, as it was and is—a sprawling mass of dealers, collectors, auction houses, artists, and runners—had first taken shape in the seventeenth century, and, at the end of the eighteenth century, London was its center.

Significant also were the artists whose works—or was it copies of whose works?—were involved: the French painter Claude Gellée, more familiar to us as Claude Le Lorrain, and David Teniers the Younger, a Flemish painter of genre scenes. Both had been dead for more than a century and the paintings of both were among the most sought after and highly priced of the period. A painting by Claude, for example, had sold a few years earlier for £2,500, many times what a major canvas by Rembrandt would then have fetched and equal, perhaps, to a quarter of a million dollars today.

Then, as now, the combination of long dead artists and very high prices had irresistible consequences. Sometimes paintings were forged; sometimes the work of a lesser hand was passed off as that of a greater one. Sometimes a painting was, in fact, "right"—as the dealers like to say—but the purchaser, infected by suspicion of the market, was still concerned that he'd been had.

One purchaser so concerned was a gentleman named Jendwine who, several years earlier, had bought two paintings from a dealer named Slade. These were a sea-piece by Claude and a scene of a country fair by Teniers. Concluding that the paintings were not originals at all but merely copies, Jendwine sued Slade for damages, claiming a breach of warranty. While both sides produced expert witnesses—who did not agree—the court neatly side-stepped the issue of authenticity and disposed of the case in the dealer's favor by holding that he had never warranted the authorship of the paintings in the first place. In the case of a long-dead artist, the court said, any statement as to authorship must be construed only to be an opinion, not a warranty. (*Jendwine v. Slade*, 170 Eng. Rep. 459 [1797].)

At the start, then, it was money—or, rather, disputes over money—that first began to bring art into the embraces of the law. Whatever else it may be in terms of human aspiration and accomplishment, a work of art is also property—a bundle of property, in fact—and the right to this property may involve considerable sums. The sequence is compelling: a growing interest in art creates a market, the market churns up activity, activity leads to abuses and contention, and the law must be called upon to remedy the abuses and resolve the contention.

So long as disputes about art could be settled by reference to some general body of law extrinsic to the art work itself, this coupling of art and law was not particularly pernicious. Throughout the nineteenth century, this was generally the case. No legislation dealt with art particularly, and the case law almost inevitably looked past the subject work of art to ground the decision elsewhere. Thus, for example, in *Zaleski v. Clark*, 44 Conn. 218

(1876), a Connecticut case, the court supported the defendant's refusal to pay for a commissioned portrait bust of her deceased husband by reference to contract law and without looking to the allegedly unsatisfactory quality of the artist's work. The contract might have been for a portrait or a pound of peas; the result would have been the same.

In the United States, the relative unparticularity with which the law approached art was nicely in accord with the general level of art activity—at least for most of the nineteenth century. For much of this period, the country was too involved with its own expansion, with questions of manifest destiny and of slavery, for art to be a matter of concern for any but a thin fringe of affluent easterners. Only in the post–Civil War period do we come to the founding of the great museums—the Corcoran in 1869, the Metropolitan Museum and the Boston Museum of Fine Arts in 1870, the Art Institute of Chicago in 1879—and to the first great American collections: Morgan, Widener, Havemeyer, Freer. The sequence we saw before was again set in motion: the newfound American interest in art created a strong market, the market—in turn—generated an ever higher level of activity, and up from this activity arose those disputes which the law must address.

This time, however, there was a difference. Concurrent with the growing American interest in art was the increasing complexity and regulation of the society in general. Such developments as a national scheme of income taxation would touch every aspect of life—art not excepted. In this changing context, the relationship between art and the law—previously arms length, circumspect, and proper—began to make a dangerous turn. It was to the work of art itself, together with the bona fides of the artist, that administrative decisions, case law, and legislation began to look.

Consider, for example, the case of Brancusi's *Bird,* sometimes called the *Bird in Space* or *Bird in Flight.* Constantin Brancusi is today acknowledged generally as one of the towering figures of twentieth-century sculpture, and the several versions of the *Bird* are among the most popular and best recognized images of modern art. And yet in 1928—when he already enjoyed a substantial worldwide reputation—the issue of whether Brancusi was a "professional sculptor" and whether the *Bird* was a "work of art" was actually litigated in the United States Customs Court. (*Brancusi v. United States,* 54 Treas. Dec. 428.)

During the mid-1920s, the American photographer Edward Steichen bought the *Bird* in Paris. On its arrival in New York, the Collector of Customs, determining that so abstract a form must be classified not as a work of art but as a manufacture of metal, assessed a duty of 40 percent; a work of art would have been duty-free. The case was tried before Justice Morrison Waite, and the government produced at least two experts—the academic sculptor Robert Aitken, now virtually forgotten, and a professor from Columbia University—who testified that the *Bird* was not a work of art. Happily, their testimony was more than outweighed by the experts who testified for Brancusi—among them the sculptor Jacob Epstein, the critic Henry MacBride, and Frank Crowninshield, a collector and the publisher of *Vanity Fair*.

Without hiding his personal doubts as to the aesthetic value of Brancusi's work, Justice Waite found (1) that its creator was, in fact, a "professional artist" and (2) that the *Bird* was a work of art. "There has," he said, "been developing a so-called new school of art, whose exponents attempt to portray abstract ideas rather than to imitate natural objects. Whether or not we are in sympathy with these newer ideas and the schools that represent them, we think the fact of their existence and their influence upon the art world . . . must be considered." (*Brancusi v. United States*, 54 Treas. Dec. 428.)

Laudatory as we may find Justice Waite's decision, a question remains. The *Bird* was a masterpiece, and it was no great trick to find impressive witnesses to defend it as such. But what if the sculpture at issue had been something less—a simply rotten work of art but, nonetheless, a work of art? Without such critical endorsement, would the court have been as easily able to resolve what essentially is an aesthetic question? It may be answered that the courts regularly resolve questions as to which they have no particular expertise beyond that which the parties can put into evidence. Why should this not be as true of art as it is of autos? The answer to *that*, I think, lies in the peculiarly subjective and self-validating way in which art must be judged. Experts may be able to project objective standards to determine whether thirty gross of rubber heels, claimed to be defective, are fit for their intended purpose. There are no such standards for art.

Let's jump into the present. In December 1974, at the tail end of the Ninety-third Congress, Representative Thomas Rees of California introduced H.R. 17613, a bill that would have amended the Internal Revenue Code by permitting collectors to deduct, within certain limits, the purchase price paid for contemporary American works of art. This bill arose from suggestions made by Artists for Economic Action, a Los Angeles–based group concerned with the great difficulty that the overwhelming number of American artists have in selling their work. The ostensible purpose of H.R. 17613 was to stimulate art sales by giving a tax break to collectors, for whom a deduction might serve as an incentive, rather than to artists who might have little or no income to be taxed in the first place.

The possibilities for abuse that such a deduction would offer are considerable. H.R. 17613 tried to meet these by limiting the availability of the deduction to the purchase of works by "professional artists." The determination of who is or is not a "professional artist" would, in turn, be made pursuant to rules to be promulgated by the secretary of the treasury or his delegate.

It is here that we begin to see the monster poking his head out of the labyrinth. The notion of officially certifying artists—of stamping them, as it were, with an Internal Revenue Service seal of approval—is troublesome. We have but to look to the Soviet Union to see what may happen when art becomes official and artists are assigned to approved and disapproved categories. Those qualities of a work of art that we looked at earlier—its quirkiness, fantasy, and intoxication, its insistence on the standards of its maker—are the very qualities least apt to flourish when art becomes official; what we tend to get, instead, are cautious copies of what has already been approved: statues instead of sculpture, pictures instead of paintings.

In passing, it should be noted that the Internal Revenue Service is, to some extent, *already* in the business of determining who is and who is not a professional artist. Such a determination must be made when deductions are claimed, most often against non-art-related income, for studio expenses and materials—allowable for the individual who pursues his art as a trade or business, but not necessarily for someone who paints as a hobby.

This trend toward administrative, legislative, and judicial definitions of art and artists is not confined to customs or tax matters. At its outermost, it may actually involve questions of criminality—not for the artist, but for those who deal with him. Commencing in the mid-1960s, a number of special statutes—intended to be protective to both artists and collectors—were enacted in New York. One of these, constituting Article 12-C of the General Business Law, regulates the relationship between "artists"—as defined in the statute—and dealers, in such a way as to transform it from the traditional one of consignor and consignee or creditor and debtor into one of principal and agent. The consequence of this change—the consequence intended by the legislature—is to transform the wrongful handling of funds by an art dealer from a civil to a criminal wrong.

Thus, if a dealer in ceramics were to run off with the sales proceeds from some handmade pots that you had sent him on consignment, you would have only a civil remedy. But if a dealer in sculpture were to run off with the proceeds from some pot-shaped sculpture that you had sent him on consignment, then it would be larceny! It is not too difficult to imagine that borderline case in which the question of whether a criminal defendant must go to jail may turn on the finding of whether the subject of a consignment was or was not a work of art—or, perhaps, was or was not a work of art beyond a reasonable doubt.

What an enormous distance we have come, since Justice Holmes first warned us of the dangers of mixing art and the law! And by what small, unintended steps. It is almost as if beauty and the beast—fully conscious of their separate backgrounds and incompatible worlds and fully determined that their innocent relationship should not ripen into anything more—have nonetheless been swept into each other's arms by the sheer complexity of twentieth-century life. As we have seen, one of the possible outcomes of this coupling—one that to me is monstrous—is the development of an official art and of all the deadening of sensibility that an official art involves.

I wonder, though, whether this story—as any good story should—may not have a broader meaning. Is it not, perhaps, a paradigm of the ways in which the most diverse—and even seemingly private—aspects of life may become entangled in an ever-increasing web of regulation and adjudication; of how—with the best will in the world, and no villain to be pointed to—we may slowly be clogging those interstitial places where fancy flourishes; of how we may be making a world just a little duller, a little grayer, and a little drier than the one we used to know?

In any chronicle of our time, this curious affair between beauty and the beast will, at best, be only a footnote; we have enough larger problems to fill the main text. And yet, as a symptom at least, it leaves some things at which to wonder.

Some Thoughts
on "Art Law" (1981)

Within the past two decades, there has been a remarkable surge of interest in an interdisciplinary cluster of legal concerns generally referred to in the aggregate as "art law." Young lawyers seem to find it particularly attractive. Scarcely a month goes by that I am not called for employment advice by a law school senior or recent graduate eager to become its practitioner. Sadly, I find myself explaining that there really is no such specific discipline, and even less of a demand for anyone to practice it more than occassionally.

To be sure, an artist might now and again run up against an unusual copyright problem or be in need of guidance through some fascinating by-way of the *droit moral*.[1] Most often, though, the disputes in which artists—like other human beings—are apt to find themselves tend to involve their landlords, spouses, or local dry cleaners. What they don't need in those circumstances, I tell my callers, is a lawyer whose chief qualification is a sensitivity to art. What they *do* need is a first-class, well-rounded attorney.

Albeit crestfallen, my callers generally persist. . . . Well, then, what about working for an art museum? Surely, things there must be different. To begin with, I have to say, there are but a few American art museums—perhaps half a dozen—that can even afford to hire their own staff counsel. Beyond that, museum counsel only rarely get to deal with "art law." Their daily concerns are far more likely to revolve about matters such as unrelated business

Copyright © 1981 by Dickinson School of Law. Reprinted from Dickinson Law Review, *vol. 85, no. 4 (Summer 1981), a special issue devoted to "art law," by permission of Dickinson School of Law. This article served as the introduction to that issue.*

income, slip and fall cases, collective bargaining agreements, and compliance with a broad range of equal opportunity regulations. What a museum needs when it hires in-house counsel is a strong generalist. The bottom line is the same. The young attorney hoping to be helpful to artists or museums would best be advised to spend his or her first precious years at the bar gaining a broad experience and not confined within so odd and only obscurely defined a speciality.

Only rarely has this advice been accepted with anything like cheer. My callers still want to be "art lawyers."

When did the contours of "art law" begin to emerge, and what might underlie its growing appeal? While stirrings of interest can be traced back to the late 1950s (and even earlier in Europe), and while the 1960s saw a sharp increase in both scholarly and legislative attention to the special problems of the art world, it was not until 1971 that the American activity in this field began in earnest.

In the East, 1971 saw the publication of *The Visual Artist and the Law,* a joint project of the Associated Councils of the Arts, the Association of the Bar of the City of New York, and Volunteer Lawyers for the Arts. Almost concurrently, across the country, Professors John Merryman and Albert Elsen of Stanford initiated a graduate level course (open to both law students and art historians) that dealt with art-related legal and ethical questions. This course, the first of its kind to be offered at an American university, proved extremely popular and has been continuously offered ever since.

An event that was to prove seminal occurred in July 1972: the presentation in New York City of the two-and-a-half-day workshop *Legal and Business Problems of Artists, Art Galleries and Museums,* sponsored by the Practicing Law Institute (PLI) and directed (in the face of considerable adversity) by Hedy Voigt. The faculty and participants included a wide range of attorneys, many of whom had theretofore been involved individually with the visual arts but who had not until then had a forum in which to share this common interest. Crippled at the start by the sudden illness of Dino D'Angelo, its chairman, the workshop nonetheless indicated that there were broad areas of law impinging on both the visual arts and museums that were in need of further exploration.

This first PLI workshop quickly engendered a series of successors. One of those in attendance was Peter Powers, the general counsel of the Smithsonian Insitution. Convinced that the growing legal entanglements in which museums were becoming enmeshed were such as to justify a separate program of their own, he went to work to establish one. The first course of study on *Legal Problems of Museum Administration* was given at the Freer Gallery in Washington in March 1973. Presented by the American Law Institute–American Bar Association (ALI-ABA) Joint Committee on Continuing Legal Education, it was cosponsored by the Smithsonian Institution with the cooperation of the American Association of Museums. Since then, this course of study has been repeated annually and in many cities throughout the country. Most recently, it was presented at the University Museum in Philadelphia in March 1981 with more than two hundred participants in attendance.

Meanwhile, encouraged by the success of its first effort, PLI organized a second workshop that was presented in New York in January 1973 and repeated the following month (to the accompaniment of an earthquake) in Los Angeles. Franklin Feldman and I were asked to serve as cochairmen. The source materials we put together for this second workshop were initially published as a course handbook, then later expanded and supplemented into the volume *Art Works: Law, Policy and Practice,* which PLI published in 1974.

As the 1970s proceeded, the hitherto sparse "art law" bookshelf began to fill at an extraordinary rate. In 1974, Scott Hodes, who in 1966 had published one of the earliest books in the field, returned with *What Every Artist and Collector Should Know About the Law.* That same year, *The Visual Artist and the Law* was republished in a revised edition, this time under the imprint of a commercial publisher. Leonard DuBoff—who had been an enthusiastic participant in the 1973 PLI workshop in Los Angeles—brought out *Art Law: Domestic and International* in 1975. His *Deskbook of Art Law* was published two years later. Tad Crawford's *Legal Guide for the Visual Artist* also appeared in 1977, as did Robert E. Duffy's *Art Law: Representing Artists, Dealers and Collectors.* In 1979 came the long-awaited *Law, Ethics and the Visual Arts* by Professors Merryman and Elsen. This past year, Aaron Milrad—also a participant in one of PLI's 1973 workshops—joined with Ella Agnew to publish *The Art World: Law, Business and*

Practice in Canada, the first comprehensive survey of the Canadian law in this field.

Supplementing these texts has been a rising tide of periodical literature. Notable issues of *The Hastings Law Journal*[2] and the *Connecticut Law Review*[3] were devoted to both the problems of nonprofit arts institutions and those involving objects themselves. *Art & the Law,* a quarterly publication of Volunteer Lawyers for the Arts, has evolved since mid-decade from a casual newsletter to a serious journal publishing some of the best writing to be found today on current art-related issues. A number of general art world publications such as the *Art Letter,* the *ARTnewsletter* and the *Stolen Art Alert* are now routinely providing up-to-day reports on legal matters. Meanwhile, workshops and symposia continue to multiply. In November 1980 the National Association of College and University Attorneys established a new section to deal with the special problems of university museums and their collections. The first meeting of this section was held in Salt Lake City this past June.

What has spurred this extraordinary growth of interest over so short a span? The conventional answer is that the explosion of values in the art market, the advent of blockbuster museum exhibitions, and the increased media attention focused on such matters as the Rothko Estate[4] and the Metropolitian Museum of Art's early 1970s deaccessioning[5] have combined to create an expanded public awareness both of art and of art-related problems. While this is probably so, I think there are several additional reasons.

To begin with, there is the art world itself—fascinating not only for the objects at its center, but also for the extraordinary *dramatis personae* by which they are surrounded. By contrast with such shopworn dyads as the vendor and the vendee or the landlord and the tenant, in the richness and variety of its characters the art world more closely resembles the *commedia dell'arte.* For Harlequin, Columbine, Pierrot, and their companions it substitutes instead such archetypes as the True Collector, the Philistine Investor, the Dedicated Artist, the Inauthentic Hack, and such supporting players as the Dealer, the Auctioneer, the Curator, the Scholar, the Critic, the Trustee, and the Archaeologist. Finally, lurking in the wings and always ready to pounce is the Tax Man.

Each of these characters is perceived as embodying certain

distinctive qualities. The interweaving of their conflicting interests is in itself dramatic. The manner in which, as their conflicts unfold, they will sometimes resort to disguises may approach the comic. And the struggle of all (the Tax Man possibly excepted) to accommodate to a system of laws not always well attuned to their special needs can often produce the most ironic of denouements.

Consider, for example, the case of the True Collector seeking to prove to the Tax Man that his activities are motivated primarily by investment purposes and that therefore he ought to be allowed to deduct the expenses of caring for his colleciton.[6] On the basis of *Wrightsman v. United States*,[7] he would be well advised to mask himself as the Philistine Investor and to play the public boor. Ideally, his collection should be left crated in a distant warehouse. Short of that, every indication of personal pleasure or enjoyment should be forcibly suppressed. He ought to sneer at art on every possible occasion, berate himself as a fool for ever buying "such junk," and ridicule the still greater fools who will one day take it off his hands at a profit. Above all, he should badger the Dealer almost daily for the latest quotations from the market. The world— or at least the Tax Man—must never discover that he is actually a True Collector.

Should the True Collector (or even the Philistine Investor) aspire to a still higher state of tax grace—one in which he might also claim deductions for depreciating his collection—he must turn things even more topsy-turvy still. He would be best off by showing that the objects in his collection were not works of art at all but simply decorations (wall or table-top, as the case might be) which, at the time of their acquisition, could have been anticipated to become obsolete after some determinable period. Taboo, under Revenue Ruling 68-232,[8] would be the ownership of anything so admirable as a "valuable and treasured art piece,"[9] Required under *D. Joseph Judge v. Commissioner*[10]—the case that dared to say that not every framed rectangular piece of canvas covered with painted marks was necessarily a work of art—would be proof of the useful life and salvage value of each of the accumulated bits of decor that constitute his collection.[11]

It should not be supposed that the advantage to the True Collector of denigrating his collection is restricted to situations that involve the Tax Man. Under California's recently enacted Art Preservation Act,[12] for example, the True Collector from whom a Dedicated Artist is seeking damages because a work of his creation has been intentionally mutilated would not be liable unless it could be proven that the work was of "recognized quality."[13] Whatever the True Collector could do to offset such proof ("Me a connoisseur? You're loco. In art, I'm just an ignoramus. I would only buy stuff by Inauthentic Hacks. And I got the witnesses to prove it.") would assist his defense. In a more extreme case, the Dealer charged in New York with larcenously converting the property of an Inauthentic Hack might have a complete defense by showing that the objects in which he deals are not "works of fine art" at all but merely items of wall decor. By so doing, he could take himself beyond the reach of the General Business Law provisions that specially define the artist-dealer relationship as one of principal and agent.[14]

The Dedicated Artist as well may sometimes have to put on a different mask in order to secure a particular legal advantage. Counterpoised against our conventional expectations of what might give meaning to his life—unswerving vision, fierce integrity, and even some carelessness of worldly things—*Churchman v. Commissioner*[15] suggests that a different set of values might serve him better if the still struggling Dedicated Artist's art-related expenses are to be deductible for federal income tax purposes. Paramount must be a craving for profit, regardless of whether the same is sought as a symbol of success (museum exhibitions and good reviews, without profitable sales, are less useful symbols) or as "the pathway to material wealth."[16] Important too is that his creative (or "recreational") activities not absorb too much of his day but that some substantial time be devoted to marketing, an activity "where the recreational element is minimal."[17] To stubbornly persist in a medium or technique despite the rebuffs of the market would not be a positive sign of profit-seeking. Far better, apparently, would be an annual change in style, preferably one based on a current survey of what is then "hottest" in the art market.

Here, again, is that awkward "fit" between the concerns of two systems—art and the law—that gives a peculiar twist to so much in this field. As a way of safeguarding the fisc against underwriting the costs of what might be only a hobby, the *Churchman* approach makes eminently good sense. To propose some alternative that the Dedicated Artist might find more appropriate—simply, for example, to put his painting or sculpture itself before a body of Critics, Curators, or peers that might pass on its merits—would be to misapprehend the issue. The Internal Revenue Code is indifferent to the quality of art. Its concern in such situations is whether expenses are merely personal or have been incurred in a quest for profit. The tilt, unfortunately, is toward the Inauthentic Hack.

Another aspect of "art law," and one that often adds to its piquancy, is the odd way in which it sometimes precipitates the courts into unaccustomed questions of artistic quality or historical authenticity. We have come a long way since Mr. Justice Holmes's familiar caution, in *Bleistein v. Donaldson Lithographing Co.,*[18] that it would be "a dangerous undertaking for persons trained only to the law to constitute themselves final judges of the worth of pictorial illustrations outside of the narrowest and most obvious limits."[19] We have even come a considerable way since the days of *Brancusi v. United States*[20] and other customs cases when the statutory question the courts had to answer was simply "Is it art?"

In *Furstenberg v. United States,*[21] for example, the United States Court of Claims found itself inescapably saddled with the task of distinguishing between the artistic merits of two paintings by Corot— one the subject (in a charitable deduction contest) of a disputed valuation and the other the "comparable" that the taxpayer had proffered in support of her claim. Undaunted, the court seized the critical gauntlet. Per curiam, it pronounced: "From the standpoint of artistic quality, however, *Girl in Red with Mandolin* is substantially superior to *La Meditation,* as the former is one of Corot's finest works whereas *La Meditation . . .* is near the average in artistic quality among the entire group of Corot's figure paintings."[22]

In *Dawson v. G. Malina, Inc.,*[23] a federal district judge found himself confronted with the demand that, as the trier of facts, he undertake the task of attributing a group of Chinese antiquities— the subject of an action by a True Collector against a Dealer for breach of warranty under one of New York's special art statutes— to their precise dynastic origins. Sidestepping any such attribution as "by its very nature an inexact science" and "necessarily . . . imprecise,"[24] the judge arrived at a more manageable approach: whether there had been a reasonable basis in fact at the time they were made for the Dealer's representations as to the origin of these antiquities, "with the question of whether there was such a reasonable basis in fact being measured by the expert testimony provided at the trial."[25] There ensued a classic battle of experts— in this instance, of Scholars—and a delightful excursion into the arcane. In the footnotes appeared such lyric poetry as:

> The fair sky is enlightened by a
>   distant sail,
> The bright moon is illuminated by
>   a pureness of the willows and clouds,
> People drift away with the flowing
>   waters but nature remains forever,
> Splashing waves play harmonious songs as
>   the water's vapor rise from the lake
>   like puffs of smoke.[26]

Such are some of "art law's" many pleasures. That it can sometimes be so diverting a field should not, however, mislead us as to the importance of what its practitioners have accomplished or what remains to be done. At the market level, special legislation adopted over the past fifteen years in such major art market states as New York,[27] Illinois,[28] and California[29] has substantially changed the relationships among artists, dealers, and collectors, largely for the better. Imbalances have been corrected, more stringent disclosure standards have been imposed, and the market (despite occasional dire predictions) has been no less robust for these changes.

At the institutional level, enormous progress has been made in better defining the responsibilities of trustees and in adding legal force to standards (applicable to trustees and staff alike) that were hitherto considered, when they were considered at all, as no more than ethical. That museums hold their collections in what is essentially a public trust is today a widely shared perception from which both they and their users have benefited enormously.[30]

By contrast, the problems of balancing competing interests in such federally dominated areas of the law as copyright and taxation[31] seem far from any satisfactory resolution. Thorny too are questions that concern the international movement of art and the protection of archaeological sites.[32] As to these, the art world itself has thus far resisted any consensus solution. A wider concern is whether the arts should receive public funding and, if so, by what means.[33] To many of these issues, the art world's diverse cast of characters (as well as the general public) brings strong and often opposing views. A major contribution of "art law" has been to help focus the terms of their debate and define the issues that must be addressed.

The arts and the institutions that embody them are too vital to our national life to be left adrift in a legal system that often treats them in too general a fashion. Attention should be paid to their special needs and even peculiarities. By assembling this special issue, the editors of the Dickinson Law Review have contributed toward that end. Hopefully, their efforts will serve to introduce a still broader public to a field of the law that—if yet too diffuse to constitute a distinct specialty and still far from able to furnish remunerative employment to my monthly callers—should long continue to provide a variety of both pleaures and worthwhile tasks for those who pursue it.

NOTES

The author gratefully acknowledges the assistance of Ms. Pamela Lajeunesse, projects editor of the Dickinson Law Review, for her assistance in the preparation of this text.

1. The doctrine of "droit moral" or "moral rights" provides that an artist has, inter alia, the right to have his or her name associated with his or her work, the right to modify and correct the work even if it is in the hands of a purchaser, the right to withdraw work after publication or display, the right to prevent others from claiming credit for the work, and the right to prevent distortion, mutilation, or other alteration of his or her work. Many of these rights have not received general recognition in the United States and must be secured by contractual agreement. See generally, Merryman, The Refrigerator of Bernard Buffet, 27 HASTINGS L.J. 1023 (1976); Comment, Artist's Personal Rights in His Creative Works: Beyond the Human Cannonball and the Flying Circus, 9 PACIFIC L. J. 855 (1978); Comment, The Doctrine of Moral Right: A Study of the Law of Artists, Authors and Creators, 53 HARV, L. REV. 554 (1946).
2. 27 HASTINGS L.J. 951 (1976).
3. 78 CONN. L. REV. 545 (1978).
4. In re Estate of Rothko, 43 N.Y.2d. 305, 372 N.E.2nd, 305, 401 N.Y.S.2d 449 (1977). At his death, abstract expressionist painter Mark Rothko left a considerable number of paintings in his estate. One of the executors of the artist's estate was an officer of the gallery to which the paintings were sold. A second executor, who acquiesced in the transactions, was himself an artist and stood to gain some special advantage from the gallery. The third executor was charged with failure to exercise his duty of reasonable care in the disposition of the

works when he suspected the personal and financial interests of his co-executors. The three were surcharged for breach of trust, and the galleries that took with notice of the breach were chargeable with the value of the unreturned paintings at the time of the court's decree.

For an account of the case by a journalist who covered the litigation, see SELDES, THE LEGACY OF MARK ROTHKO (1978).

5. "Deaccessioning" refers to the removal of a work of art from the official collection of an institution. For an account of the Metropolitan's deaccessioning activities, see Bator, *Letter to the Editor,* N.Y. Times, Jan. 23, 1973; Cunningham, *Letter to the Editor,* N.Y. Times, Feb. 3, 1973; Metropolitan Museum of Art, Report on Art Transactions 1971–73 (June 20, 1973), *reprinted in* J. MERRYMAN & A. ELSEN, 2 LAW, ETHICS AND THE VISUAL ARTS 7-111, 7-712, & 7-114 (1979).

6. IRC § 212 entitles the taxpayer to deductions for "ordinary and necessary expenses" incurred "for the production . . . of income" or for the management, conservation, or maintenance of property held for the production of income.

7. 428 F.2d 1316 (Ct. Cl. 1970). In *Wrightsman,* the court denied the deduction of expenses incurred by the taxpayers in maintaining their collection, finding that although investment was a prominent purpose, it was not the *primary* motivation.

8. Rev. Rul. 68-232, 1968-1 C.B. 79.

9. The official position of the Internal Revenue Service regarding the depreciation of art work is set forth in Revenue Ruling 68-232 *(Idem)* is as follows:

A valuable and treasured art piece does not have a determinable useful life. While the actual physical condition of the property may influence the value placed on the object, it will not ordinarily limit or determine the useful life. Accordingly, depreciation of works of art generally is not allowable.

10. 38 T.C.M. (CCH) 1264 (1976).

11. *Idem* at 1273.

12. The California Art Preservations Act, 1979, CAL. STAT. ch. 409, § 1 (codified at CAL. CIV. CODE § 987 (Deering Supp. 1981)).

13. The California Art Preservation Act defines "fine art" as "an original painting, sculpture, or drawing of recognized quality," but excludes "work prepared under contract for commercial use by its purchaser." CAL. CIV. CODE § 967(b)(2) (Deering Supp. 1981).

14. N.Y. GEN. BUS. LAW § 219-a (McKinney Supp. 1980–81).

15. 68 T.C. 696 (1977). In *Churchman,* the Commissioner argued that the taxpayer-artist was a "hobbyist," that she did not engage in her artistic endeavors for profit, and that therefore IRC § 183 applied. Section 183 allows deductions for ordinary and necessary expenses arising from an activity not engaged in for profit only to the extent of the gross income derived from the activity less the amount of those deductions, such as taxes and interest, that are allowable regardless of whether or not the activity is engaged in for profit. The court held for the taxpayer, however, and allowed the deduction in full of her art-related expenses under sections 162 and 165.

16. Churchman v. Comm'r, 68 T.C. 696, 703 (1977).

17. "While petitioner's artwork involved recreational and personal elements, her work did not stop at the creative stage but went into the marketing phase of the art business where the recreational element is minimal." *Idem* at 702.

18. 188 U.S. 239 (1903) (application of copyright laws to three chromolithographic circus advertisements).
19. *Idem* at 251.
20. T.D. 43063, 54 Treas. Doc. 428 (1928).
21. 595 F.2d 603 (Ct. Cl. 1979).
22. *Idem* at 608.
23. 463 F. Suppl. 461 (S.D.N.Y. 1978).
24. *Idem* at 467.
25. *Idem.*
26. *Idem* at 470 n. 10.
27. *See, e.g.,* N. Y. GEN. BUS. LAW §§ 219 & 219-a (McKinney Supp. 1980–81).
28. *See e.g.,* ILL. ANN. STAT. ch. 121½ § 316-69 (Smith-Hurd Supp. 1981–82).
29. *See e.g.,* CAL. CIV. CODE § 1740-45 (Deering Supp. 1972).
30. *See* Marsh, *Governance of Non-Profit Organizations: An Appropriate Standard of Conduct For Trustees and Directors of Museums and Other Cultural Institutions,* 85 DICK. L. REV. 607 (1981).
31. *See* Comment, *Tax Incentives for the Support of the Arts: In Defense of the Charitable Deduction,* 85 DICK. L. REV. 663 (1981).
32. *See* McAlee, *From the Boston Raphael to Peruvian Pots: Limitations on the Importation of Art into the United States,* 85 DICK. L. REV. 565 (1981).
33. *See* Comment, *Mechanisms for Control and Distribution of Public Funds to the Art Community,* 85 DICK. L. REV. 629 (1981).

Resale Royalties:
Nobody Benefits
(1978)

That American artists should, through their own creative efforts, be able to sustain themselves—and to sustain themselves with greater dignity and more adequate means than many can do today—is not merely socially desirable. It is a national necessity. In an environment that increasingly stresses corporate accomplishment and technical skills, the importance of artists becomes correspondingly greater. They are among the last role models we have of free imagination, transcendent aspiration, and—above all—individual effort and responsibility. Beside whatever contributions their work can make to our accumulated cultural heritage, artists in their own selves are more than ever vital to maintaining the balance of our national life.

Recognizing that artists require a more adequate support system than American society now provides, legislators at both the state and the federal level have shown increasing interest in finding other means to help them. One proposal, strongly championed by a number of artists and by many artists' groups, would do so by the establishment of resale royalties.

To question, as I shall, both the principles underlying this proposal and, regardless of the soundness of these principles, the utility of any legislation that would establish such royalties is to risk being misunderstood as indifferent or even hostile to the well-being of artists. I hope that I am neither, and I would hesitate to raise such questions publicly were I not convinced so strongly, first, that the establishment of resale royalties, far from helping

Copyright © 1978 by ARTnews Associates. Reprinted from ARTnews, vol. 77, no. 3 (March 1978), by permission of ARTnews Associates.

artists or having only a neutral impact, would in fact be positively harmful to their interests and, second, that it is critically important that those who wish to help artists take advantage of this current surge of legislative interest by concentrating their efforts on alternative measures that would increase—rather than, as resale royalties threaten to do, diminish—the funds now available for the purchase of contemporary art.

Analogy and image. Underlying the proposal for artists resale royalties are an analogy and an image.

The analogy is to the means by which authors and composers have traditionally been compensated. Implicit is the suggestion that, by reason of their right to receive royalties, these other creative workers enjoy an advantage that visual artists are denied. This was clearly expressed in one of the seminal documents of the present campaign for resale royalties, the Art Proceeds Act proposed in 1966 by Diana B. Schulder in the *Northwestern University Law Review.* Section 2 provided: "Since a painter or a sculptor who creates a unique work of art does not benefit from the fruits of his labors as does an author or composer who derives royalties from the reproduction or performance of the work, this act, by allowing an economic right upon re-transfer, is intended to ensure to artists a parallel benefit."

The image coupled with this analogy is that of a collector who, having purchased a work of art for relatively little, resells it for a great deal more, pocketing the entire profit and leaving the artist, whose effort first created the work and whose subsequent accomplishments may have contributed to its increase in value, with no part of such increase. It is the image of Robert Rauschenberg and Robert Scull in tense confrontation after the 1973 auction at which Scull resold for $85,000, a work for which he had originally paid Rauschenberg less than $1,000.

If the establishment of resale royalties is to be founded upon some sound principle, then, at the outset, two questions must be asked. Is this underlying analogy correct, and does this underlying image—unquestionably distressing in its suggestion of a collector unjustly enriched at an artist's expense—reflect some common situation or only an occasional, albeit highly visible, anomaly in the market?

Painters, poets, and others. Would the grant to visual artists of some continuing economic interest in their work, the realization of which would be dependent on the resale or successive resales of such work, in fact be a "parallel benefit" to the royalty rights now enjoyed by other creative workers? Clearly, it would not. The royalties that authors and composers receive are based on the multiple initial sales of their infinitely reproducible efforts. For each additional copy of a novel printed and sold, the author may receive additional compensation. So may the composer for each additional performance of a musical composition. For that matter, so too may the visual artist who elects to sell additional copies of an infinitely reproducible *image* of a work of art rather than the unique object in which the work itself is embodied.

This is not the case with a resale royalty. In the case of a resale royalty, no additional example of the original work is being brought into being nor is the work itself being put to any broader use. The event that would cause the proposed royalty to be paid would, instead, be the substitution of one owner for another. It would be as if Norman Mailer could claim some further payment for each copy of *The Naked and the Dead* resold in the secondhand book market above the $4 price at which it was originally published in 1948 or as if an architect could claim some share of the proceeds when a house he designed was subsequently resold at a profit. No such right exists today.

What is proposed here, then, is the establishment of a *new* right—one very different from a royalty and one that does not extend naturally from existing concepts of property and ownership. Whether such a special right should be established for artists is a larger, open, and arguable question, but not one that can be answered by a simple analogy to the royalties payable to authors and composers.

Might the establishment of this special right be justified, then, on the ground that the traditional method by which artists have been compensated places them at a disadvantage to other creative workers? It might, if this were so. It appears, however, not to be so. If we exclude such supplementary income-producing activities as teaching, lecturing, or wholly unrelated employment—none of which relates to the question of royalties and some of which normally supplement the art-derived income of most creative individuals—and exclude as well the grotesquely inflated earnings of such mass-appeal entertainers as rock stars or gothic novelists, visual artists would seem to be consistently better compensated for their creative effort than their peers in the other arts.

To make such comparisons is awkward. Real names must be used, and virtually no one will agree with particular comparisons. Nevertheless, if you compared the probable art-derived income of creative individuals of comparable seriousness, achievement, and popularity, how well would visual artists fare? Consider Pablo Picasso in relation to Igor Stravinsky or Thomas Mann; Marc Chagall to Vladmir Nabokov or Béla Bartók; Henry Moore to Benjamin Britten or W. H. Auden; the fifth best earner of the Castelli Gallery to the fifth best earner among the Yale Younger Poets. Make your own comparisons. If you do it fairly, I believe you will find that the earnings of visual artists—no matter how inadequate such earnings may be in themselves or how poorly they may compare with those of individuals outside the arts—are nevertheless consistently above the earnings of those of their peers who are compensated by royalties.

There are reasons why this should be so. That a work of art is traditionally embodied in a tangible, physical object rather than— as in the case of literature or music—expressed through such infinitely reproducible media as words or sounds has more than aesthetic implications. Beyond the fact that their value is influenced—if not largely determined—by scarcity, works of art do not require the same level of demand as do works of literature or music to secure their creators a living. A painting needs no initial market larger than a single buyer in order to be sold. Two potential buyers, by themselves, can provide the basis for a successful auction. A hard-core audience of two hundred faithful collector-buyers might guarantee an artist's livelihood. By contrast, a poet or novelist—able, perhaps, to realize a two-dollar royalty on the sale of each hardcover copy of a book—would require thousands, if not tens of thousands, of reader-buyers to earn any continuing support from the sale of his work.

If this is so—and if the difference in the way in which they have traditionally been compensated has been an advantage, rather than a disadvantage, to visual artists—then we must look elsewhere for some basis by which the establishment of a resale royalty might be justified.

The argument of unjust enrichment. We know that there are

collectors who, from time to time, have made a great deal of money from buying and reselling works of art. We know too that some artists whose work has been involved in these transactions feel that they have been "ripped off" as a result. What we do not know, however, is whether this happens very often. That is only the tip of our ignorance. Confining our consideration to works of art by living American artists, we also do not know, for example:

• The annual dollar volume, number, and price level of primary sales (sales from the artist or dealer to a first collector).
• The ratio these bear to the overall market for art, antiques, antiquities, and other competing "collectibles."
• The number of those works sold in the primary market that are ever resold in the secondary market, and the interval between such sales.
• Of the works resold in the secondary market, the number that are sold at more and the number that are sold at less than their initial price and, in each case, the dollar volume involved.

Beyond this, we have only the haziest idea of how many American artists there are for whose work there even is a regular primary market, of how many of these artists also have a secondary market, of how many buyers "collect" art in any significant way, and of how many such buyers ever resell the works they buy.

We remain, thus, stalled at our original question: How common is the situation that provoked the Rauschenberg-Scull confrontation? Is it one that is constantly repeated across the country, with large numbers of collectors reaping "windfall" profits by reselling the work of a large number of artists? Or is the resale market for contemporary art confined largely to the work of a relatively small group of well-known artists whose work is bought and sold chiefly by "blue-chip" collectors?

Certainly, if it proved that some substantial number of transactions were involved, and if there were general agreement that the ability of collectors to reap such windfall profits had within it an element of unfairness, there might be some warrant for adopting national legislation that would impose some additional tax— which need not necessarily be one payable to artists—beyond the state and federal income taxes to which such profits are already subject.

Even here, though, it would be difficult to know what, except in the most extreme cases, would be meant by a "windfall" or even—always a problem in calculating taxes—what would be meant by a "profit." If, between the time he bought and resold it, the net after-selling-cost value of a painting in a collector's hands increased by no more than the current rate of inflation, was he unjustly enriched? What if the increase just equaled the interest paid on funds that he might have borrowed to purchase the painting in the first place? What if the increase just equaled the expenses incurred during ownership for insurance and/or conservation? What if he bought and sold two paintings by the same artist, profiting as much on one as he lost on the other?

And what if all of these—inflation, interest cost, the expenses of ownership, and offsetting gains and losses—occurred together? While something may be sensed as unfair in a collector buying a work of art for $10,000 and selling it the next year for $50,000, to what extent do we sense it unfair if a painting, or anything else with a secondhand value, is bought for $10,000 and resold for $15,000 some ten years later?

To justify a resale royalty on the basis that it would ameliorate some widespread injustice done by collectors to artists would require considerable information beyond what we now have. Moreover, to achieve acceptance as fair and reasonable, it would require a mechanism more sophisticated than those proposed thus far to determine when, and in what amount, such a royalty might be appropriate. If windfall profits from the sale of contemporary art are, in fact, a substantial problem, that problem should be addressed by some measured response and not by a dramatic gesture that, regardless of any immediate satisfaction it might give, could neither be justified to those it would affect nor be of benefit to those on whose behalf it was made. Frustration and anger, real as they may be, are not a sound basis for national legislation.

The one-way connection. A further argument made in support of resale royalties is that their establishment would give legal recognition to—as well as symbolize—a continuing connection between the artist and a work of art after it had once been sold. In so doing, it would move American law closer to those Continental systems that recognize a *droit de suite*, from which the concept of resale royalties was first derived, as well as a *droit moral.* Their right to receive resale royalties would, in effect, be the "umbilical cord" through which artists would maintain an ongoing relationship with their work.

The justice of this argument fades, however, when we realize how one-sided this ongoing relationship would be. It would not require the artist to bear any part of a collector's ongoing expenses, such as those for insurance or conservation. Neither would it impose on the artist any greater liability than heretofore for the instability or failure of the materials or workmanship he might have employed in his work. Above all, the proposed umbilical cord would only carry gains, carefully filtering out any losses that collectors might incur on the resale of those works to which the artists would otherwise remain connected.

Certainly, no one seriously proposes that the artist—or the artist's heirs for fifty years after death—should be liable for a refund of five percent of the initial purchase price whenever a collector is unable to resell a work of art for the amount it originally cost. For many artists, the contingent liability might well exceed their total worth. At the same time, however, it is difficult to accept as just a proposed form of partnership in which one of the partners would bear all of the risks while the other enjoyed the luxury of sharing in profits only.

Art in a commodity market. To all of the foregoing, it may in some fairness be replied: so what? If resale royalties would, in reality, benefit artists generally, that fact alone, regardless of any infirmity in the supporting arguments, might be reason enough to consider their establishment. As I said at the outset, however, I have come to believe exactly the opposite: that resale royalties would be neither of any benefit nor even neutral in their impact but would in fact do enormous harm to the already not-very-well-being of contemporary artists.

Unpalatable as it may be to many, works of art—once out of an artist's hands—become commodities. They are articles of commerce. As such, the prices at which, and the numbers in which, they are bought and sold in both their initial and resale markets are influenced by those same considerations that affect the level of prices and sales of any commodity in any market.

No matter how else it may be characterized, a resale royalty would function as a tax. As a tax, it could—as we know from long experience with other taxes—substantially influence the behavior of those to whom it applied. If contemporary art were as much a necessity for collectors to buy as it is for artists to make, this might not matter. Unhappily, though, no matter how bravely we proclaim "ya gotta have art," nobody "gotta" have art, and especially contemporary American art.

If contemporary works of art are to be the subject of a discriminatory tax—one that would not be equally applicable to such alternative "collectibles" as nineteenth-century American art, twentieth-century European art, contemporary crafts, Ming vases, shares of IBM, or condominiums in the Bahamas—there is every reason to believe that some number of collectors would choose alternative investments. Ironically, these would most likely be those very same collectors who most distress artists by considering works of art primarily for their investment possibilities rather than as a personal commitment. Without greater knowledge of the art market, we do not know what this number and their impact might be. What we do know is that to impose a greater tax on one commodity than on another that can readily be substituted for it is to alter the pattern of demand and that, in any market, a reduction in demand must inevitably be followed by a reduction in either or both the level of prices and the volume of sales.

As it is, contemporary works of art are, for the most part, poor investments already. While some may increase in value, the greater number can never again be resold for what they initially cost. Those that do increase in value must increase substantially before any significant return can be realized. Unlike securities, for example—on which a stockbroker's commission may be less than 1 percent—the expense of reselling a work of art through a dealer or at auction will often be 15 to 25 percent. To this, before a profit can be realized, must be added any intermediate costs of ownership: insurance, conservation, and shipping. A security that increases in value by 20 percent can, on resale, yield its owner a profit. A work of art that increases by only the same amount will more likely yield its owner a loss. And, unlike a security, neither such loss nor any intermediate cost of ownership is generally deductible for tax purposes.

Into this already fragile situation, the resale royalty would introduce a further disincentive. Its impact—if calculated on the basis of gross proceeds rather than, as in the case of an income tax, on profit alone—would be far greater than the generally proposed figure of 5 percent at first suggests.

Assuming an average expense of 20 percent, a collector cannot—even before any resale royalty—resell a work of art for less than 125 percent of its original purchase price without incurring a net loss. By adding a resale royalty of 5 percent of gross proceeds, the minimum breakeven point would rise to 133 percent. In the case of a painting bought for $10,000 and resold for $13,000, leaving a net of $10,400 after the payment of expenses, the collector—his remaining profit having been already wiped out—would have to pay a substantial portion of the $650 resale royalty directly from his own pocket.

As resale prices began to exceed 133 percent of the original purchase price, the impact of the royalty, while no longer confiscatory, would still remain high in comparison to other taxes. Thus, if the same painting were sold for $14,000, the resale royalty—$700, to be paid out of the net profit of $1,200 remaining to the collector after expense—would equal an income tax of 58 percent. If the painting were resold for $20,000, the royalty of $1,000 would—after deducting expenses of $4,000—still equal a tax on this profit of more than 15 percent. Even with a three-times appreciation—the original $10,000 painting resold for $30,000—the royalty, calculated on gross proceeds, would equal a tax of more than 10 percent of the net profit remaining after the cost of sale. Beyond this, the collector would still, of course, be required to pay state and federal income taxes on whatever remained.

To make contemporary American art so disfavored an investment can only affect the level of demand in its primary and secondary markets. While diminished demand might initially affect volume, it would sooner or later be reflected in prices as well. If the prices and sales of well-established artists were the first to weaken, then those of almost-as-well established artists would inevitably follow. The process would continue until it affected the sales and prices of the least established of all.

Less now, more later? Acknowledging that the market might be thus affected, some proponents of resale royalties have argued that artists would nevertheless make up, and ultimately surpass, any initial depression in their primary selling prices by the resale royalties they would earn in later years. Surely, there are some who might: the well-established artists, those with regular resale markets and, for the most part, substantial primary markets as well.

For the greater number, though—the 90 or 99 out of every 100 whose work never increases substantially in value, who may have no resale market at all, and who might far better be the focus of legislation intended to benefit artists—no subsequent royalties would make up for this initial deficiency. In the end, what the establishment of a resale royalty would do is what most regressive legislation does: the rich might—or might not—get richer, but the poor would certainly get poorer. As Monroe and Aimée Price concluded in their 1968 *Yale Law Journal* article analyzing the distribution of benefits under the comparable *droit de suite* legislation in France: "to those who have shall more be given."

When gross sales proceeds are used as the basis for computing royalties, this balance is tilted still further—to those who have the most shall the most be given. Artist A, young and unknown, sells a painting for $1,500. Several years later, primarily as a result of A's steadily growing accomplishments and reputation, the painting is resold for $15,000, a tenfold increase. At five percent, Artist A will receive a royalty of $750 to add to the $1,500 he received on the original sale. Artist B, mature and well established, also sells a painting. The price is $18,000. After the same several years, it too is resold. The price is $20,000, a moderate increase reasonably attributable to the intervening inflation. Artist B will receive a royalty of $1,000 to add to the $18,000 that he received on his original sale.

Results such as these are inherent in the gross proceeds formula. They make an awkward fit with the argument that justifies the establishment of resale royalties as rectifying an injustice done to artists when collectors sell their work at very large profits. In fact, the artists who already have the strongest primary markets, and generally the strongest secondary markets as well, would be those likely to benefit the most from this formula. For them, only a moderate percentage increase on resale would be necessary to trigger a substantial royalty. For newly established artists, a many-fold increase might not bring them nearly as much.

Alternatives. The most serious economic problem facing most contemporary artists is the lack of any broad initial market for their work—not such abuses as may occur in the resale market.

What would benefit these artists most is an increase in the funds available to purchase works of art. This is the basic flaw in the resale royalty. It does not seek to increase these funds, but, at best, would merely redistribute—ostensibly from collectors to artists but, as a side effect, also from the less-established to the better-established artists—some portion of the inadequate funds already in the market. At worst, by imposing a discriminatory tax on contemporary art, it would reduce such funds.

In Europe, where it originated, the resale royalty has not produced any substantial returns for the great mass of artists. In some countries it has been rejected, in others it is unenforced, and, at its best, it favors only a few. In California, the resale royalty established last year [1977] has thus far served only as a divisive element within the art community and has produced virtually no tangible benefits for artists.

Given the limited, and possibly transient, attention that Congress can focus on this problem, it would be far bolder and more productive if artists and those who would help them channeled their energies behind legislation that would have an effect exactly opposite to that to be expected from royalties—that would increase, rather than diminish, the potential funds available for the purchase of contemporary art.

Most effective would be legislation that, instead of making art a less favored form of investment, would do just the contrary and give it a special and favored status. That is a route that other special-interest groups have taken with advantage. There might, for example, be a provision parallel to the present Section 1034 of the Internal Revenue Code, which defers to a later time any capital gains tax otherwise payable on the sale of a taxpayer's residence provided that the proceeds realized are used to purchase a new residence. By giving collectors an incentive to use the entire proceeds from the resale of a work of art—both their initial investment and any profit realized—to purchase additional works of art, substantial additional moneys could be brought into and kept in the market for contemporary art.

Such a provision could include many refinements. It might limit qualifying new purchases to the work of living American artists. It might require that all such purchases be made directly from artists and not in the secondary market. To benefit a broader group of artists, it might require that no single purchase could exceed some particular price or some particular portion of the amount to be reinvested. Whatever the formula, the object would be to provide an incentive for recycling back into the market—and thus back to artists—100 percent of the funds invested in every kind of art, ancient and modern, domestic and foreign—and not merely 5 percent of the resale proceeds from contemporary art.

Another alternative that has been suggested is the establishment of an art bank similar to that which now exists in Canada. Should an art bank be considered desirable, there is no reason why it need be, as some have suggested, connected with—or financed through—resale royalties. While no one has yet estimated what level of funding would be necessary to establish, supervise, and enforce a nationwide resale royalty, it must be considerable. Instead of using these funds to provide more jobs in Washington, why could the same funds not be used as the initial capital for an art bank? Its benefits could flow to artists immediately—not in five or ten years hence, as would be the case if resale royalties were to be used for its financing. Moreover, such funds would be "new money" in the market—not, as would be the case if an art bank were financed through royalties, simply a redistribution of the funds already there.

"Percent for art" legislation has only recently begun to receive the stronger backing that it deserves. Where it does not yet exist, it can be brought into being. Where it already exists, there may be the possibility of seeking higher percentages. At the federal level, Representative Gladys Spellman of Maryland has taken this course with the introduction this past summer of H.R. 7988, which would require the General Services Administration to double to 1 percent the percentage of construction funds to be used to commission or purchase works of art.

One enormous advantage of "percent for art" legislation is that it can coexist at the federal, state, county, and municipal levels. In some local jurisdictions, substantial percentages have been achieved. San Francisco has established a 2 percent rate, Miami Beach has a 1½ percent rate, and a 1 percent rate will become effective in Colorado this coming July [1978]. Above all, legislation of this kind at the local level offers the broadest group of artists not only the possibility of improving their livelihood through the sale of their work but, beyond that, the opportunity to see their work woven into the public fabric of the communities in which they live.

Whether these or other devices, alone or in combination, represent the best possible approach, what they share is the purpose of increasing the demand for contemporary works of art by injecting into the market new funds that could be channeled toward their purchase. Rather than serving to divide, such measures could enlist the enthusiastic support of all elements within the art community and, in the most practical way, offer what artists presumably want most from any legislation passed on their behalf: an increased opportunity to earn dignified livelihoods through their own creative efforts.

In the end, we would all be the beneficiaries.

Afterword

In the summer of 1977 a group of artists, collectors, and others—I was an "other"—were invited to an informal meeting on Capitol Hill to exchange their views concerning resale royalties for visual artists. In the background was California's recently established Resale Royalties Act, the first such law in the country. Conceived and pushed forward by local activists who believed it would primarily assist the "struggling" artist, it had passed the California legislature—critics said "snuck quietly through"—in September 1976 and taken effect the following January 1. In the foreground was the possibility that our host, Congressman Henry Waxman of California, might introduce a bill in the House of Representatives to establish resale royalties on a national basis. This article was adapted from a written statement I submitted at that meeting.

For such militant advocates of artists' rights as Rubin Gorewitz, the New York accountant who served as President of A.R.T. ("Artists Rights Today"), Inc., the adoption of California's Resale Royalties Act had been celebrated as the first giant step on the road to the New Jerusalem. Although parallel legislation had quickly been introduced in New York, Pennsylvania, and Ohio, and similar measures were being discussed in Florida, Texas, and several other states, it was generally agreed by proponents of the resale royalty that federal legislation would be far more effective than a patchwork pattern of local laws. On the other side were some who thought such legislation could only be damaging to the art market generally and others who questioned whether the benefits to be derived from resale royalties would be channeled almost entirely to those least in need. For its opponents, the passage of the California act had come as an unpleasant surprise—"It was the best kept secret in the state of California," said Harry Anderson, one of the Bay Area's most prominent collectors—and they were determined not to be surprised again.

All extremes were represented at the meeting. The discussion—heated, though not uncivil—made it clear that any effort to introduce a national resale royalty would face a badly divided art community. Congressman Waxman's staff, which may have initially thought this would be a reasonably popular proposal, showed an appropriate concern. Over the next few months staff members tried to negotiate away some of the sharper differences. What if the royalty were to apply only to works of art that an artist initially sold after its establishment, exempting whatever a collector already owned? What if some of the proceeds were diverted to fund an art bank that could purchase the work of younger artists? Would the royalty be more broadly acceptable if it was measured as a percentage of the profit instead of the gross selling price?

Finally, in March 1978, Congressman Waxman—joined by Congressmen Robert Drinan of Massachusetts and Frederick Richmond of New York—introduced H.R. 11403, the Visual Artists' Residual Rights Act of 1978. The bill, as introduced, was considerably milder than the proposal discussed the previous summer. In his accompanying remarks, Congressman Waxman suggested a course that was milder still—that the House not rush into action but first carefully examine the scope of the primary and secondary markets for works of art and consider whether and to what extent these might be affected by such legislation. The bill was referred to the Committee on Interstate and Foreign Commerce, where it expired with the end of the Ninety-fifth Congress. No hearings were held, and the congressman—discouraged, perhaps, by the acrimony that this foray into the genteel world of the arts had triggered—has yet to introduce such a proposal again.

Meanwhile, back in California, some of those who had come to Washington to testify against the national resale royalty were organizing themselves into Collectors, Artists and Dealers for Responsible Equity (CADRE) with the purpose of challenging the local Resale Royalties Act in the courts. Howard Morseburg, a Los Angeles art dealer, agreed to be the plaintiff in a test case, and, with CADRE's backing, *Morseburg v. Andre Balyon* was commenced as an action for declaratory relief. Morseburg asked that the California act be ruled invalid on three grounds: that it dealt with a matter preempted by the Federal Copyright Law as it was then in effect and that it violated both the contract and the due process clauses of the United States Constitution. In 1978 all three arguments were rejected by the United States District Court. On appeal, they were again rejected in a decision of the Court of Appeals for the Ninth Circuit handed down in June 1980. A final appeal was taken to the Supreme Court. This, too, failed. In November 1980 the Court denied Morseburg a hearing. CADRE pressed no further and quietly withdrew from the fray.

Thus triumphant, the California Resale Royalties Act still stands, but it stands alone. The flurry of state-level activity that followed its original adoption appears to have subsided, at least for the moment. At the federal level, likewise, all is now quiet.

In the meantime, though, the economic problems of artists are little relieved. While growth in the number of alternative spaces may have increased their opportunity for exposure, it has not necessarily brought substantial new funds into the market. As the ranks of artists swell faster than those of collectors—there are innumerable schools that support themselves by producing the former, but only the hope of more disposable wealth to create the latter—the imbalance threatens to grow worse. Whatever hope there may have been in 1977 or 1978 that more public funds could be injected into the system—whether through the establishment of an art bank or increased "percent for art" legislation—must today be seen as dimmed. The seventies' upward surge in public funding for the arts has run its course, and no one knows how soon—or whether—we will have such a surge again.

If the chronic distress of artists is to be ameliorated, it is im-
that whatever assistance is given be focused where the
on the broad group of painters, sculptors, and others
ggle for some steady share of a slender market. Resale

royalties do not meet this criterion. As hitherto projected, they tilt almost entirely toward the handful of artists who are already self-sustaining. An estimate quoted in the February 1, 1982, issue of *Forbes* suggests just how far these better-known American artists have already advanced from their once chilly garrets. It comes from Kenneth S. Friedman, publisher of the *Art Economist*, who calculates that there are twenty to thirty contemporary American artists with gross annual sales of $1 million or more and at least another one thousand who—taking into account teaching or other outside income—now have annual incomes of $100,000 or more.

Of two hundred thousand American artists (a Department of Labor estimate), that's not many—less than 1 percent. It should be enough, however—when compared with the situations of poets, composers, and other creative workers—to challenge the assumptions of those who claim that, under the present system, even the most successful visual artists are exploited beyond those of their peers who are compensated through royalties. Rather than such assumptions, what is truly needed, and what we have never had, is a thorough study of the art market that could serve as a sound basis for determining some appropriate remedies.

The "Moral Right"
Comes to California
(1979)

I n 1938 Alfred Crimi was commissioned
to paint a mural for the Rutgers Pres-
byterian Church on West Seventy-third Street in New York City.
In 1946 the church was redecorated and the mural painted over.
Crimi sued, demanding that his mural either be restored or be
removed from the church. In the alternative he asked for damages
of $150,000. The court could find no American precedent to sup-
port the proposition that, following the unconditional sale of a
work of art, the artist retained any continuing interest that might
serve as the basis for a judgment in his favor. Crimi got nothing.

In 1958 a private collector donated Alexander Calder's mobile
Pittsburgh to Allegheny County, Pennsylvania, for installation in
the Greater Pittsburgh International Airport. The mobile was originally painted black and white. Without the artist's prior knowledge, it was repainted green and gold, the official county colors.
Also changed was its configuration. Despite his continuing (and
reportedly furious) protests, the work was never—during the 18
remaining years of Calder's life—properly restored. Only later,
after the situation had received national publicity in *ARTnews*
(January 1978), were the commissioners of Allegheny County finally induced to return the mobile to its original condition.

In 1960 David Smith learned that, subsequent to its sale, his
sculpture *17 h's*—originally painted cadmium red—had been
stripped of its color. A new owner preferred it shiny. Frustrated
by his inability to compel its restoration, Smith dispatched a series
of angry letters disclaiming his authorship. To *ARTnews* he wrote,

Copyright © 1979 by ARTnews Associates. Reprinted from ARTnews, *vol. 78, no.
10 (December 1979), by permission of ARTnews Associates.*

"I renounce it as my original work and brand it a ruin." And to *Arts:* "I ask other artists to beware. Possibly we should start an action for protective laws."

Rare as such instances may be, they are nevertheless common enough to be of concern, and of particular concern to American artists. Troubled that our laws have never recognized an artist's legitimate interest in the continuing physical integrity of a work that he or she has created—a work that may embody months or even years of effort—artists and their supporters have urged with growing insistence that some legal remedy be provided to prevent or ameliorate such situations. "Would it not be appropriate," the late Thomas B. Hess asked in these [*ARTnews*] pages in 1960, "to press for legislation that would give the American artist at least a part of the legal protection and proprietary rights that are enjoyed by his colleagues in civilized countries?"

To fill this void, some artists sought protection through contracts with the collectors who bought their work. In the early 1970s covenants against destroying or modifying a work of art were included in the widely circulated Artists Reserved Rights Transfer and Sale—or so-called Projansky—Agreement as well as the gentler sequel that Charles Jurrist proposed after collectors resisted other terms of the Projansky Agreement as too harsh. In 1974 the Seattle Arts Commission agreed to include a "non-destruction" provision in the contracts issued to purchase works of art for public places. Several artists—the sculptor Jackie Winsor for one—had meanwhile devised their own individual forms of contract to provide similar protection.

Increasingly, though, artists have come to recognize that the most practical solution—one that would not require the agreement of some second party to be effective—would be legislation such as that proposed nearly twenty years ago by Smith and Hess. As models, they have cited the *droit moral*, or moral right, laws long in force throughout the European and other civil law countries. While these embrace a number of elements and differ slightly from country to country, they commonly include, as one of the artist's principal rights (a right that, under France's frequently cited Law of March 11, 1957, is *"perpetuel, inaliénable et imprescriptible"*), the "right of integrity of the work of art." The failure to grant artists a similar right in the United States has been termed by Professor John Henry Merryman of Stanford University, a lead-ing authority on moral right, "an unworthy and intolerable hiatus in our law."

The campaign to fill this hiatus has now produced its first significant victory. On January 1, 1980, the California Art Preservation Act will take effect. With it, moral right—or, at least, a homespun frontier equivalent—will make its full-fledged entry into American law. Meanwhile, legislation to establish moral right on a national basis has been introduced in Washington.

The Art Preservation Act was sponsored by State Senator Alan Sieroty, who also introduced the California Resale Royalties Act several years earlier. Mindful, perhaps, of the sharp division his earlier legislation had caused among artists, dealers, and other concerned professionals, Sieroty this time consulted broadly within the art world as the Art Preservaton Act was being shaped toward its ultimate form. An initial draft was circulated in the spring of 1978 and, after the bill was first introduced in the California senate on April 6 of that year, there were repeated amendments through two legislative sessions before the assembly gave the act its final approval this past [1979] summer. The version that Governor Brown signed into law on August 1 should be readily acceptable both to artists and to collectors.

While similar in many respects to the various moral right laws, the California act is both broader and more restrictive. It goes well beyond the French law, for example, by including the *destruction* of a work of art among the acts that are prohibited. (The French theorize that, while an altered or mutilated artwork can be prejudicial to the honor or reputation of an artist, a work that has ceased to exist cannot.) On the other hand the protection it offers is neither *inaliénable*—the act specifically provides that an artist may sign an instrument waiving his rights—nor *perpetuel*. The rights granted run only for the lifetime of the artist and for fifty years thereafter. Though only two of the several elements of moral right are covered, they are the two that American artists will probably find most valuable: the right to claim or disclaim authorship, as in Smith's renunciation of *17 h's*, and the right of integrity.

Where the Art Preservation Act most differs from the moral right laws, however, is in its legal approach. It has, literally, an American accent. Rather than proclaiming a cluster of inalienable and imprescriptible rights, the act carefully defines certain conduct that, if occurring within the state of California, can serve as the basis for a legal action by the artist or the artist's heirs.

Key to understanding the act is realization that much of this conduct might be proscribed in any case. A museum that deliberately destroyed works from its collection would likely be subject to investigation by the attorney general. A framer who mutilated a collector's painting would normally be subject to the collector's claim for damages. What is novel in American law is that California's new act gives a supplementary right to the artist or, if the artist is dead, to his heirs, legatees, or personal representatives. Under the act, the framer—already answerable to the collector for the mutilation of his physical property—could have a further liability to the artist for whatever damages were caused by the loss of his artistic effort. So too might a vandal be held responsible both to a museum whose painting he slashed and to the artist whose efforts brought it into being. New entirely, though, is the potential liability to the artist of a collector who intentionally damages or destroys a work from his own collection.

Explicitly covered by the act are original paintings, sculptures, and drawings. While these must, to fall within the act's protection, be physically located in the state of California, there is no requirement that the artist himself be a resident. Implicitly excluded are prints, collages, photographs, and crafts. Three other exclusions are specific: (a) works of art created under a "contract for commercial use," (b) works of art so integral to a building that they cannot be removed without being damaged or destroyed, and (c) because of the limited duration of the rights granted, works of art by an artist who has been dead for fifty years or longer. There is a final exclusion—certain to be one of the act's most controversial features—exempting from the act's coverage any work of art that is not of "recognized quality."

To many who followed its evolution, this last exclusion seemed essential to prevent the act's abuse by claims that were essentially frivolous or self-promotional. Without such an exclusion, there would have been no barrier to such colorful plaintiffs as the disgruntled Petaluma barfly whose favorite graffiti has been erased from a lavatory door or the contentious Orange County mother who yearns to sue a local kindergarten teacher for throwing away her daughter's finger painting.

"Recognized quality" is to be determined as a question of fact.

The act, however, does not abandon the question to the unassisted sensibility of the judge or jury. It specifically provides that expert witnesses must be heard. Under Section 1(f), these witnesses are to be "artists, art dealers, collectors of fine art, curators of art museums, and other persons involved with the creation or marketing of fine art." While this may invite the traditional battle of experts, there is no reason to believe that "recognized quality" should fare any worse in the courtroom than such other commonly contested abstractions as "insanity" or "malpractice." The law cannot accord a special status to art without also providing some mechanism for tracing its boundaries.

Assuming that a work of art does avoid these various exclusions—that it is, to take the simplest example, an original painting of recognized quality by a still-living artist that hangs in the home of a Fresno collector—what violations of the work's integrity would give rise to a cause of action? The key provision is Section 1(c)(1), which prohibits anyone other than the artist from intentionally defacing, mutilating, altering, or destroying a work of art covered by the act. Two points should be noted. Unlike various of the European laws, where the right of integrity may also protect the artist from an allegedly inappropriate or grotesque use of either an original work or its reproduction, the California Art Preservation Act deals only with the physical integrity of the original work. Whatever remedies the artist may have against such other use must be found under copyright or general tort law. Beyond this, the violation of the work's integrity must—with one exception—arise from the commission of some intentional act and not merely as the result of negligence.

The omission of this test of intentionality from early drafts of the act had concerned a number of commentators who feared that without such a limitation, the act might provide too broad a license for harassing collectors, dealers, and museums. The courts of California would have had no choice but to hear—and defendants no choice but to assume the expenses of defending—claims as wide-ranging as that an artist's work had been damaged because a collector knowingly kept too rambunctious a dog in his home, because a dealer's premises lacked adequate climate controls, or because a museum—attempting, perhaps, to make its collection more accessible to the visually impaired—was maintaining too high a level of lighting in its galleries.

Negligence, however, may still be the basis for a cause of action if a work of art is damaged or destroyed in the course of framing, restoration, or conservation. The specialists who perform such services—whether as individual entrepreneurs or within a gallery, museum, or other institutional setting—are charged by the act with a higher degree of responsibility than is the general public. Such negligence must, however, be "gross negligence," defined in Section 1(c)(2) of the act as "the exercise of so slight a degree of care as to justify the belief that there was an indifference to the particular work of fine art."

The act provides a broad range of remedies. If the violation of a work's integrity can be cured (as might have been the case with Calder's *Pittsburgh*), there may be injunctive or such other relief as "the court deems proper" to effect such a cure. If the violation cannot be cured (as in a case of total destruction), compensation may be given in the form of "actual damages." Additional provisions permit the award of attorneys' and expert witnesses' fees and of punitive damages. (To assure that punitive damages are not too tempting a bait for speculative lawsuits, any such damages would not be awarded to the plaintiff but rather to such art-related California charitable organization as the court might select.) The act also has its own statute of limitations: a suit must be commenced "within three years of the act complained of or one year after discovery of such act, whichever is longer."

The measurement of "actual damages" will present difficult questions. Since the injury to a work owned by somebody else would cause no immediate out-of-pocket loss to the artist, and since nothing suggests it was ever intended to compensate him for any emotional distress he might be caused by such an injury, what are his "actual damages"? They must, presumably, relate to some future economic loss he can be expected to suffer because of the present (or ongoing) injury to his work.

If such a loss is claimed as arising from damage to his reputation, would the mutilation of a painting valued at $5,000—a collector might have trimmed it by several inches so it would fit better over his new couch—have more (as the French believe) or less damaging consequences than its total destruction? On the other hand, could additional damages be awarded if the artist also claimed that learning of the painting's mutilation had caused him such mental anguish as to force the cancellation of a forthcoming exhibition from which he had expected substantial sales? In any case, would the $5,000 value be an upper limit to his recovery or might the ownership of a work of art—or even a museum visit with an unruly child—leave a defendant open to unlimited liability? What actual damages could an artist's heirs suffer if they no longer had works by the artist left to sell? In a case of total destruction, could damages be mitigated by arguing that the increased scarcity of his work had enhanced rather than diminished the artist's well-being?

Together with such questions, the California courts may also have to address a constitutional issue. Since the Art Preservation Act covers works of art acquired at any time—not only those that were first acquired from the artist on or after January 1, 1980—it may be argued that its provisions amount to an unlawful deprivation of some property right hitherto enjoyed by California collectors. In most instances, the right so asserted—"I paid for it and, by Jove, if I want to paint it purple, I'm entitled"—may seem trivial. In the case of a work that is integral to a building, though, the stakes may be substantial. Consider, for example the situation of a retiring Los Angeles entrepreneur whose only offer for the purchase of his disco—now adorned with erotic murals of "recognized quality"—is from a local Methodist congregation intending to convert it into a sanctuary.

The act has elaborate provisions to meet this situation. As noted earlier, it does not protect works of art that are so integral to a building that they cannot be removed without being damaged or destroyed. If a work *can* be removed without substantial damage, then the owner still has no obligation (assuming he chooses not to remove the work himself) beyond making a diligent effort to notify the artist that the building is to be renovated or demolished. Thereafter the choice is the artist's: to abandon the work or to pay the expense of removal. If the artist actually pays for removal, compensation is provided by returning the ownership of the work. On the other hand, if the artist cannot be found, or being found, fails to have the work removed within 90 days, the provisions of the act no longer apply and the work is no longer protected.

Complex as the California Art Preservation Act may appear on first encounter, it is doubtful that so large a segment of the art community would have found it acceptable had it been cast in simpler or less qualified terms. Assuming that its chief beneficiaries were intended to be artists, its purpose would surely have been defeated had its provisions been so draconian as to expose collectors to unlimited liability for even the most accidental damage to a work of contemporary art. The collector whose valuable marble sculpture has just been smashed by his frisky German shepherd might well—on learning that his already substantial loss was to be compounded by a claim for damages from the deceased artist's nephew in Budapest—consider whether there was not something less burdensome he would prefer to collect. Artists, moreover, would be little helped if a developer could no longer commission artworks for a building without the risk of substantial liability if the building should subsequently be renovated or demolished. Legislation failing to balance so nicely the various interests comprising the art world could only further narrow the already slender market for contemporary art.

Where do we go from here? So long as the rights created by the California Art Preservation Act relate only to conduct prohibited within a single state, they will have a certain evanescence. Without violating the act, the collector with the new couch may still ship his oversize painting to Nevada for trimming and bring it back to California thereafter. If national coverage is to be achieved on a state-by-state basis, the California act—with such changes as experience may show to be desirable—could well serve as the basis for a model act. Since Sieroty currently serves as chairman of the Arts Task Force of the National Conference of State Legislatures, he is clearly well positioned to champion such an approach.

The alternative would be federal legislation. This past January [1979], Representative Robert Drinan of Massachusetts introduced H.R. 288, which would append a moral right provision to Section 113 of the revised Copyright Act. (A similar bill was introduced in the last Congress but died in committee.) By contrast with the detailed and conduct-centered approach of the California act, the bill, which follows the language of the Berne Convention, is confined to a general statement of principle:

> Independently of the author's copyright in a pictorial, graphic, or sculptural work, the author or the author's legal representative shall have the right, during the life of the author and fifty years after the author's death, to claim authorship of such work and to object to any distortion, mutilation, or other alteration thereof, and to enforce any

other limitation recorded in the Copyright Office that would prevent prejudice to the author's honor or reputation.

There is, however, some question as to whether the copyright clause of the Constitution—little else would authorize Congress to act in this area—is broad enough to encompass such legislation. (Paradoxically, too strong an assertion that moral right is a component of copyright might suggest that whatever right California might have originally had to adopt its Art Preservation Act was preempted by the Copyright Revision Act of 1976.) Beyond this, artists may find the right merely to "object" an insufficient remedy for the mutilation of their work while collectors, museums, and dealers could justifiably complain that the bill is too vague in defining the duties and liabilities to which they might be subject.

Although focused mainly on establishing the artist's "right of integrity," both the California act and the proposed Drinan legislation have the incidental effect of furthering the general public interest in preserving important works of contemporary art. Unsolved by either, however, is the problem of protecting the privately owned art of earlier centuries. (Publicly owned art can be protected through the state's general supervisory power over public institutions.) Two approaches, neither of which seems satisfactory, are generally suggested. By one, the moral right could, following the European pattern, be extended in perpetuity, thus leaving responsibility for protecting such works forever in the hands of the artist's heirs. The other would accord certain works of art a status akin to that of "landmark" buildings and charge some public body or official with responsibility to assure that their integrity was maintained.

The grant of perpetual rights to an ever-widening circle of remote heirs would be both antipathetic to our legal system and ultimately impractical. As the size of the plaintiff class grew, and the value to each of its members of this inherited right correspondingly shrank, there would be little means or incentive for enforcing such rights. Moreover, as Professor Merryman has noted, there is no assurance that the interests of an artist's heirs will always coincide with those of the public. At the other extreme, it is doubtful that private collectors would accept, as a necessary adjunct to public enforcement, the establishment of a "Fine Arts Flying Squad," empowered to demand entry to their homes and monitor the care of their collections. Landmarks are generally in plain view. A Marie Laurencin pastel that hangs in the boudoir is something else.

The initial draft of the California Art Preservation Act, seeking to address this problem while avoiding such unpalatable extremes, provided that, in the case of an older work of art, the right to claim a violation of its physical integrity could be exercised by "any person acting in the public interest." In essence, this would have given standing to bring suit to just about everyone (kooks included) who for any reason (grudges included) wanted to bring to trial—or press for a settlement from—any museum, collector, dealer, framer, or conservator in the state of California. After strong (in some cases, horrified) objections were voiced, an intermediate amendment narrowed this provision to apply only to works of art of "substantial public interest." Eventually the provision was dropped entirely [it was restored in part in 1982] and the act's coverage limited basically to the art of this century. (Not entirely, though, since Picasso's work of the late 1890s will remain protected until 2023!)

While this and other problems, particularly those concerning the measurement of damages, must still be resolved, the California Art Preservation Act is an important and brave beginning, one that can only be welcomed by those who believe that works of art have a value beyond their function as commodities. In the first test of the constitutionality of California's earlier Resale Royalties Act, United States District Judge Robert M. Takasugi characterized it as "the very type of innovative lawmaking that our Federalist system is designed to encourage." That description could be applied with equal justice to the new Art Preservation Act.

Afterword

In February 1982 the New York State Assembly's Committee on Tourism, Arts and Sports Development [sic] held a hearing in New York City on a proposed Artists' Authorship Rights Act that Assemblyman Richard Gottfried of Manhattan had introduced with several cosponsors in the state legislature the preceding month.

Among the witnesses testifying in favor of the act was the sculptor Isamu Noguchi.

Noguchi's testimony was based on his own bitter experience. In 1974 he had been commissioned to create a site-specific sculpture for the New York office of the Bank of Tokyo Trust Company. The work, *Shinto*, was in the form of a rhomboidal solid and fabricated in stainless steel. Seventeen feet long, it was suspended point-downward in the bank's main lobby. Critics were enthusiastic. The staff of the bank was not. Some contended that it looked like a guillotine—a poor image, they said, for a bank. Others thought it might be unsafe.

In April 1980—without consulting, or even notifying, the artist—the bank took a torch to *Shinto*. Too large to be removed through a door, it was cut into pieces ("We tried to make the pieces as big as possible," a faintly embarrassed vice-president told the *New York Times)* and carted to a warehouse. "Vandalism," said Noguchi, "and very reactionary." But, he sadly concluded, there was nothing he could do. "As long as they paid for it, I have no legal right." The bank agreed. There had been no need to consult with the artist, a spokesman explained, because "the sculpture is the property of the Bank."

It was in that same year, 1980—also the year California's Art Preservation Act took effect—that an effort to introduce some equivalent of the moral right into New York began. Instead of adopting the carefully crafted California model, though, the New York proponents initially set out to write an ambitious grand omnibus of a law that would preserve the art of both the present and past, establish parallel schemes to permit—depending on the circumstances—either private or public enforcement, and grant to artists an array of moral rights that were intended to run in perpetuity.

The version introduced in 1982 (and ultimately passed by the State Assembly but not the Senate) was considerably less grand. After further study and several intermediate drafts, the sponsors apparently concluded that the legislation would stand a better chance of passage if its public preservation aspects were temporarily set aside. To be emphasized instead were the individual artist's rights of authorship. These were described as the right of the artist to "claim or disclaim authorship for a work of art" and the right to "object to the alteration, defacement, mutilation or other modification of his work which may be prejudicial to his career and reputation."

With respect to "paternity"—the right of the artist to claim authorship or, "for just and valid reason," to disclaim it—the most recent New York proposal, although somewhat finer in detail, generally follows the California act. In almost every other respect, however, its approach is different. Lurking in those differences is the possibility that—at least in its most recent version—it could open the way to niggling litigation while accomplishing little of any real substance.

The California act limits its coverage to "painting, sculpture, or drawing of recognized quality." New York would expand this considerably by omitting the criterion of "recognized quality" and widening the class of covered media to include prints and photographs "of a limited edition of no more than three hundred copies" as well as, by implication, work "prepared under contract for advertising or trade use." By so broadly extending this coverage, the New York proposal would potentially offer its remedies—and a day in court—to virtually anybody who had ever put brush to canvas, pencil to paper, or eye to camera. Democratic as this appears to be, it also poses a consequent danger of courtroom clutter.

Where the Artists' Authorship Rights Act becomes most diffuse, however, and appears headed toward new territory entirely is in its departure from the California pattern in defining the conduct to be proscribed. The California law is direct: what anyone in California is forbidden to do, at the risk of having to pay damages, is intentionally and physically *deface, mutilate, alter,* or *destroy* a work of fine art. While New York originally began on a similar track, at some point in 1981 it changed direction. The acts proscribed in the most recent New York proposals are entirely different: they are to *publicly display* or *publish* a work of fine art, or a reproduction thereof, in an altered, defaced, mutilated, or modified form if "damage to the artist's reputation could result therefrom."

Noteworthy is the fact that actual physical damage to the work itself is not a relevant factor. Neither is intention. The critical elements, instead, are (1) public display or publication in an altered, etc., form, and (2) the possibility that the artist's reputation might thereby be damaged. The California act would, for example, be triggered if an individual deliberately slashed into ribbons a contemporary painting that was part of his own collection. Under the most recent New York approach, such an act would not in itself be a violation unless the painting was subsequently displayed to the public in this mutilated condition *and* the circumstances were such that this could damage the artist's reputation. By contrast, the proposed New York act might be invoked if a museum, for example, was negligent in publishing a poor color reproduction of an artist's work or if a scholar or editor chose to use a detail of an artist's work to illustrate an article. In either case, New York would give the artist a cause of action if he could show that his reputation might thereby be damaged. These are not at all the sorts of conduct that the California act addresses.

The case of Noguchi's *Shinto* poses the contrast most starkly. Under the California act, the Bank of Tokyo Trust Company would have been obligated to offer the artist an opportunity to remove the sculpture at his own expense and, if he chose to do so, to reconvey to him its ownership. In fact, this apparently would have involved little more than the temporary removal of a window frame and the employment of some riggers. Having failed to do this, the bank would be liable for damages. Under the New York act, the bank would not be under any such requirement. Its only obligation would be to assure that the work—assuming its fragments could be reassembled—was not thereafter publicly displayed or published in a manner that could be damaging to Noguchi's reputation. In other words: so long as it threw away the pieces, the bank was off the hook.

In essence, the California act is concerned with the physical preservation of important works of contemporary fine art. The legislation working its way forward in New York began with that aim, but its focus changed en route. What it seeks principally to protect now is the artist's reputation. While this is surely a worthy goal it should nonetheless be understood at what a considerable distance it lies from California's accomplishment in adopting its Art Preservation Act in 1979. In some respects, what is being looked at in New York is no more than an enlargement—albeit a sympathetic one—of the existing laws of libel and slander.

Meanwhile, at the federal level, things remain as they were. The bill that Representative Robert Drinan introduced in the Ninety-sixth Congress to add a moral right provision, Berne-style, to the

Copyright Act died—as had its predecessor—in committee. With Representative Drinan's retirement, the mantle of sponsorship passed to his successor, Representative Barney Frank, who introduced a similar bill, H.R. 2908, into the Ninety-seventh Congress in March 1981. The immediate prospect for it was equally dim. The issues are complicated, and the special interest groups affected—artists, collectors, dealers, framers, conservators, and museums, among others—are many.

If the moral right is to be more deeply implanted in American law, it may well be the case, at least for the moment, that it must make its way on a state-by-state basis until there is a sufficient national consensus to permit federal legislation. If so, then every effort ought to be made to develop a uniform statute so that the rights of artists would not be so arbitrarily dependent on the happenstance of where their work might be found at any particular moment. As New York struggles to formulate its own unique (and now watered down) solution, the California act looks better than ever as the model from which such a statute might be developed.

Prices—Right On!
(1972)

Parke-Bernet's auction of postwar and contemporary art this past [1971] November 17 was like a high-wire act: suspenseful and glittering, but not nearly so risky as at looked.

Several weeks earlier, publication of the catalog had sent tremors of fear rumbling down Madison Avenue and into Soho. To be offered were sixty-one lots—the work of thirty-seven artists. Big names abounded: Stella was to be there with six entries, Warhol with five, and Louis, Noland, and Smith with four each. Gorky, Gottlieb, Hofmann, Rothko, Calder, and de Kooning would represent the older generation; among younger artists would be such salesroom novices as Poons, Flavin, and Andre.

Rarely had there been a sale offering so much so new. The average age of the works was only ten years, and more than a dozen had been executed after 1966. Would American art (meaning, in this case, the prices galleries were asking) survive? Would the German dealers, those legendary gnomes who snatch up neglected paintings and bury them in the Black Forest, arrive in time? Would Oldenburg prove to be a soft South Sea Bubble? Or—oh, comforting thought—would contemporary American art achieve record highs?

What did in fact happen on the evening of November 17 was what almost inevitably had to happen, i.e., not very much. While skillful publicity and the tension of the salesroom—the unnerving possibility that *anything* might happen—give auction its standing

Copyright © 1972 by Art in America, Inc. Reprinted from Art in America, *vol. 60, no. 1 (January-February 1972), by permission.*

as a spectator sport, the underlying mechanics of the market considerably minimize its chanciness. An auction of contemporary painting and sculpture should, on average, produce reasonably predictable prices. And so it was with Sale No. 3268.

Of the forty-eight lots that were sold—the remaining thirteen were bought in—nineteen fell within Parke-Bernet's presale estimates, fourteen were above estimate, and fifteen below. The dollar figures are even more striking. The aggregate low estimate for the forty-eight works sold was $643,000; the aggregate high was $788,000. The total price received at the sale was $752,000— not quite right down the middle, but close enough: the average deviation from the midpoint of Parke-Bernet's high and low estimates was less than $800 per lot! There is nothing occult in this. Both the top and bottom estimates for the works of well-established artists can be calculated with some accuracy by reference to the prices of similar works which are otherwise available.

In theory, at least, the top estimate should be somewhat less, perhaps 10 or 20 percent, than the price a gallery would ask for a similar painting or sculpture. (For its higher price, the gallery may provide a range of works from which to choose, a chance to try works at home on approval, guarantees of authenticity and condition, and even extended payment terms and the right to make a later exchange.) Only when no similar works are otherwise available is there no limit (other than the underbidder's self-imposed one) on how high an auction price may soar. Then there may be runaway bidding, as happened with the Titian *Death of Actaeon* and the Velázquez *Juan de Pareja*. Since the greatest likelihood that a supply of similar work will overhang the market occurs in the case of contemporary art—and especially art that tends to run in series, such as Warhol cans or Noland stripes— the well-publicized prices dealers are asking for such similar works act as a brake on bidding and limit how high a price may be obtained at auction.

On the other side, there are factors that limit how low a price may fall. Reserves provide the first line of defense, but beyond the reserves (and especially in the case of contemporary art) there is the further protection of well-stocked dealers who may feel it necessary to protect the value of their inventories, or even to add to them if this can be done at a favorable price. They—together with the corps of Big Name bargain hunters that seems particularly attracted by contemporary art—provide an extra cushion buoying bids up past the disaster level.

The thirteen lots bought in on November 17 were a special situation. Ten of these (along with at least twelve other lots that were sold) came from a single consignor, subsequently identified by the *New York Times* as Dayton's Gallery 12, operated by the department store in Minneapolis. The works had largely been purchased by Dayton's from New York dealers who showed little inclination to buy them back and some indignation over the store's approach to reducing its inventory—not unlike a pre-Thanksgiving turkey sale. Reserves had obviously been set too high, and Parke-Bernet's agreement to this (normally, it will refuse consignments rather than litter an auction with too many works that may not be sold) was perhaps attributable to the bargaining power Dayton's derived from consigning two dozen works at once.

If the November 17 sale lacked surprising prices, it nevertheless had its share of human interest and humor. The former was supplied by Governor Nelson Rockefeller, who sent five paintings to auction. Pre-sale disgruntlement ("Why should *he* make money out of art?" "Couldn't he have done as well giving them to a museum?") was not reflected in the bidding. All five sold above their estimates (in three cases at record prices), possibly proving that a glamorous provenance is still worth a few extra bids in the salesroom.

Humor erupted during the bidding of Lot 29: Oldenburg's *U.S. Flag—Fragment*. This seemingly fragile sculpture of painted muslin, plaster, and wire was displayed on stage in a rickety plexiglas case supported awkwardly by two attendants. In the midst of spirited bidding, there was an ominous cracking sound—whether of the sculpture itself or just the case was not immediately clear. Auctioneer John Marion lost not a second in bringing his hammer down and announcing "sold." Happily, it was only the plexiglas that cracked; Oldenburg's sculpture, together with the price structure of contemporary American art, survived the evening intact.

Review of *Money and Art: A Study Based on The Times-Sotheby Index* by Geraldine Keen (1971)

Money and Art: A Study Based on The Times-Sotheby Index. By Geraldine Keen.

Published by G.P. Putnam's Sons, New York, 1971. 286 pp. 168 black and white illustrations and 12 color plates.

Since 1967 Geraldine Keen, working with representatives of Sotheby's, has compiled for the *Times* of London a series of indices intended to show (in the same manner as a stock market average) the annual rise or fall in the world auction prices recorded for twelve categories of art, objets d'art, and books. Now she has prepared what purports to be a "study" of the six of these indices which deal with paintings, drawings, and prints, covering their movement from January 1951 through June 1969.

Money and Art is, however, scarcely a "study." It is, rather, an elaborate advertisement puffing the financial joys that purchasing fine art may still bestow and the advantages of a London salesroom as the place to make such purchases. Packaged with this puffery is a brief history of Western art from Cimabue forward, tidbits of connoisseurship, and hot tips on likely growth candidates—in short, everything the novice investor might need to know to make his first move in the market.

The novice investor might, of course, feel intimidated. Art is said to be pretty heavy stuff, and artists have long been considered a strange breed. Miss Keen is reassuring. It is the collector and his money, not the artist, who brings art into being: "most of the great art of the past, which is now venerated, studied and considered a precious heritage, came into existence following the normal economic laws of supply and demand." This is not to say that the "rich collector" must buy the art of his own time to bring

Copyright © 1971 by The Print Collector's Newsletter, Inc. Reprinted from The Print Collector's Newsletter, *vol. 2, no. 3 (July-August 1971), by permission.*

it into being. Buying art of the past will do as well. "In seeking out the finest artistic achievements of the past, he is also providing the artists of his own time with a new inspiration, and helping to extend the cultural heritage for future generations."

Having established the role of Maecenas as a creative one, Miss Keen goes on to assure her readers that it will be profitable as well. Notwithstanding the two-decade boom her book describes, it's not too late to catch the boat. In a key paragraph of *Money and Art*, one that reads as if drawn from the prospectus for a pyramid club, she explains why it's *never* too late to catch the boat, at least for contemporary art.

> The logic of this is fairly simple. Year by year, the number of wealthy people is increasing, as is their total wealth. Thus the amount of money potentially available to spend on modern pictures is steadily increasing. At the same time, museums, by their purchases of modern art, are continually removing good paintings from the market. It is natural in this situation that the value of most accepted artists' work should continue to rise and that new artists should be "discovered" in order to provide enough "art" to go round.

The remaining questions, then, are where and what to buy. As for where, the unsurprising answer is London. Although the *Times-Sotheby* Index is based on "prices recorded at auction in all the world's major salesrooms," not merely at Sotheby's, there is scarcely a reference to any Continental auction house and references to American auctions are restricted to Parke-Bernet, taken over by Sotheby's in 1964. Such major European auctions as those at Lempertz and Ketterer are not mentioned at all; the firm of Kornfeld and Klipstein appears only in the acknowledgements. Should the novice investor, however, discover that there *are* Continental sources, he might still prefer to shop in London. The difficulties he might encounter with European export and tax laws are described by Miss Keen at gleeful length and to clinch the matter, at least for her American readers, there is this:

> Furthermore, the British are by tradition considered more straightforward in their business dealings than their Continental neighbours. The American, therefore, feels safer with an English dealer and less likely to be sold a fake or grossly overcharged than he might be elsewhere in Europe. There are, of course, crooked dealers in London, just as there are scrupulously honest dealers in Paris, Geneva, or

Rome; but by and large the English market is conducted on more straightforward lines than the market on the Continent.

As for what to buy, Miss Keen's tips are suitably hedged. But you might try Victoriana, "a fascinating field . . . which offers excellent opportunities for backing one's own judgment" or some minor Impressionists, "an interesting speculative venture for anyone with a certain amount of time and money on his hands."

The first three chapters of *Money and Art* describe the mechanics of the art market, the relationship between patronage and art, and the impact of changing fashions on the relative values of different schools and media. Discussing the factors that may go into establishing the value of a work (artist, quality, relationship to other works, scale, medium, subject, period, condition, strength of attribution, provenance, etc.), Miss Keen makes the interesting observation that scarcity, past a certain point, may be a negative rather than positive factor. There must be enough of something to collect in order for collecting it to become fashionable and for its price to rise.

The remaining six chapters consider in greater detail the six areas covered by the specific indices: Old Master paintings, Old Master drawings, Old Master prints, English paintings of the eighteenth and nineteenth centuries, Impressionist paintings, and twentieth century paintings. Each chapter is in two parts. The first gives the historical background; the second is tersely subtitled *What Costs What*.

How this works may be seen by examining the index for Old Master prints (defined as "Gothic to Goya") which shows a 38 times increase in value from the beginning of 1951 through mid-1969. This index is, in turn, based on seven subindices: Gothic prints (up 15 times), Dürer prints (up 26 times), prints after Peter Bruegel (up 97 times), Rembrandt prints (up 40 times), Canaletto prints (up 30 times), Piranesi prints (up 33½ times), and Goya prints (up 19½ times). The lustrous increase in the value of Hieronymus Cock's engravings after Bruegel is somewhat dimmed by learning that it reflects a price rise from an average of about $10 in 1951 to $970 in 1969. A 97 times increase somehow sounds more dramatic than a $960 profit.

In compiling the indices, Miss Keen and her co-workers from Sotheby's were careful to take into account the effect of quality, scale, condition, and other factors on the prices which particular works fetched. An elaborate system of adjustments—many of them admittedly subjective—was utilized to bring various examples of an artist's work into an equivalence which would permit price comparisons to be made. Thus, if a major Renoir nude preceded a scrappy Renoir sketch to the salesroom, a ratio of estimated value was established between them in order to determine in which direction their successive (and dissimilar) prices would push the Renoir index.

No adjustment, however, has been made for either inflation or the 14 percent devaluation of the pound in 1967. Assuming the purchasing power of the pound was not quite half in 1969 of what it was in 1950 (Miss Keen's own estimate), then her general figures—a five to ten times increase in fields of traditional interest and a twenty to forty times increase in fields where "a new collecting fashion has been at work"—are not so spectacular as they seem at first. In the first field, adjusted for a constant pound, the average increase in value from 1951 to 1969 would be four times; that is the equivalent of little more than 8 percent compounded annually. For a nonincome producing investment (and one, moreover, that has to be insured), that does not seem extraordinary. Her high fliers (paced by Chagall, up 50½ times, and Italian seventeenth century drawings, up 45 times) do better. Deflating their average multiple of 30 to 16 for a constant pound, their yield of about 16 percent compounded annually is certainly rewarding, if not quite so glamorous as the indices would at first indicate.

Not one of Miss Keen's indices move down for the entire period. English sporting pictures, historical portraits, and Dutch genre paintings do display sinking spells, but each index save one ends happily. The exception is Fantin-Latour who shows a decline from 1968 to 1969; a note cheerily explains that this is due to one exceptionally high sale in 1968, not weakness in 1969, and "is not significant." When she discusses a field where prices have fallen— French seventeenth-century prints—no prices are quoted and no index is given.

The novice investor relying on Miss Keen must nevertheless be wary of some errors and omissions. Regarding American tax law, her innocence is dangerous. The value of charitable gifts is deductible from income and not, alas, from taxes, as she several times insists. Since January 1, 1970, the ceiling on certain types of charitable deductions has been 50 percent of income, not the 30 percent she claims.

A more serious error mars Miss Keen's discussion of the "universal consciousness of what is the maximum conceivable sum to pay for a picture." Using Leonardo's portrait of *Ginevra de' Benci* as her touchstone (her manuscript was presumably completed before the sale of Velázquez's *Juan de Pareja* this year) she reports its purchase by Washington's National Gallery at £5 million ($14 million). At the time of this sale, the price was widely reported to have been about $5 million and, unless Miss Keen has new information, this slip between pounds and dollars has added $9 million to what such a "maximum conceivable sum" might be. In a "study" which is claimed to be both scientific and businesslike, $9 million is a lot of mistake.

Some omissions are interesting. None of the indices includes sculpture, and there is only a passing reference to it in the text. Also omitted from the indices is American painting. The twentieth century index (up 29 times) is based entirely on seven artists: Picasso, Braque, Bonnard, Chagall, Vlaminck, Rouault, and Utrillo.

One omission is especially serious. Miss Keen gives no figures as to the impact of higher prices on the volume of sales. At one point she asserts that volume has been "notable," but there is nothing else. Volume figures would seem as essential to making *Money and Art* a true "study" as they would be to interpreting a Dow Jones average. Is buying interest substantially as widespread as it was at lower levels, or do such prices reflect the willingness to pay of only a diminishing handful of wealthy collectors? The art market is not, after all, a "market" in the same sense as that for oats or office space. Except for death or economic distress, there is rarely any *need* to sell and virtually none to buy. Paintings don't spoil, and five van Gogh's would not a good auction make.

While other faults abound—an irritating failure to list most dimensions so that we know only that a specific example brought a high or low price because it was "huge" or "tiny" or of "unmanageable size," poor color plates, and even poorer proofreading—the chief vice of Miss Keen's book is her uncritical assumption that constantly rising prices are, per se, a good thing. Except for a brief caveat as to the unsettling effect that art investment trusts might have on the market by pouring too much money in too quickly, she generally cheers each upward move with all the enthusiasm of a track fan watching a record-breaking high jump.

More, however, may not necessarily be better for everyone concerned with art. For museums, notwithstanding Miss Keen's theory that higher values eventually lead to greater charitable giving, the first effect of ever higher prices is to reduce the purchasing power of already dwindling acquisition funds. Even when such funds are available, the public purchase of multimillion dollar paintings begins to raise some uncomfortable questions about social priorities. Museum visitors too are affected; as the insurance values underlying loan exhibitions soar, the number and scope of such exhibitions must be curtailed.

The serious collector faces the same problems of diminished purchasing power and higher insurance costs. In addition, sharply increased values may ultimately create so great an estate tax liability as to require dispersal of his collection. Even to the living artist, ever increasing prices can be a mixed blessing. They may thin the market and cut down a potential purchaser's willingness to please his taste or gamble on an unknown or simply indulge a *jeu d'esprit*. Certainly, there is a substantial question whether the health of the art community would not be better served if each $50,000 available for purchase were put into fifty works at $1,000 each instead of a single gilt-edged canvas.

Miss Keen is not concerned with this. Neither the museum, the serious collector, nor the artist is the audience at which *Money and Art* is aimed. It is the novice investor she is seeking to lure to a London salesroom with its dazzling prospect of ever higher prices. And while she may well be right that prices must rise in the long run, the long run can be very long indeed; uncritical reliance on *Money and Art* might in the short run cost the novice far more than its twenty-dollar price.

Afterword

The *Times*-Sotheby Index proved to be transient. It expired quietly in the early seventies. The art market boom it was intended to document also turned out to be transient. After reaching a peak as the eighties began, it promptly went flat. Enduring, though, was humankind's urge to quantify. In the fall of 1981, Sotheby returned with a new and more sophisticated model. It was chastely titled the Sotheby Index.

In the United States, the Sotheby Index appears monthly in *The Collector-Investor* and weekly in *Barron's*. The latter is published by Dow Jones and Company—itself no mean compiler of indices—and the new art index to some degree resembles those familiar averaging devices by which the movements of financial markets have long been charted.

Whereas the original *Times*-Sotheby Index was derived entirely from the prices fetched by whatever objects might happen to turn up at auction, this new index is based on the periodic reappraisal of an art "market basket" hypothetically filled with hundreds of "representative" objects. These objects, which remain constant, are divided into twelve categories. Five are composed of paintings, two each of ceramics and silver, and three of furniture. Each category, in turn, is first given a weight that reflects its share of Sotheby's total business and then combined on its weighted basis into an aggregate index intended to measure the market as a whole. In compiling the aggregate index, the five categories of paintings are weighted at 60 percent. Impressionist/postimpressionist and Old Master paintings are the two heaviest categorical indices, together accounting for 35 percent of the aggregate.

In constructing the Sotheby Index, the year ending September 30, 1975, was chosen as the base. For each categorical index, as well as for the weighted aggregate, the total estimated prices of the objects it contained was assigned an initial value of 100. Estimates of annual price changes were then made for the years ending on September 30 of 1976 through 1981. Since October 1981 these estimates—still covering the same group of objects, and made by Sotheby's in-house experts in London and New York—have been updated each week. Valuations are based on current auction results (at all houses, not just Sotheby's) for comparable objects and also on dealer transactions.

Assuming there was an American collector-investor who in 1975 had spent 100 (the base) to "buy the market" (in this case, the "market basket"), the index lets us follow his changing fortunes. The first two years were good. By September 1976, his basketful was worth 111. A year later it was up to 128. The next three years were even better. By September 1978 its value had soared by 28 percent to 164. With nearly a similar gain for 1979, it reached 217. By September 1980, it was a giddy 253.

And there it stopped. According to the Sotheby Index, the overall art market has been stagnant or worse ever since. While the more philistine of our hypothetical collector-investor's friends were pulling down 15 percent and more in interest from their money market funds and inflation was raging in double digits, he sat and watched the worth of his zero-yield basket begin to dwindle. By September 1981 it had slipped to 244. A year later, not significantly changed, it had inched back to 251. For the moment at least, the boom was over and the moment to sell had long since passed. The index suggests that for the art market—no less than any other—timing may be all.

Assuming the index to be accurate, what does it tell us about the recent history of art as an investment? With the most impeccable timing, our collector-investor would have sold out in 1980. His gain would have equalled a return of just over 20 percent per annum, compounded annually. Adjusted for inflation—the Consumer Price Index rose at a rate of 9 percent, compounded annually, during the same period—this seems a solid improvement over the 8 percent annual compound increase that the *Times*-Sotheby Index recorded for 1950–69 in collecting fields of traditional interest. Certainly, it was far better than he might have done with a similar "basket" in one of the conventional financial markets. While the art investment figure must, as always, be tempered by factoring in the high transaction costs for both purchase and sale, the foregone yield, and the costs of insurance and transportation, the 1975–80 result would still seem a good one.

With greater selectivity and a well-timed switch, though, our collector-investor could have done even better. While the weighted aggregate was growing from 100 to 253, seven of the twelve underlying categorical indices underperformed the aggregate, and two barely stayed even. It was Chinese ceramics—with a hefty weight of 10 percent and a more-than-hefty jump from 100 to 462—that powered the average through 1980. With a nimble jump off his T'ang horses and into impressionist/postimpressionist paintings, he might have kept his winning streak going. Up from 206 to 255 in the two years after September 30, 1980, it was one of the few categories (along with modern paintings and American painting for the period 1800–1939) that kept the aggregate index from sinking further. If timing isn't everything, selectivity is the rest.

In general, the Sotheby Index seems a vast improvement over the original *Times*-Sotheby Index. The use of a constant "market basket" eliminates much of the happenstance factor of what might or might not be offered at auction as well as the need for elaborate adjustments to bring the prices of disparate objects into equivalence with one another. Moreover, the use of "representative" examples avoids the distortions caused in the earlier index by the occasional sale of a spectacular object that fetched a blockbuster price. That the index still retains an element of subjectivity—particularly in the choice of comparables—might be considered a weakness, but one that is probably unavoidable in any method of measurement based on appraisals.

There are several other flaws, though—all of them carried over from the original *Times*-Sotheby Index—that do seem curable. One relates to volume. The index gives no indication whether its values are derived from a thriving multitransactional market or from one that is thin or even dormant. In theory, at least, a market could dry up entirely, and the index would show little or no change until the obduracy of either buyers or sellers gave way. Second, there is the matter of inflation. No adjustment is made for it, and yet inflation accounted for nearly half of the increasing values that the index reflected for 1975–80. One has only to compare the Dow Jones Industrial Average adjusted for inflation with the unadjusted average to understand what a startling difference it can make. Finally, some clarification might be in order about how currency differences are being handled. Depending on whether pounds are being translated to dollars or vice versa—the values are all expressed by numbers, not in any currency—the results might vary considerably with any wide fluctuations in foreign exchange.

One question remains. The present market, as viewed through the Sotheby Index, is not one likely to appeal greatly to either consignors or investors—essential ingredients of Sotheby's business. What, then, are we to make of its timing in bringing out the index when it did? Work on the index began in early 1979 when the market was still roaring—base 100 was heading toward 217 on its way to 253—and the firm was in the midst of its greatest expansion. By 1981 the market had stalled, and by 1982 Sotheby itself was forced into a surprising and painful contraction. Clearly, someone had failed to heed the *caveat* that accompanies the index; the past ought not to be relied on to predict (much less to guarantee) the future. Across the board, Sotheby must simply have misread where everything was headed. Once again, though, the art market itself may provide its own comfort. Things sooner or later turn topsy-turvy, and there is little that keeps moving the same way for long.

Review of *The Economics of Taste: Volume III, The Art Market in the 1960's* by Gerald Reitlinger (1972)

The Economics of Taste: Volume III, The Art Market in the 1960's. By Gerald Reitlinger.

Published by Barrie and Jenkins Ltd., London, 1970. 695 pp.

In Volumes I and II of *The Economics of Taste*, Gerald Reitlinger traced the fluctuating market values of paintings, sculpture, and objets d'art from the middle of the eighteenth century through the 1950s. From this study of salesroom records, earlier publications, and newspaper accounts (together, now and then, with a bit of gossip), he reached two conclusions: that there have always been art objects in such demand they could only be bought for what, in their time, were thought to be outrageous prices, and that the identity of such objects has been as susceptible to change as any other fashion.

With the publication of Volume III, Reitlinger has brought his research up through the 1960s and substantially supplemented and corrected many of the entries in the earlier volumes. While those were divided almost equally between historical narrative and chronological price lists arranged by artist, school, or class of object, Volume III is made up entirely of price lists—each preceded by a brief introduction. These lists are not intended to demonstrate price movements in any rigorous way; except when the same object reappears for sale, successive entries are far too disparate in quality, authenticity, condition, medium, and scale to permit exact price comparisons. Rather, when taken together with their introductions, these lists provide a general impression of what changes the 1960s brought to the art market.

These were, for the most part, changes in price rather than taste. Fashions in art move at a stately pace, and the period of a decade covered by Volume III was simply too short to encompass

Copyright © 1972 by The Print Collector's Newsletter, Inc. Reprinted from The Print Collector's Newsletter, vol. 2, no. 6 (January-February 1972) by permission.

many changes in the relative values the market assigned to Old Masters. Prices, however, were up sharply, more sharply than the general cost of living. Whether this signaled a long-range trend or was simply a case of the art market anticipating further inflation is not yet clear. During this century, the prices commanded by "star" paintings (or those regarded as "star" class when they were bought) have remained relatively constant. In 1901 J.P. Morgan paid $484,000 for Raphael's Colonna Altarpiece, Czar Nicholas broke all records when he bought Leonardo's *Benois Madonna* in 1914 for $1.5 million, and Duveen succeeded in obtaining $620,000 from Henry Huntington for Gainsborough's *Blue Boy* in 1921. Adjusted for inflation on a table provided by Reitlinger, these purchases translate into a range of three to ten million dollars— figures comparable with the seemingly spectacular prices of recent years.

Prices for the last available paintings by currently enshrined masters should not, of course, be taken too seriously. The market for Leonardo, Velázquez, or Raphael is like a supernova, flaring up in brilliant farewell—then collapsing into extinction as the last major works are tucked safely away in museums. Reitlinger's lists make clear how thin this market was, at least to public knowledge, in the 1960s.

More indicative of the generally upward trend of prices are those lists covering artists of whose work substantial numbers reached the market during the 1960s. There are nearly two hundred of these lists for individual painters—more than a quarter of them English—together with a further twenty-two lists grouping less frequently marketed painters by schools. Sculpture is dealt with more briefly; most of the entries are by schools, with only thirty-four sculptors, none earlier than Daumier, covered individually. Prints are not listed at all. On the other hand, prices are reported for an extraordinary variety of objets d'art: ninety major lists range from arms and armor through Majolica to watches; subordinate lists cover such esoterica as Jacobite glass and mounted coconuts and ostrich eggs.

The Economics of Taste is not, however, nearly so solemn (nor always as accurate) as might be expected of a reference work. Reitlinger is possessed of a wicked humor and a fair number of prejudices running against things so diverse as soft currency, American art, and paperweights. In Volume III, he deals with contemporary American painting for the first time and manages, in a stretch of four pages, to misspell the names of Newman, Rothko, de Kooning, and Still; to identify Calder as a painter; and to pause midway in his otherwise deadpan listing of prices to snortingly describe a painting by Rothko as "plain oblong, slightly tinted." A Tiffany stained glass window panel, sold in New York in 1969, is described by Reitlinger as diffusing "a dim religious light through a Walt Disney landscape that only needs an electric cinema organ of the period, a small extra item on a bill that already approaches £9,000, as if the window had come out of Chartres Cathedral."

While Reitlinger was, in the earlier volumes of *The Economics of Taste*, merely curmudgeonly, in Volume III he occasionally becomes shrill. Fabergé works in "the Snow White and the Seven Dwarfs tradition, that facet of the Swiss genius which created all those bears and cuckoo-clocks"; Chagall is obsessed "with violins and roses, brides and Christmas-cracker colors"; and John Hoppner "surely holds the title of the most overrated old master ever known to the art market." Samuel Palmer is "a kind of William Blake without tears."

No matter; in the end, it is neither in these grumbling appraisals nor in the mass of data he provides that Reitlinger's greatest value lies. It is, rather, in his wry appreciation of the profound changes that time can work on artistic taste. The short-term changes he discusses are relatively familiar. They are, after all, the material from which artists spin their sustaining myth: that death, or at least death plus fifty years, will bring a fair accounting—the unjustly praised will be unmasked as mediocre (Meissonier, Bonheur), and genius ignored in its time (van Gogh, Cézanne, Gauguin) will emerge truimphant.

More illuminating are those cases in which one or more reevaluations of an artist's work have occurred over a long period of time. History, as read from the market by Reitlinger, does not render a final verdict but, rather, one that is ever changing. And while the market may not be a perfect gauge—high prices may stem from a short supply as well as a large demand—it is still a strong indication of how artists are publicly ranked.

It seems odd today that, in 1880, the most expensive art object ever sold—more expensive even than any painting—was a German parcel-gilt standing cup for which Meyer Rothschild paid $150,000.

Will the objects that fetched record-breaking prices in the 1960s seem equally strange a century hence? Perhaps not. Canons of excellence may now have been so firmly fixed by art history and the museums—both relatively recent inventions—that the "official" masters will reign in the market so long as their work is in adequate supply. *The Economics of Taste*, though, makes this seem dubious; the wheel of fashion turns slowly, but it does turn.